one &
done

The Guide to Raising a
Happy & Thriving Only Child

REBECCA GREENE, MSW, LMSW

one &
done

FAMILIUS

To Alex, my wonderful one and only

Published by Familius LLC, www.familius.com
PO Box 1249, Reedley, CA 93654

Familius books are available at special discounts for bulk purchases, whether
for sales promotions or for family or corporate use. For more information,
contact Familius Sales at orders@familius.com.

Library of Congress Control Number: 2022942635

Print ISBN 978-1-64170-744-2
Ebook ISBN 978-1-64170-832-6

Printed in the United States of America

Edited by Laurie Duersch, Peg Sandkam, and Shaelyn Topolovec
Cover and book design by Brooke Jorden

10 9 8 7 6 5 4 3 2 1

First Edition

Foreword by Jessica Myhre

"Will my child be spoiled if he doesn't have a sibling?"
"Am I going to regret not having more children someday?"
"Everyone says my only child will be lonely."
"This isn't what I thought my family would look like."

These are concerns I hear each and every day from parents who, whether by choice or by circumstance, have one child. They were also some of my first thoughts when I considered stopping at one child after my own daughter was born. The rampant stereotypes about only children and the lack of support for parents were my reasons for creating a podcast called *Only You: A One and Done Podcast*. When I learned about this book, *One & Done*, I knew it would be an incredible resource for so many, including myself.

I am one of five children, and I dreamed of having a large family for most of my life. When it was my time to try for a baby, pregnancy came quickly and easily, and was (for the most part) uneventful. I assumed I would be doing it several more times in my life and tried to rise above the intense anxiety and discomfort it brought me. When I was suddenly diagnosed with severe preeclampsia at thirty-five weeks and wound up with a premature baby in the NICU, almost immediately I started revisiting the expectations I put on myself. Why, exactly, did I assume becoming a parent meant I had to have more than one child?

It was then that I began searching for support. I read any article I could find on single child families, listened to parenting podcasts, and asked friends for advice. For the most part, people told me not to have an only child. They would lecture me with anecdotes about spoiled children who couldn't share and the lonely fate of a child without siblings. I was told I would change my mind and that I was too young and too early in my motherhood journey to be thinking about being done.

Research, on the other hand, did not support these negative biases. Every study I found disproved the stereotypes I was hearing, and I started wondering why they are so enduring. When I spoke to only child adults, I heard the kinds of stories you would expect to hear from any person's childhood. Some parts were great, others were hard. And in the end, it had very little to do with how many siblings they had and a lot more to do with how involved their parents were. Lonely children are unfortunately a consequence of a lack of emotional support from their parents. While siblings can help bridge that gap, it's the parents' job—not a sibling's—to meet their child's emotional needs.

For the most part, the people I talked to who grew up without siblings were very happy with their lives and had great relationships with their parents. The more I learned, the better I felt about having one child. Coming from a large family, it actually began to sound quite nice. We would have more resources and time for our daughter, I wouldn't have to go through pregnancy or childbirth again, and I had time and space to heal from the trauma it caused me. I could once again focus on my career, my marriage, and my life.

Despite all of this, I still needed to find a community. As a new mother, I was scouring every corner of the internet for advice on this topic, but there was a complete lack of discourse on being one and done. I found that mom groups weren't as accepting of only-child parents. It felt inappropriate to talk to other moms about how complete my family felt with just one kid. Every conversation felt like a defense, and the ups and downs of parenting one child were considered insignificant in comparison to those with multiple children. Every so often an adult who grew up as an only child would chime in, but even their positive experiences would be met with rebuttals and horror stories.

By the time my daughter turned six months old, I was finally coming out of my postpartum fog and socializing with friends and family again. That fleeting moment of personal freedom was cut short when the COVID-19 pandemic disrupted my plans, and our fate as a one child family was sealed. Through quarantine, isolation, unemployment, and the constant triggers of medical trauma from our NICU days, I knew in my heart I couldn't have another child.

I created my *Only You* podcast because I felt there was a great need of support for parents of one child. The show gained traction more quickly than we ever imagined! Hundreds of parents reached out to me and told their stories of birth trauma, infertility, adoption, postpartum depression and anxiety, and so many other components that led them to being one and done. Others reached out to tell me about all the amazing aspects of having one, how it had always been their dream, and how they don't understand why they are criticized for that choice. While I am happy to lead this conversation and hold emotional space for parents, there is still a great need for literature on the subject.

I hope this book finds you when you need it, and that it helps you feel heard and understood for the unique set of circumstances that come along with having one child. One of the reasons I advocate so strongly for parents of one is that we can never truly know how each family came to be. So many parents out there are suffering in silence, feeling isolated, and wishing their family could look like the ones they see around them. For every proud and confident only child parent, there is one who is aching for a second child they may never have. We have to do better for parents.

One of the first steps in doing so is to give them the tools they need to be successful, no matter what their family looks like. Having a book devoted to raising only children is such a gift, and *One & Done* is sure to leave parents with everything they need to thrive and to enjoy exactly what they have. I know this book is the kind of resource I have really needed during my parenting journey.

Jessica Myhre
Creator of *Only You: A One and Done Podcast*

Introduction

One and done.
Only-child family.
Single child family.
Triangle family.

There are many ways to describe a family with an only child. Most likely, you picked up this book because you are a family with one child, you have decided to remain one and done, and you're interested in learning more about how to best raise an only child in today's parenting landscape. You may be eager to discover parenting tips and suggestions specific to only children but have struggled to find books or online resources specifically tailored to an only-child family. If so, look no further—you have come to the right place!

One & Done is written for parents, grandparents, mental health professionals, educators, and anyone else who wants to help only-child families thrive. In these pages, you will find practical parenting information and advice, interviews with mental health professionals, and helpful statistics and conclusions from relevant research studies.

We will explore a variety of topics pertinent to raising an only child, including an exploration of the reasons why you have an only child, a focus on the many benefits of having an only child, how to build a strong village for your only child, how to create new and exciting family traditions that are perfect for a family with one child, tips on how to maintain strong ties with extended family to benefit only children, how to tactfully handle hurtful comments and inquiries about why your child is an only, navigating difficult questions from your child about lack of siblings, and debunking the idea of the lonely only and other stigmas surrounding only children.

A few years ago, when we made the decision to be one and done, I began a quest to seek out all the information I could find about how to best raise an only child. To my surprise, I came up relatively empty-handed after an exhaustive search. According to census data, only-child families are the fastest growing family structure in the United States, but there is a dearth of print, online, discussion forum, and other supportive resources dedicated to raising an only child. This leaves a huge gap that needs to be filled.

I decided that I wanted to help fill this gap and write the definitive parenting guide for raising a happy and well-socialized only child, from birth through age eighteen. In fact, it became my mission. And I felt like I was the right person for the job, given that I have the unique perspective of being an only child who is raising an only child. Additionally, I am a mental health professional who works with kids, teens, and parents. I began talking with other only-child families across the country about the need for a book specifically tailored to our parenting journey and realized that so many of us share the same hopes, dreams, concerns, and worries for our families. They shared their stories and perspectives with me, which became the foundational interviews for this book.

With so many families having a single child, whether by choice or not by choice, there is a growing demand for practical, hands-on information on how to best raise an only child. There are plenty of general parenting guides on the market, but surprisingly few tailored to the unique concerns and needs of families with only children. Judging from the large number of only-child family groups on social media, each with thousands of members, parents of only children are eager for this type of customized parenting advice.

This book may have also piqued your interest because you don't know any other families who are one and done, and you may be seeking support and community. It's interesting that the largest growing family unit in the United States over the last forty years is the family with one child, with around 22 percent of US families having this dynamic, according to Pew Research Center data. This national percentage of only children is set to grow in the next decade as more families consider the many benefits of having a single child. However, despite the fact that only-child families are so prevalent, you might not personally know a single one.

This lack of community with other only-child families can lead to feelings of loneliness and isolation during your parenting journey. One of my goals in this book is to help you connect with other only-child families, both in spirit (by reading their stories) and in real life, by encouraging you to join online only-child family support/social groups or form your own group in your local area. By joining together with other only-child families, you will build your support network and grow a village of other like-minded parents.

If you're like many only-child families, the decision to be one and done was not an easy one. Perhaps you knew right away that you wanted to have a single child. Some families proactively make the decision to have one child and consider themselves "one and done by choice," which is amazing! But other families have the decision made for them, due to such factors as infertility, advanced maternal age, health/pregnancy risks, divorce, or financial concerns, among others. These families consider themselves "one and done, not by choice," and many are plagued by insecurity, self-doubt, and guilt as they ruminate about their family size. These families seek reassurance, validation, and a sense of community with other parents in the same situation as they try to make the best out of challenging circumstances.

Regardless of whether only-child families are "by choice" or "not by choice," what we all share in common are several unique struggles, which we will explore in detail in this book. Only-child families may have a constant concern about their only child feeling lonely, or nagging guilt that they are not providing their child with enough socialization and companionship to meet their developmental needs. They may also worry about their only child being alone as an adult without much family support, and worry incessantly about the future when their only child is tasked with all the eldercare responsibilities.

Parents of only children may also struggle with fitting into their social circles and school/religious communities where most other families have multiple children. They may harbor feelings of inadequacy or dejection when they are left out of social events because they have just one child, or when they are the only parents in the preschool pick-up line without another child in tow. They often feel judged for their family size and endure intrusive questions from strangers and close family members about why they're not having more children. They also worry that they aren't legitimized by society as a "real" family because they only have one child.

That's where this book comes in. *One & Done* stands out in the sea of general parenting books because it truly understands and addresses the needs, problems, and struggles of today's only-child family. In these pages you will not only learn about how to best raise an only child and how to address parenting concerns specific to only children (like what to do if your only is lonely, or if your child constantly asks for a sibling), but you will also hear from other only-child families around the world about how they handle specific parenting challenges. You will learn important tips, such as how to create a village for your only child, what to do when your child is lonely, how to best nurture friendships for your child, how to plan new family traditions, what to do to manage the guilt about depriving your child of a sibling bond, and how to deal with insecurities you may feel about being one and done, among others.

My hope is that you will come away from this book with a variety of new parenting tips, suggestions, inspiration, and ideas for making your only's childhood as meaningful and fulfilling as possible; with new knowledge about online resources (including support groups) so you can connect with other parents of only children; and with a feeling of support and reassurance in knowing that you are not alone.

This book is for all only-child families, both those who are one and done by choice, and also for those who are one and done, not by choice. It celebrates all only-child families and is as inclusive as possible in order to represent all facets of the only child parenting journey. While we all have different reasons why we came to have an only child, what we have in common is the goal of giving our only child the best possible childhood. This book is a roadmap to show you how.

May the ideas inside this book, and the self-dialogue you engage in from being inspired by its words, empower you to raise a happy, well-adjusted, and thriving only child.

Warmly,
Rebecca Greene, MSW, LMSW

P.S. I love to hear from readers and am eager to hear your thoughts and experiences about being an only-child family, along with what has been most meaningful to you in your parenting journey! Please get in touch with me:
Rebecca Greene, MSW, LMSW
OneandDoneBookFamilius@gmail.com

Contents

Section I:
All about Your Family

CHAPTER 1

The Story of Us: How You Came to Be One and Done

E very family with an only child has a unique story. What is yours? How did you decide to have one child? Families with only children generally fall into two categories: those who are "one and done by choice," and those who are "one and done, not by choice." In this chapter, we will explore the many different reasons why a family might choose to have a single child. These can include, but are not limited to, a personal choice, secondary infertility, advanced maternal age, prior pregnancy/health issues, prior miscarriages/losses, financial concerns, lack of family or childcare help, strained marriage/divorce, single parenthood, lack of emotional support, and even environmental reasons. All of these reasons are valid and are part of your family's journey. Once you have made the decision to be one and done, or had the decision made for you, it's important to own this choice and move forward with confidence.

One and Done—by Choice

Many only-child families consider themselves to be OAD (one and done) by choice, and they are very happy with their family dynamic. While there is no data on the percentage of families who are one and done by choice—compared to one and done, not by choice—when I think about the many only-child families I personally know, most fall into the one and done by choice group. These parents have made the affirmative choice to have a single child and are thrilled with their decision. These families are confident in their choice, and don't spend much time worrying about the negatives of having an only child. They also seem to be the happiest and least stressed out, and have the best work/life balance of all the families in my social circle.

These families made an active decision to have an only child and celebrate in knowing that it's the best choice for their family. And there are many reasons why they made this choice. If you fall into this group, think about when you first realized that having a single child was the best choice for your family. Did you already know you wanted an only before you got married? Did you and your spouse agree on this family size before getting pregnant? Or did you decide to become one and done after you had your child and experienced parenthood? Here is a list of common reasons why parents choose to have an only child. Do any of these reasons resonate with you?

- They want to give all their love, time, and resources to one child.
- They were an only child themselves, loved it, and wanted to create the same experience for their own child.
- They are not close with their own siblings and place a low value on the sibling relationship.
- Financially speaking, it makes the most sense for their family to have one child.

- They have a health issue that makes it more practical to have a single child.
- They have very little social support/lack of a village.
- They have a spouse who works very long hours or is unsupportive; thus, they are the main parent, so one child makes the most sense.
- They feel they can only handle one child.
- One child allows for the best work/life balance.
- They are a single parent and feel that one child is more manageable.
- Their housing situation works better for one child (small city apartment or condo).
- They prefer a calm, quiet home with less chaos.

One common reason why many one and done by choice families choose to have a single child is that they feel they can be the best parent to one child and would be stretched too thin with multiple children.

Alejandra from France felt this in many ways. She said that her desires to be a stay-at-home mom and provide her daughter with the best educational opportunities were the main reasons why she decided to have an only child. She explained, "When my daughter, Maya, was born, I tried to be an educated mom and respond to her needs. I wanted to put all my knowledge and patience into her so I could create a good person. I also worried that if I had another baby, it would bring more pressure to my mental health. I decided I wanted to stay home with my daughter [and] help her learn good social skills. She makes friends so easily and they attach so well to her."

Stretching yourself too thin can be a challenge physically and emotionally, but it can affect you financially as well. Raising a child is incredibly expensive. Recent data show that it costs $233,610 to raise a child from birth through age eighteen. Some parents might want to dedicate all their resources—time, love, education, and finances—to a single child in order to give them the best possible opportunities in life.

Alejandra continued, "Here in France, there is not as much opportunity for gifted kids, and we want to focus on her education, which is a lot of money." By focusing all their resources on their only child, parents are more likely to have extra money for lessons, extracurricular activities, sports, and summer camps—all of which can help foster their child's talents and interests.

Some parents decide that having one child works best for their family dynamic, their level of support, and the nature of their parenting village.

Keren, an Australian mom, made the decision to have an only child due to a lack of a local support system, as well as a daughter with a spirited temperament that resulted in an especially challenging infancy and toddler period. Experiences and realizations built upon each other until Keren and her husband decided that one child was best for their family.

"It was always our intention to have two children, as we each have one sibling. And quite simply, it's just the norm in our culture. My pregnancy was a breeze, but an induction due to a long pregnancy resulted in what I believe was an unnecessary emergency C-section. This experience was followed by six months of our daughter screaming in the car until she was almost blue in the face. This made life incredibly difficult, as we were an hour [away] from any major shopping centers and the majority of our friends and family. Then our daughter went from typical newborn sleep of three- to four-hour chunks to waking every thirty to sixty minutes to feed, all night long, which only improved when I weaned her at age three.

"All these issues, combined with no nearby help and a very spirited child who was intensely clingy and never napped, we decided by the time that she was two years old that we were OAD. We were so confident in our decision that we sold our large five-bedroom home and downsized into a much smaller three-bedroom home."

Perhaps you feel that your specific lifestyle is more conducive to having one child because you travel often, have a time-consuming hobby, prefer a tranquil home environment, or have a demanding career. These are all aspects that hold an important weight in the decision to be one and done.

Keren agreed when she said, "My partner and I have many hobbies, and as introverts, we desperately crave alone time, as well as quality time as a couple. Starting all over again with a newborn would only prolong our ability to do the things we need to be happy as individuals. We feel stretched enough as it is with one. We want to be the attentive, patient, loving, present parents that our daughter deserves, and we only have the capacity to do that with one child, so being OAD is the smartest decision for our family."

Besides a family's immediate needs, some parents may have chosen to have an only child based on personal experiences growing up. If you feel similarly and are in this category, you may have grown up in a family with a sibling or two but were never close as children or adults. Or perhaps you had rocky experiences with your sibling(s) that negatively colored your perception of the sibling bond. You might even be estranged from a sibling and feel you would have had a better childhood if you'd been an only.

Another situation might have been that during your childhood, your parents had to deal with the needs of multiple children pulling them in several different directions, and you craved more parental attention, thus contributing to your inclination to be a more involved parent with your one child.

Or perhaps you had one child and felt immediately fulfilled, knowing you don't need or want a second. Maybe your partner is adamant about having just one child, and you decided together that this was the best overall fit for your family. Alternatively, some parents of only children were only children themselves. You may have grown up as an only child and loved the experience, so you want the same for your child.

Different situations in life also affect the decision of family size. You may have started trying to have a child later in the childbearing years and decided that with advanced maternal age, being one and done is the best choice. Or you might have decided that adoption is the best path for your family and have adopted your only child. Some of you are single parents by choice, and one child might be the best option because of the many challenges involved in single parenting.

Jessica from Virginia, a queer single parent by choice, who is also one and done by choice, shared that she got pregnant with a sperm donation from her gay best friend and is raising their daughter by herself. "When I was twenty-five, I was unlucky in love, and my best friend and I made a pact that at some point if I wanted kids, he would donate to the cause. At thirty-five, I was still single and really wanted a kid. I felt I was running out of time, so I said, 'Let's do this' . . . and he said okay.

"We found a clinic . . . and I found out I have all sorts of issues that I didn't know about. It took six unsuccessful IUIs, then an egg retrieval and two miscarriages, then the third egg retrieval, which was my daughter. The whole process took four years. I had a complicated pregnancy and was lucky to have my child."

Another single mother by choice in Virginia, Rashmi, said that being a single mom with an only child can be challenging in a variety of ways, and so having one child was the best fit for her family. "I don't have the typical support system. . . . As a single parent, you're [your child's] entire world, so that's difficult. Without having a partner, I don't have someone else to be a sounding board, and that can be really challenging. It would be nice to have someone else to run ideas by so that you're not the only one making critical decisions. I can discuss some things with my parents, but there's a generational gap too.

"The day-to-day is . . . hard from a childcare standpoint. I'm fortunate that I have my parents living in the same household with me for childcare help. But during the [COVID-19] pandemic, it was especially challenging because I had no choice but to work, and with schools not being open, it was stressful. Then there is the financial aspect too, because as a single parent, *you're it* as far as finances go."

Families have a variety of reasons for why they decide to have an only child, but each reason is right for each family. It can be helpful to take time to reflect on the reasons why you chose to have an only child, and celebrate those reasons every day. When challenges arise and you question whether having a single child was, in fact, the right choice, looking back on your reasons can be helpful in reinforcing that you made the right decision for your family.

One and Done—Not by Choice

Other families consider themselves one and done, but not by choice. For them, the decision to have an only child was made for them, and this can come from a variety of circumstances. These parents may have originally wanted a larger family, but because of reasons such as secondary infertility, health issues, lack of spousal support, or advanced maternal age, were unable to have more children. They may struggle with feelings of inadequacy, shame, regret, and bitterness as they make the best of challenging circumstances. They love their only child, but at the same time grieve the loss of the larger family they always dreamed of.

If you fall into this group, think about how you felt when you realized you would be one and done, not by choice. Did you feel disbelief? Anger? Disappointment? How have you coped with these feelings? Here is a list of common reasons why parents become one and done, not by choice. Do any of these reasons match your situation?

- You struggled with secondary infertility and were unsuccessful in having a second child.
- You had a difficult pregnancy or delivery and were advised to not get pregnant again.
- You had a traumatic pregnancy or delivery and couldn't go through that process again.
- You have a health condition which would make pregnancy or delivery too risky.

- You have a mental health condition which would make raising another child too challenging.
- You had a miscarriage or stillbirth and don't want to go through that emotional pain again.
- You are of advanced maternal age and were unable to get pregnant again.
- Your spouse/partner changed his/her mind about having another child.
- Your spouse/partner is not an equal or involved parent, and one child is all you can handle.
- You got divorced and are not able to have a second child.
- You don't have any support system.
- You couldn't afford to have a second child.

Some couples have struggled with the pain of primary infertility for years, finally able to have one child, but then couldn't have any more. Or maybe they got pregnant easily the first time and struggled with secondary infertility, ultimately unsuccessful the second time around.

Other only child parents may have originally planned to have more children, but after a challenging pregnancy, realized that they didn't want to risk pregnancy complications again. And others may have had health issues that prevented them from becoming pregnant again, so now their family size is smaller than they originally pictured.

Rebekah from England said that it took her a long time to get to the point where she is accepting of her one and done, not by choice, status. She said, "I got pregnant with my daughter very quickly when I was twenty-nine. I had a good pregnancy, but she came early at thirty-three weeks. It was a very quick and sudden birth, and she was taken from me to the NICU. . . . It was quite traumatic.

"The next few weeks were a daze, and then we went home from the hospital. I always wanted [multiple] children, but that first year was hard. Harder than I would have thought. I have trauma in my background that I thought I had dealt with, [but] the emotional needs of a baby were massive, and I think I found that incredibly hard. It's on reflection that I can see I was probably a bit depressed, and that my own experiences of childhood meant that I became depleted quite quickly.

"Still, my partner and I spoke about having more children; however, there was always something holding me back, and I watched my friends have those seconds with a growing sense of wanting it, but not wanting it too. . . .

"As time goes by, I have slowly grown to the point of being accepting of one and done. . . . I think I would say I am 85 percent accepting of where I am at, but a year ago I would have said 60 percent, and a year before that, 20 percent. It has taken a long time to accept this position and see the beauty and benefit of being one and done. I am much more able to let that go than I ever was, and allow myself to have a little cry without that deep, deep searing pain. I think I realized I had to see this process as grief and allow it to take its course. When I had the realization that at whatever point you stop having kids you grieve a bit, knowing that even if I had another, I would go through a process of loss as they grew up, that really helped me weather the pain."

In Missouri, Erin had her own experience of a difficult pregnancy, then afterward was busy with her son's health complications. This made the decision for her to be one and done. Erin said that when she and her husband first found out they were pregnant, they were over the moon. She said, "I have PCOS (polycystic ovarian syndrome), and knew I didn't ovulate normally. I was taking my first round of Clomid, a drug commonly used to induce ovulation, and I got a positive test on the first round . . . something we were not expecting.

"Everything was going well until I was about fourteen weeks. [I] began having intense pelvic pain and was subsequently diagnosed with Pubic Symphysis Dysfunction. The Pubic Symphysis Dysfunction continued to get worse, and my sacroiliac joints started to move more than the typical person, causing almost unbearable pain. By the time we were starting to register for gifts for our baby shower, I was using a walker.

Soon after, I had to use a wheelchair to get around. I had to take a leave from my job, something I was not prepared to do.

"Every day was full of never-ending pain, and then migraines began to develop . . . and I was rushed to the hospital by ambulance one evening to make sure I was not having a stroke. I also started showing signs of an auto-inflammatory condition. . . . What was supposed to be one of the most wonderful times of my life was beginning to become a nightmare.

"By the time I was thirty-five weeks, I was in unbearable pain from all the maladies that only just began with my pregnancy. My blood pressure started to spike, and I was monitored for preeclampsia. At thirty-six weeks and two days, I was back at the hospital and the decision was made . . . to do a C-section the next morning. What we were hoping to avoid was now putting my life and the life of my unborn baby in jeopardy.

"My son was born the next morning. . . . Because he was almost four weeks premature, he was rushed to the NICU, because he was having trouble breathing. I was so worried about my brand new baby, the brand new baby that I didn't even get a chance to hold. In the recovery room after my C-section, all the other mothers were holding their babies, and I was lying there in agony.

"It was almost the next day before I was stable enough to visit the NICU to finally spend some time with my son. He was perfect and thriving. . . . When he was finally discharged from the NICU . . . I thought everything was fine and that our journey was finally on the right track. Boy, was I wrong.

"I ended up back in the hospital with a uterine infection about a week after I was discharged. Then one evening, my husband was changing the baby's diaper and noticed his stool had a red tinge to it. We called in the nurse that was caring for me, and [she] said it was indeed blood and to take him to the ER immediately. It was determined that he had necrotizing enterocolitis, [a serious gastrointestinal problem] . . . and he was immediately admitted to the hospital. I have never been so scared in my entire life. This little perfect person just arrived, and now his life [was] in jeopardy.

"He recovered by the grace of God, and we finally took him home after two weeks. My husband and I had been through so much in the last year, and we knew we could not do this again.

"I . . . was told that if we had another child that I could go through this whole ordeal again. As much as we knew we wanted more children, we knew that my body just could not go through this again. We knew we were so lucky to even have our son, so we decided to be one and done. Do I wonder about what it would be like with another child? Sure, but I know we made the best decision for us, for our family. I love having one child. It is a blessing!"

What families who have one child, not by choice, have in common is that they might feel sad and disappointed that they have a smaller family than they originally dreamed of. They might feel envious of friends who got pregnant easily with several children. They might feel left out when they're the only one at preschool drop-off or pick-up without a younger child in tow. These feelings can be challenging to process.

What can help is having a support network made up of other families who also have an only child. If you can't find a local, in-person support network, consider looking for one online. There are many only child groups on Facebook and other social media platforms that you can join and connect with other one and done families located all over the world. If you're finding that you need extra help to navigate this difficult journey, consider finding a therapist who can support you and help you process your feelings. These trying circumstances in life can be difficult, but with time and support, you *can* find peace in your situation.

A family with one child is very common in the media. Countless books, movies, and TV shows feature an only-child family. In fact, did you know that most superheroes are only children? Here are some examples in the media that depict families of all shapes and sizes raising an only child:

» Annie from *Annie*
» Bastian Bux from *The NeverEnding Story*
» Cher from *Clueless*
» Harry Potter and Hermione Granger from the *Harry Potter* series
» Peter Parker from *Spiderman*
» Hiccup from *How to Train Your Dragon*
» Moana from *Moana*
» Timothy Green from *The Odd Life of Timothy Green*
» Mary from *Three Men and a Baby* and *Three Men and a Little Lady*
» Punky Brewster from *Punky Brewster*
» Christopher Robin from *Winnie-the-Pooh*
» Coraline Jones from *Coraline*
» Nemo from *Finding Nemo*
» Charlie Bucket from *Charlie and the Chocolate Factory*
» Clark Kent from *Superman*
» Rory Gilmore from *Gilmore Girls*
» Anne Shirley from *Anne of Green Gables*

Sharing Your Story

If you're content with your decision to be one and done, you may love to tell your story, happy to share your journey. If you're one and done, not by choice, and are still processing your decision, it may be emotionally difficult and too painful to share your experiences with others, so you don't share it with many people.

Regardless of which group you're in, it can be helpful to reflect on your one and done journey. If sharing with others does not feel like an appealing idea at this time, or even if you've readily confided in others, it's helpful to think about how your experiences have shaped your family into the loving, supportive unit it is today. So ponder the *story of your family*, and consider the following questions to help you think about your parenting journey from new and different perspectives.

REFLECTION QUESTIONS

1. Reflect back to when you first started to think about having children. Did you know right away that you wanted one child, or did you envision yourself with a larger family? Did your vision change after having a child? If so, what do you think contributed to your change in perspective?

2. If you are one and done, not by choice, what feelings have come up for you as you process not having the family size you originally dreamed of? How have you coped with these feelings?

3. Have you shared your parenting journey with others? Have you found a community of other parents who have similar experiences?

4. Is raising one child harder or easier than you expected? What makes it easier or harder?

CHAPTER 2

Exploring the Benefits of Having (and Being) an Only Child

" **I** honestly wish more people would consider having only one child. There are so many advantages," said Beth of Georgia, a mother of an only child and an adult only herself. There are so many wonderful benefits in deciding to have an only child, both for the parent(s) and the child. More time to spend with your child, less stress overall, a quieter home, more time for your marriage, and more free time for yourself are just a few of the most common benefits. In addition, only children enjoy having their parents' attention all to themselves, not having to deal with sibling rivalry, and being able to do more activities. Having one child also ensures a better balance between work and family life.

Many families believe that having an only is the most ideal family size. Let's more deeply explore why having an only child is the best choice for many families.

Benefits for the Child

If you ask only children what they think about being onlies, most are highly enthusiastic about the experience. Because what's not to love? Only children get all their parents' attention—100 percent of the time— because they don't have to share Mom and/or Dad with another sibling. This is beneficial because when children feel that their parents are paying attention to them, supporting them, and spending quality one-on-one time with them, it strengthens their self-esteem and self-confidence, and helps them feel emotionally connected.

Only children also tend to have more opportunities and resources to pursue their interests and talents because their parents have more time and money to spend on a single child. Logistically, it's easier for parents to schedule around one child's interests and not have to divide their time between multiple children. The result is that only children usually get to do more activities of their choice and pursue their individual interests more often than kids with siblings do. Because their parents can focus all their financial resources on a single child, they often have more unique experiences, like specialty summer camps, private school, or extracurricular classes. They get the best of the best because all their parents' resources are utilized just for them, which can have long-lasting benefits into adulthood.

When I think back to my childhood of being an only, what stands out as one of the biggest benefits was being able to pursue any activity I wanted, which helped make me a well-rounded young person. My mother didn't mind driving me all over town to different activities because she only had one child's schedule to manage. In middle and high school, I did pretty much every extracurricular activity that my school offered because I was able to stay after school or on weekends for meetings and events. In the summers, I participated in different summer camps and volunteer opportunities. My friends who had multiple siblings were often frustrated that they were limited to one activity each because of the difficulty of coordinating multiple siblings' schedules.

If your child has special needs, another benefit of being an only child is that there will be more time to devote to your child's therapies and treatments, which can have tremendous benefits in helping your child make positive progress.

Danielle Peters, LMFT, a therapist in California specializing in emotionally supporting parents of kids who are neurodiverse and kids with special needs, said that one of the benefits of being an only child who has special needs is having one-on-one support from parents. "A child who has special needs has their parents' focused attention all on them. Their parents also have more time to go to IEP meetings and learn more about their child's disability, and they have more time to take their child to therapy and medical appointments. In a family with multiple children, those things also get done, but sometimes those things get put off or the parents are overwhelmed. Additionally, with one child, the parents' stress level is lower, so that benefits both the parents and the child."

Many only children feel comfortable around adults, because they are around grown-ups so much at home. This can lead to strong verbal skills and vocabularies (because they're primarily talking to parents), self-confidence in sharing their opinions and perspectives, and overall greater maturity than their peers.

Amy Weber, LCSW, is a licensed clinical social worker with a private practice in New York who specializes in therapy for children and their families. She noted that the only children she has worked with in her practice are very comfortable around adults, saying, "They are able to easily navigate different relationships with adults, and that's a really important skill—a skill other peers may not have. . . . Only children are used to relating to adults."

Weber said that this skill translates well to working with teachers in the middle and high school environment and, later, with co-workers in the workplace. "It has a great practical application because in middle and high school you have several teachers, you have a different teacher for different subjects, as well as coaches, and engaging with different adults and having that confidence around adults will allow only children to be more confident to raise their hand, be more comfortable going to office hours, and be better able to advocate for themselves and ask for help. The only children I've worked with in my practice have been incredibly creative, smart, funny, engaging, and really a pleasure to work with."

Another advantage of being an only child is that they get the entire spotlight. At the dinner table, everyone wants to hear about their day and their thoughts, and they don't have to share the stage with anyone else. They don't have to worry about their day-to-day experiences being compared to those of a sibling, which can lead to sibling rivalry when kids feel like they're being compared (because, invariably, one child feels they don't measure up to their sibling). Not having to share the spotlight can lead to only children having higher self-confidence and self-esteem.

Additionally, an only child inevitably receives more one-on-one time with a parent, which leads to closer relationships and can benefit kids through adulthood. That is a huge positive! I think about all the quality father/son time my son has with his dad, and how much he loves the time they spend together fishing, biking, skiing, and playing sports. Having this quality time together with a positive role model has really strengthened my son's self-confidence and has nurtured a strong father/son bond.

Some parents of multiple children don't have as much time or resources to spend individually with each child. It's more challenging for each sibling to spend quality one-on-one time with a parent, and kids can become resentful of other siblings who seem to get more time and attention. This is something I see often in my work as a mental health therapist. When children resent their siblings for getting more parental attention, it can cause long-lasting hurt feelings that can turn into deep rifts in adulthood.

Children thrive when they receive ample, individual time with a parent. Only children get to spend as much exclusive, quality time with their parents as they need. Many onlies have extremely close relationships with each parent, while some children with siblings don't have the same opportunity to spend as much one-on-one time with their parents. As a result, one could argue that only children tend to have closer relationships with their parents. Our onlies are extremely lucky in this regard!

This one-on-one time also allows parents to be more responsive to their child's needs, strengthening the relationship between parents and child in a different way. When you're able to focus on just one child, not being pulled in multiple directions, you have the energy to give more time and undivided attention to your child.

Keren in Australia believes that having only one child allows you to parent more responsively, as you do not need to divide your time or attention among multiple children. "If we had had a second child . . . I would never have had the energy or patience to breastfeed my daughter to three years old, or bedshare with her. I don't believe I could have been the calm, gentle, responsive parent that I am . . . and I certainly don't believe we would have the strong bond that we share now."

Another benefit of being an only child is that there's plenty of time for onlies to explore their interests and hobbies because they have a lot of time to themselves. Without siblings in the home to keep them company, when a parent is unavailable, only children usually spend time alone. While many people equate being alone with being lonely, there's actually a distinct difference between loneliness and solitude. "Solitude" is when you're alone, but you're enjoying your own company; whereas "loneliness" is when you feel alone and isolated, even if you're surrounded by others. When you're feeling lonely, you want to connect emotionally with others, but are unable to. Many only children enjoy their solitude and spend their time alone engaged in various creative pursuits or use the opportunity for introspection and self-growth.

The alone time onlies experience is not necessarily a lonely time because they learn to make the most of it and find productive and creative ways to keep themselves busy or entertained. Only children learn to play by themselves very early in life and become experts at entertaining themselves. When I think about my own childhood, where I spent many hours in my room creating all sorts of imaginative stories, I didn't find that to be a lonely time. I made the most of my time alone and truly credit it to honing my creativity. My son can play alone for hours, which has really nurtured his imagination and allowed him lots of time to strengthen new skills, like building incredible structures out of LEGOs. And that kind of creativity can be a huge benefit to only children as they grow up because it can lead to them becoming extraordinarily creative and innovative thinkers.

This time to one's self can also teach kids self-reliance and resourcefulness, which are helpful, positive traits that will benefit them in the future. Only children often grow into self-sufficient adults who usually do not mind being alone because they get so much practice with it as children. Being comfortable with solitude is an important life skill, and as an adult, it allows you to be satisfied with just yourself for company, and you can do things like comfortably sit alone in a restaurant with a book and not feel sad or lonely.

What about adult only children? How do they feel about their childhoods growing up as onlies? Most of the adult only children I spoke with for this book have very positive experiences of their childhoods.

Nikki is an adult only child from Minnesota. She said that the best thing about being an only child was the flexibility of being able to do the things she wanted and having space and time to herself when she needed it. "I am also extremely grateful for the financial benefits of having been raised as an only—no college debt and the ability to enroll in the activities I desired. I never thought that I would end up choosing to have an only, but after my daughter was born, I quickly realized that I wanted to devote all of my love, time, and patience to her."

Danielle is an adult only child from Florida who also doesn't mind being an only child. She said, "My parents divorced when I was only two, and I think that was a big part of me being an only. But I always had a good relationship with them both growing up, and even now. I'd say my childhood was good and perfectly normal. I would have liked to have not split time between my parents, but other than that, no real complaints. As for traditions, my mom was able to take me on vacations more often than my friends went on. We did a lot of cruises, which I fell in love with, so I hope to take my son on a ton as he gets older. Something my mom did a lot was let me bring a friend on trips we went on, and I loved that. If possible, I'll let my son do the same."

As you can see, the benefits to a child of being an only are tremendous. The majority of only children grow up to be well-adjusted, well-rounded, and resourceful adults, lucky to have had such special childhoods that taught them so many valuable life skills, along with close relationships with their parents.

Benefits for the Parents

Having an only child also has many benefits for the parents. Did you know that a research study in the journal *Demography* (2016) recently found that the happiest and most satisfied moms have just one child? A second study found that having their first child makes both parents happier; however, when women have a second child, their overall life satisfaction and well-being goes down. Other research studies have also found that having just one child seems to be the ideal number for overall life satisfaction among moms. Why might this be?

Having one child means you get to be a parent and experience all that parenting has to offer, but you don't have the additional stress and chaos that comes with having multiple children. In my work as a mental health therapist, I have found that parents, and mothers in particular, experience more stress when they have their second child.

Some moms complain that there is very little downtime once they have multiple children, which can lead to overwhelming exhaustion, especially if their partner isn't stepping up. If one parent is shouldering the lion's share of parenting responsibilities, and the other parent is doing little to nothing, this can lead to burnout and resentment over time. This is especially the case when both spouses/partners work full-time and there is very little free time. Parents' stress levels tend to rise, and the balance between work, life, and family starts to topple. Some parents in this situation wish they had stopped at one child, when their lives were less stressful and when they didn't feel so pulled in multiple directions.

Let's face it—parenting can be completely overwhelming! Some parents feel drained from having just one child. Parenting is very hard work, and if you're overwhelmed, you may not be able to be the parent you want to be. Some parents feel that one child is all they can handle, especially if they don't have much support from their spouse or family. Having one child really does allow you to experience all the meaningful aspects of parenting without the added stress that comes from having multiple children.

Jessica from Virginia said that she is the only one in her network of friends and family who has an only child. "I do not have friends or family who also have only children, most have two to three kids. I hear a lot of the struggles of my friends with multiple children—finances, marriage, even the concept of college is upsetting for them. Then I think to myself, 'it's great that I only have one. We are lucky that I only have to pay for one daycare, plan for one college tuition, pay for one set of activities and the logistics of that.'"

With only one child, you get to experience every milestone of parenthood without being pulled in multiple directions. There's enough time to be an involved parent, nurture your marriage, take care of yourself, and have a good work/life/family balance.

The concept of having better work/life/family balance overall when you have one child is another major reason many families choose to have an only. And it's easy to see why. If you're like many working parents, you feel crunched for time every minute of every day. When you add in caring for your child—plus necessary household chores, errands, and appointments, not to mention recovering from the long work-day—you've probably found that there isn't much time left for family or hobbies. Having a better work/life/family balance is something that I certainly appreciate now that we are definitely one and done. Both my husband and I are able to work, have quality family time, attend our son's school events/programs and sports games, nurture our marriage, participate in a few hobbies, and still have some free time left over. It can be exhausting to work *and* have a fulfilling family life, but it's more achievable when you have one child.

Keren in Australia said that having only one child meant the best possible balance for her family. "We can tag-team, allowing the other parent some free time to pursue their own hobbies, or simply for self-care activities. Having that time to 'fill our cups' means we are not as stressed out, resentful, or tired. We have the energy to give our daughter quality family and on-on-one time, and the ability to deal with any misbehavior with patience and care, rather than resorting to yelling or punishments. There is also the added benefit of having more money to set aside for holidays, team sports, education, and more."

Nikki from Minnesota, who is an only child raising an only child, said that growing up as an only child felt very natural, as though it was the best choice for her parents. "Both of my parents had demanding careers, and my dad would not have been able to give me nearly the love and attention I received had they had another. My mom was very focused on her career and had little, if nothing, left to give when she was not working. That being said, I did truly enjoy being an only and feel like it helped shape me into the person I am today."

Coordinating schedules is another part of family life, and when you have multiple kids, it's much more difficult to do than when it's just for one child. These days, with many kids participating in several activities each, there can be a lot to coordinate, which means a lot of driving around to activities and lessons, as well as juggling multiple commitments. This can be stressful for parents who need to shuffle through and organize multiple kids' schedules. Additionally, if your child has special needs, there can be a lot of additional appointments and therapies. But if you just have one child, it's much more straightforward to coordinate the logistics of all your child's activities, appointments, playdates, and birthday parties.

My son does a few extracurricular activities, some on the week-nights and some on weekends. Not to mention the birthday parties, school events, and playdates that also fill up the calendar. It would be a lot harder to coordinate all the logistics if I had another child who was also doing similar activities, requiring me to be in two places at once. There's just more flexibility in your schedule when you have an only. Also, you and your spouse/partner can make sure to be at all your child's games or events without having to split up, where one parent goes with one child and the other goes with another.

When you have one child, there's also more time for you! Parents of onlies generally have more time to themselves than parents of mul-tiple children. Without additional children to care for, when you do have free time and your only is at school or engaged in her own play, you can choose to spend it however you'd like. What will you do with that time? Will you finally write your novel, learn how to paint, take up yoga, or become an expert in gardening? You can spend that time on your personal development, which helps to make you a more well-rounded person, as well as a more fulfilled individual.

This additional time gives you the opportunity to focus on your own goals and projects. And your child gets a happy, fulfilled parent who is modeling inspiring goal-setting behavior. When your child sees you working to achieve your own goals, he or she will also be motivated to work on his or her own goals and dreams too.

Kristie from California said that having one child will allow her to accomplish all of her career goals. "I want to get my master's degree. I feel like with one child, I would be able to raise my child and do everything I need to do to support his growth. I don't want to put my goals aside to have another and try to do that balancing act. I want to continue on with my education, have a child, and have my own life too."

You'll also have more time for self-care with an only. Self-care is extremely important for parents, no matter how many children they have, because without self-care, we burn out quickly and can't parent as effectively. Moms are often so busy taking care of everyone else and shouldering the brunt of the housework and schedule coordination that they frequently feel overwhelmed and exhausted. Regular self-care helps you focus on your own well-being and feel more balanced.

There are so many ways to engage in self-care routines, and even as little as fifteen minutes a day of focusing on your needs alone can make such a difference. In the evenings, after your only is in bed, you might have some time to yourself to take a bubble bath, read, do yoga, bake, or do a mini spa at home. These self-care routines can help you feel well taken care of and centered, enhancing your overall well-being.

Also in the realm of self-care, when you have one child, you get your normal sleep schedule back sooner. I remember how rough it was when my son was having multiple night wakeups between birth and around age three. I was always exhausted from waking up multiple times a night to tend to him. When you have one child and get through the nightly wake-up stage, you get your sleep schedule back sooner, and you will feel much more refreshed during the day. As someone who doesn't do well on minimal sleep, I think it would be very challenging and exhausting to go through many years of continuous nightly wake-ups with multiple children.

There are also little pockets of time here and there that you can claim for yourself when your child is busy with playdates or other activities. The nice things about these little pockets of time is that you can get a lot done in these small chunks, which add up to increased productivity for you. Parents of multiple children usually don't have this luxury because they are usually busy with the other child or children. When your child is old enough to participate in activities independently, you'll have time to yourself to use however you'd like while they're at the activity.

For example, I loved having an hour to read a book or catch up on emails while my son was having his own fun at soccer or swim class. I could watch him do his activity, but also have some free time to myself to accomplish some things on my to-do list. It was a small, but helpful, weekly pocket of time that helped me feel refreshed during a busy day. In the waiting area of the activity, I would see other moms trying to entertain a sibling or two, who many times looked fussy or bored and didn't want to be waiting for their brother or sister to finish up. I was grateful for those quiet moments all to myself!

When your child is old enough for drop-off playdates, parties, and sleepovers, you'll have even more time to yourself. Having an extra two hours to run errands or work on your novel while your child is happily playing at a friend's house is wonderful. Some families arrange their weekends so that on a Saturday, one parent watches the child for a few hours while the other parent gets some time to themselves. Then they switch on Sundays. This is something that is much more challenging for families with multiple children to accomplish because it's harder for one parent to watch multiple kids while the other parent has leisure time.

My husband and I worked it out so we each get a few hours to ourselves on the weekends to sleep in and do whatever we want—he takes Saturday mornings and I take Sunday mornings. Then we do things all together as a family for the rest of the day. This gives us a great balance between family time and alone time.

You also have more time for personal hobbies when you have one child, which goes along with self-care. Hobbies are important, and they help you grow and become proficient in something that's meaningful to you. With one child, parents are more easily able to give each other the time needed to enjoy their hobbies.

It's also beneficial to involve your child in your hobby. For instance, if you like art, you could work on art projects with your child. This can become one-on-one time you spend together while teaching your child the importance of self-care and the fun in working to achieve or create something. A win-win for everyone!

With an only, you also have more time to spend with your own friends because it's easier for your spouse/partner to watch one child while you go out. Some moms with multiple kids seem to have a harder time leaving them with their partner/spouse while they have a night to themselves or out with friends. (Probably because they think it's unfair to leave their spouse to handle all the kids while they are out having fun.) But it's easier to get away with just one, whether it's for a ladies' or gents' night out, or a weekend away with your college friends. If friendships are important to you, having this time to spend with friends can enhance your overall well-being.

For introverts who need a lot of alone time to recharge, having one child may be a better choice. I've heard from friends with multiple children that there really isn't any downtime because one child always needs something. That might be tough for introverts to manage, because without downtime to recharge, introverts can burn out quickly. Introverts thrive on having an only-child family dynamic because it allows for plenty of quiet moments to themselves.

Having a quieter, less chaotic home can be the result of having an only child. Now some of us do have only children who seem to have the energy level of several kids combined. Your child may be rambunctious and spirited, constantly talking, running, and keeping you on your toes. But in general, a home is more chaotic the more kids you have. Some of us do much better with less chaos and more quiet, especially if you are someone who needs extra time to recharge. When you need more mental space and time alone, you will find more of those opportunities to enjoy that kind of solitary time when you have a single child.

You also will have more opportunities to nurture your marriage or relationship when you have an only. Parents with multiple kids are often exhausted because every ounce of their energy goes to the kids. When you're that drained, there's often little left over to sustain your marriage. But with an only, you have more time and energy to focus on your relationship, which is vital to keeping it strong and healthy.

A strong partnership is the backbone of a family. As a therapist, I often see clients who don't nurture their relationship after they have a child. They may find that they become distant from their spouse or partner or don't have much in common anymore, and that can lead to problems within a partnership. But putting in the effort to spend time with your spouse or partner, as just the two of you on a regular basis, goes a long way toward keeping your relationship healthy.

Jennifer Sotolongo, LMHC, a maternal mental health therapist in Florida, said that having one child can have many positive benefits for a marriage. In her counseling practice, she finds that having one child creates much less stress on marriages. She points out that when it comes to childcare or travel, it's much easier for a married couple to count on family to help out with an only child versus multiple children.

"The mothers I see with multiple children often say that the support system they had back when they had one child no longer shows up for them once they have multiple children. It is very common to see both parents reporting less stress when they only have one child to think about, one child to worry about, and one child to plan a future for. Planning a future for a child is often what creates the most stress for many parents, in terms of finances and time. Parents do report less stress when there's only one child to take care of."

Along with prioritizing time to nurture your relationship, it can be challenging (and expensive) to find a babysitter. If you don't have the luxury of having local family who can watch your child while you and your spouse have a date night, it can feel like a huge undertaking to find a sitter you trust who is also reliable; however, with some creativity, you and your spouse can find opportunities to spend quality time together that doesn't involve finding a sitter for a weekend date night. Take advantage of the opportunities when your child is engaged elsewhere. For example, when your child is over at a friend's house, at an extra-curricular activity, or asleep for the night, you and your spouse/partner can spend those moments in quality time together. Use these pockets of time when your child is occupied with something else to strengthen your marriage.

For example, when my son was at a friend's house on a Saturday morning, my husband and I would take that time to go out for brunch. Or if we both had the same day off, we would do day dates when my son was at school. We would get takeout and eat at a local park, go for a hike, or take a walk around a lake. And we'd have the entire day together—no sitter needed because our son was at school. Taking this time for our marriage was helpful and kept our marriage going strong.

Some lucky families have grandparents who live nearby and are will-ing to take their grandchild overnight for occasional sleepovers. I have a few friends with onlies whose local grandparents take the child over-night once every weekend. They get an automatic weekly date night, which must be a great benefit to their marriage. Other friends have grandparents who are willing to watch their child for a whole weekend, or even an entire week, while they go out of town and have a child-free vacation with their spouse. They are certainly lucky to be able to do this!

Parenting can be stressful—it's certainly been so for parents during the COVID-19 pandemic with virtual school, quarantines, fewer play-dates and activities, and the constant fear of their family contracting the virus. As a therapist, I see so many parents who have severe decision fatigue from having to weigh every minor decision with the risk of their family getting sick. Over time, this constant vigilance and the stress it causes can take its toll on our physical and mental well-being.

In normal day-to-day life, it's stressful when kids are sick, when they have a health concern, when they're misbehaving, when they're having problems at school or with friends—the list goes on and on. Kids can be needy and demanding, and they often do things that frazzle parents, like staying out too late, not listening, and not doing what they're supposed to. When you multiply that stress by multiple kids, it's easy to see why many parents are stressed out and overwhelmed all the time. When you just have one child, you have lower stress than you would with multiple kids. And less stress is a positive in general!

Another advantage to having an only child is that you only go through the hard parts of childhood once. There are definitely very challenging parts of growing up. Some aspects of parenting are tedious and unpleasant for many people, such as the terrible twos, teething, little kids who get sick all the time, sleep regressions, and the rebellious teen years. As the parent of an only child, you experience those difficult aspects just like all parents, but having to go through them only once can be a blessing!

Another benefit of having one child is that you don't have to worry about sibling issues, such as favoritism, which can make things easier on parents. Sibling favoritism can be a contentious issue among siblings, with lasting effects even decades later. Sometimes parents show favoritism consciously or unconsciously. If one child truly believes that Mom or Dad favors another sibling, it can have major repercussions on that child's self-esteem and can wreck their relationship with their siblings, sometimes for years. Many adults with siblings remember feeling that their mom or dad liked the other sibling better, which caused friction within the family. When you have an only, you don't have to worry about this issue because your child always knows that he or she is your favorite!

Having an only child also means that you don't have to deal with sibling rivalry or break up sibling fights. Many adults with siblings remember fighting with their brother or sister as one of the defining moments of their childhood—your brother slamming your door so

hard that it cracked, or your sister always taking your favorite
toys—these things can cause a
lot of stress for kids growing up.
While parents always hope that
their kids will have a harmonious
relationship, sometimes, despite
the best efforts made on all ends,
siblings just don't get along. And it
can cause tremendous stress in the
home. With an only, you can have
a quieter, more peaceful home
without having to deal with the
stress of siblings arguing.

What do you call your one
and done family? There are
many terms to describe an
only-child family. Do any of
these resonate with you?

» One and done
» Triangle family
» One and done by choice
» One and done, not by choice
» Single child family
» Only-child family

Having only one child can also be a more economical choice.
Everyone knows that raising a child is expensive! The most recent sta-
tistic from the US Department of Agriculture is that it costs $233,610
to raise a child born in 2015 from birth through age eighteen. That is a
staggering amount of money—and that doesn't even include the cost of
college! Many families simply can't afford to raise multiple kids. When
you think about the clothes, toys, food, extracurriculars, healthcare,
lessons, private school (if applicable), vacations, college, etc., and you
multiply all that by multiple kids, you can see why it's more economical
to have just one child.

Conclusion

As this chapter has described, there are countless benefits of having and
being an only child, for both the parents and the child themselves. So
if, like many parents of onlies, you have wondered from time to time
whether your child will be happy as an only or whether you've made the

right choice, rest assured that for most families, the positives of having a single child far outweigh the drawbacks.

REFLECTION QUESTIONS

1. Reflect back to when you first decided to have one child. Did you know right away that having one child was the right fit for your family, or did you spend some time thinking about the benefits of having a single child? Did your thoughts about the benefits of having an only change after becoming a parent?

2. Some parents like to make a list of all the positives of having one child, which they reflect back on during times when they question whether their decision to have an only was the right one. Which benefits would be on your list? Write them down to refer to when you need the encouragement.

3. Consider asking your child (if old enough) what he thinks are the benefits of being an only child. His answers may surprise you! He may come up with some positives that you hadn't considered!

Section II:
Dealing with Issues
Common to Only-Child
Families

CHAPTER 3

Fact or Fiction: Common Stigmas about Only Children

We've all heard the detrimental, cliché stereotypes: only children are lonely, spoiled, maladjusted, and do not share well with other children. You've probably heard others, like only children have behavioral issues, poor social skills, don't play well with other kids, and are bossy. Society at large seems to view having *just* one child as an inadequate choice. Many people will ask you in disbelief, "How can you have just one?" You might have been on the receiving end of some of these stereotypes, either as a parent or as an only child yourself.

These stereotypes about onlies are harmful, sweeping generalizations about an entire demographic of children, and can make parents feel anxious, guilty, and constantly on guard. We, as these parents, are unfortunately on the receiving end of many of these outdated and damaging beliefs about onlies, but we can also do our part to debunk these harmful stereotypes whenever we hear them.

If you've met one only child, you've met *one* only child—every child is different and has their own unique set of characteristics, quirks, hopes, and dreams. Children's personality types and qualities are a combination of nature and nurture, and are not determined by the number of siblings they have. How they're raised and the relationship with their parents is much more of a determinant of their personality traits than whether or not they have a sibling.

Nikki from Minnesota echoes this sentiment. She is an only raising an only, and said that she definitely had trouble sharing her space as a child and young adult. "My daughter, on the other hand, shows none of these characteristics. I think parenting is the determining factor in this, much more than birth order or sibling presence."

Only-child families are becoming more and more common, while larger families have usually been the norm. Families with one child are currently the largest growing family unit in the United States. Around 22 percent of all US families have one child, according to Pew Research Center data, and many of these families are concentrated in the largest US cities like New York, Los Angeles, and Seattle. In New York City, 30 percent of families have an only child. These percentages will grow in the next decade as more families consider the many benefits of having a single child.

Global trends also show that families internationally are increasingly embracing having just one child. In the European Union, 47 percent of families have an only child, with Portugal being the country with the most only children. In Canada, 38 percent of families have an only child, and in the UK, it's at 42 percent. With these growth trends in the OAD family, you would think that society would drop the outdated stereotypes of onlies and more warmly embrace the only-child family. However, this seems to be happening at a snail's pace.

Danielle from Florida is an adult only child. She has heard stereotypes of only children, both as an only child herself and as a parent. "I've heard a lot of people say only children are spoiled and lonely, but that wasn't the case for me. . . . So far, we've had some family members make comments that we should have another kid to give our son a sibling so he's not lonely. . . . We're both only children, so we can say we weren't lonely, and we've turned out fine. If they still insist on it or say we'll change our minds, I usually just shrug it off and say, 'Who knows.'"

Keren in Australia said, "I think the greatest challenge of raising an only child is dealing with the guilt. Society has deemed it unacceptable to have 'just one' child. Whenever we have shared that we are OAD, we have been met with negativity. Repeatedly hearing the stereotypes about only children has often made me question whether we are doing the right thing by our daughter. While we have very legitimate and practical reasons for being OAD, and we have zero yearning for another child, it's the idea that we are doing her a disservice by not giving her a sibling that continues to weigh on my mind."

I don't know about you, but I have certainly had random strangers make hurtful judgments about my family size—often at the grocery store or at restaurants. A person in line at the grocery store might ask if my child has siblings, and when I say no, they will often comment that it's unfair of parents to deprive their child of the sibling experience, or that an only child is always going to grow up spoiled. They might also comment that every child needs a sibling, or that an only child is destined to always be alone. They might imply that having *just* one is inadequate, saying things like, "I could never have just one" or "How can you have just one?" These comments are rude and judgmental, and I've always wondered how many only children the person making these negative statements actually knows.

What can you do if you're on the receiving end of these kinds of hurtful comments? How can you respond if someone tells you that your only is doomed to grow up spoiled, selfish, or socially awkward?

Amy Weber, LCSW, a licensed clinical social worker in New York who specializes in therapy for children and their families, believes that parents can cope with these types of comments by being armed with research that shows only children do not have behavioral problems more often than children with siblings do. She said, "There's a way to say this to a teacher or principal or coach or anyone you're encountering. You can say, 'The science says that this is not true, but I'd love to do some problem-solving with you around what's going on in the classroom,' and letting them know that you're on their team, but you're not going to put up with those comments."

You may wonder if teachers or therapists are able to determine who is an only child and who has siblings solely based on personality or behavior. The answer is no! Amy Weber, LCSW, provides some insight on this question. Weber said that in her therapy work with children, she does not notice any significant differences between only children and children with siblings. While she is aware of the common stereotypes of only children, she finds that in her practice, only children don't struggle with those issues any more or less than children who have siblings do.

Today many people, across a variety of countries and cultures, unfortunately carry negative preconceptions about only children. And a family with two children is still seen as the ideal family size. But many researchers have demonstrated that only children actually exceed their peers with siblings in many areas, including intellectual abilities, leadership, and social skills. So the good news is that being an only child is actually a huge advantage in many areas!

In light of this research, it's puzzling why today so many people still attribute negative qualities to only children. Where did the idea even start? Back in the late 1800s, a well-known psychologist named Granville Stanley Hall started the idea that only children are lonely, deficient, inadequate, and have poor social skills, all based on a study he supervised in 1896 called "Of Peculiar and Exceptional Children."

Hall said that "being an only child is a disease in itself." Unfortunately, this negative view of only children stuck stuck and was mentioned over and over again in books, newspapers, and journal articles. People seemed to latch on to the idea that there was something fundamentally wrong with having and being an only child. And ever since then, even today, only children have had to grapple with a plethora of unfair stereotypes.

Sarah from England, who is an adult only child herself, said that she was on the receiving end of some only child stereotypes when she was growing up. "I've had a few people ask me when I was at school if I was spoiled when I told them I was an only." She continued that the only comments she hears now are from her mother-in-law. "She voiced her concern that it would be hard on my daughter when my husband and I are old, as she'll be the only one to care for us with no other siblings to help share the burden. But I just brushed it off and said that hopefully she'll be away living her life and we'll pack ourselves off to a home."

One would think that as more families decide to have a single child, the negative attitudes around only children would change for the better. Hopefully with time, these attitudes will fade into obscurity. It's unfortunate, however, that society still harbors these damaging stereotypes that make only-child families feel inadequate and insecure.

Kristie from California believes there is a stigma to having an only child. Kristie has felt considerable pressure from multiple people when they ask, "Why aren't you having another one?" or "What do you mean that he won't have a sibling? That's so sad!" She continued, "I had my child when I was thirty-four . . . when we were more established. Becoming a new parent when you're older, you feel this pressure to have another one in two years. We thought we were going to have two, but decided we're not going to do it. People try to guilt you into having another child, but why is having one not okay?"

Next we will discuss the most common stereotypes of only children and how you can turn each one into something positive.

Stigma #1: Only Children are Spoiled

While it's true that many only children are given a lot of great material things because the family budget is less stretched out, that doesn't mean that only children are spoiled. There's a big difference between being spoiled, which means getting everything you want and being ungrateful for it, versus being provided with many resources and appreciating all that you have.

Being spoiled means that a child expects to get whatever they want, whenever they want, and has no gratitude for what they get. Think of the "spoiled brat" concept, where a child gets exactly what they want and still asks for more. An image that comes to mind is Veruca Salt in *Charlie and the Chocolate Factory*. I imagine that very few parents of only children give in to their children's every whim and allow them to have everything they want. Instead, most reasonable parents provide everything their child needs, like food, clothing, education, and shelter, and some of what their child wants, like toys, video games, and vacations. Reasonable parents who are raising appreciative children also likely emphasize gratitude so that their child appreciates what they do receive.

If you think your child might be "spoiled" and you want to turn things around, then consider having your child work for the things they get more often. For example, think about how often your child gets new toys. If it's every week and they're starting to expect a new toy often, you might consider cutting back or reserving a new toy as an occasional reward for a job well done at school or with household chores.

If your child is adamant that they want a certain toy, let them know that they may get that toy for a holiday or birthday rather than right away, or they can earn the toy for doing a good job with schoolwork or chores around the house. If your child is older, they can earn money from an allowance and put that toward a treat. When a child earns something they want through their own hard work, they tend to value it more, and this reinforces the idea of working hard for a tangible benefit.

Only children are no more or less spoiled than other children with siblings. When children are raised to have reasonable expectations, express gratitude for what they receive, do chores around the house to earn money for things they want, and understand the value of volunteering and giving back to others, they grow up to be well-adjusted children.

Stigma #2: Only Children Don't Know How to Share

So many parents of only children hear this stigma, especially in the early childhood years. They hear that "little Timmy doesn't like to share his toys with anyone; it must be because he's an only child." People seem to automatically assume that when you grow up without siblings around, you don't have any opportunity to learn valuable social skills, like how to share toys and possessions with others. Many people hold the stigma that only children are territorial about their things and that they don't want others using their stuff.

While it's true that only children grow up in a house where they get their toys and games to themselves most of the time, they still have many other valuable opportunities to practice the art of sharing. Very few children are raised in an isolated bubble where they don't interact with anyone at all. The majority of only children are well socialized and interact with other children often at school, at playdates and when having friends over, when participating in extracurricular activities, and when playing with their parents at home, so they learn important social skills like sharing through these avenues.

What can you do if you feel that your child needs some work on their sharing skills? You can set up more playdates so your child gets additional practice interacting and sharing with peers, or sign them up for extracurricular activities where they can practice these skills with other kids. A class like robotics, where kids work together to build collaborative structures, an art class where kids need to share materials, or even a regular playgroup can all be great opportunities for kids to improve their sharing skills.

If your child is hesitant about other kids coming over and playing with their toys, you might even set special or prized toys aside at play-dates so that your child is more comfortable sharing regular toys with other kids. For example, before playdates, I ask my son if there are any of his LEGO creations that he doesn't want other kids messing with, and I put those away in his closet. I figured this out after one disastrous playdate where another child started disassembling my son's prized LEGO creations (ones that took days to build), and he got very upset. After that, it was simpler to just put those special kinds of toys away.

Lastly, if you think your child could benefit from more practice sharing, consider enrolling them in a social skills group. School guidance counselors might have some recommendations, or you can look for counseling practices in your area that offer after-school or weekend social skills groups. Many social skills groups focus on sharing as one of the key skills they teach.

Stigma #3: Only Children Have Poor Social Skills

This is one of the most common stereotypes of only children, and one that bothers me the most. Similar to the inability to share, people often assume that when they're not raised with siblings, only children have poor social skills by default. What they don't realize is that only children aren't raised in complete seclusion.

Only children go to school and summer camp, do playdates, and participate in extracurricular activities, and they learn valuable social skills in these settings. Even just going to school provides a strong foundation for learning the most important social skills because kids learn from other kids. If they're homeschooled, only children usually have many social outlets where they can be with other kids, like homeschool groups, playdates, co-ops, and meetups. Our onlies learn social skills from being around other kids regularly, figuring out like every kid does how to navigate a social environment.

As long as your only child has plenty of opportunities to socialize with other kids, their social skills should be just fine. It is important, however, to make sure your child has lots of opportunities to socialize in early childhood. Recent research has shown that learning social skills early on is incredibly important. A study spanning two decades found that kids who have strong social skills in kindergarten are more likely to become successful adults. So if you are worried about your child's social skills development, or if you feel they need a bit more practice, focus on helping your child gain those vital social-emotional skills that will be extremely important for her long-term well-being.

To start, think about all the ways they can socialize with other kids outside of school. Consider signing them up for some social extracurricular activities after school, like a team sport or dance class, where they will see the same kids long-term and interact with them frequently. Are there neighborhood kids your child can play with? Are there opportunities for him to socialize through local moms' groups or parenting groups?

If your only has special needs, they might benefit from additional social skills practice, and there are usually many local social skills classes and camps that can be of help. Your pediatrician, therapist, or school may be able to recommend some wonderful resources for you.

Stigma #4: Only Children Don't Know How to Stand Up for Themselves

Since only children don't experience the rough and tumble childhoods of siblings fighting with them, taking their toys, pushing them around, and teasing them, many people think they will have difficulty standing up for themselves. They might feel that only children don't get enough practice with self-advocacy if they aren't growing up around siblings, so when they're faced with a child saying mean things to them or taking their lunch money, they will just stand there like a doormat because they don't know what to do or say.

This does not have to be the case for your child, however. The school environment, extracurricular activities, and even just running around on the playground with other kids are great ways for your child to learn self-advocacy skills and how to stand up for themselves.

If you notice your child doesn't seem to understand how to react to common childhood situations where another child says mean things or teases them, do some role-playing at home to teach them how they might be able to respond to such situations. You can come up with a few common situations that they're having difficulty responding to (such as another child teasing them or telling your child they're not allowed to play), and say to your child, "If another child says this, how can you respond? How would you handle the situation? What are some things you can say and do?" You can do this over and over until your child feels more confident.

You can also find board games and children's books that discuss problem-solving and decision-making skills, such as the *What Should Danny Do?* book series by Adir Levy and Ganit Levy, or the board game "What Should You Do? A Game of Consequences." Real-life examples in literature and the media can also help your child understand what to do when they encounter similar situations.

Reaching out to your child's teacher or school counselor can also be helpful if your child is having difficulty with mean kids or bullies at school. He or she can work with your child to more specifically address how to deal with bullies or stand up for themselves in the school environment.

If you feel your child could benefit from additional self-advocacy skills or problem-solving practice, a social skills group or meeting with a therapist might be helpful.

Stigma #5: Only Children Are Lonely

It's a common stereotype that all only children are lonely all the time, so naturally one of an only child's parents' greatest worries is that their child is chronically lonely. When people talk to you about why you should have more kids, usually the number one reason they give is because, without siblings, an only child is always going to be lonely. This stereotype annoys many only-child families who know this is definitely not the case!

Like all children, some onlies are lonely from time to time. But it would be a huge disservice to them to say that all only children are constantly lonely. Most only children have a full schedule where they interact with others for most of the day—they go to school, do extra-curricular activities, play sports, go on playdates, and hang out with kids in the neighborhood. And if they're not doing those things, they're often interacting or playing with parents. In other words, most only children are not sitting in their rooms and feeling all alone in the world. They are usually surrounded by people who care about them, including parents, grandparents, other extended family, teachers, classmates, and neighbors.

Occasionally I will hear my own son say that he's feeling lonely or that he would like some company. When he does say this, I make sure to spend time with him right then doing something he likes to do. If he says he's feeling lonely, I might also suggest we video call the grandparents, arrange a playdate with a friend, or even get out of the house and go somewhere where there are other kids, like a playground, because he can usually find someone there who wants to play. Just being around other kids can help a child who is feeling lonely.

There are plenty of things you can do to make sure your only feels well supported if they tend to mention feeling lonely often. Some ideas might include getting them a pet so they have regular companionship at home, making sure they're connecting with grandparents and extended family (over video calls, if needed), scheduling regular playdates or get-togethers with their friends, and enrolling them in social extracurricular activities, like a team sport. If your only is still battling feelings of loneliness after you've tried several of these ideas for a while, consider meeting with a therapist who might be able to offer some additional suggestions specific to your situation.

Stigma #6: Only Children Have "Only-Child Syndrome"

One type of stigma that many parents of only children hear about often is the dreaded "only-child syndrome." This isn't a real syndrome, but a made-up stigma about only children that only serves to paint them in a negative light and further the misguided idea that only children have poor social skills.

"Only-child syndrome" involves any kind of a conglomerate of negative, spoiled, entitled, or bad behavior in a child that others chalk up to being "an only child." So if your only is having behavioral problems at school, the teacher might call you and tell you that they are acting this way because of "only-child syndrome." Or if your child is having difficulty sharing on the playground, another parent might point out it's because of "only-child syndrome." It has become a catch-all phrase for any kind of behavioral or personality flaw that someone sees in your child. And this can be extremely frustrating!

How can you respond if someone makes a comment to you or your child about him having "only-child syndrome"? Because it's a made-up disorder, one thing you can do is explain that what the person is saying is an untrue stereotype of only children, and that it's both hurtful and unhelpful to make a generalization like that. You can put the person on the spot and say something like, "Wow, that was a very unkind statement (or broad generalization). What exactly did you mean by that?"

You can also try to educate the person about the fact that only children have the same blessings and challenges as all other children and shouldn't be subject to sweeping and hurtful generalizations. Educating someone about why a statement like that is both hurtful and offensive can, over time, help change minds and attitudes in your community to be more kind and accepting of all children.

Stigma #7: Only Children "Need" a Sibling

Many parents of onlies hear this one a lot, especially from random strangers in the grocery store. Usually the conversation starts out innocuously enough, but once they hear your child is an only, they start in with how your only "needs a sibling." If you ask why they "need" a sibling, the person will usually rattle off one of the aforementioned stereotypes about only children, like about how they needs a sibling because otherwise they will be lonely/not know how to share/be doomed to have deficient social skills forever.

"Here in France," Alejandra, the mother of an only child, said, "they still carry the old ideas that having numerous kids is the better way." While this stigma can come from people of all ages, Alejandra said that it's mainly the older generation who tend to voice this stereotype.

She continued, "I get comments often that my daughter is going to be lonely. I get asked that uncomfortable question, 'When will there be another one?' And people ask without knowing the pain and the stress you may carry. . . . Especially the older generation. . . . [They] come into the grocery store and tell my daughter, 'You need a brother or sister.' The older generation doesn't see an only child as a positive, but the newer generation does. . . . I see a lot of young families looking out for the future and having only one child."

If you are the recipient of this kind of statement, it can really sting. It presumes that only children are deficient in some way, like they are not complete unless they have a sibling. This idea that only children "need" a sibling devalues only children because it makes it seem like they're not good enough on their own. This kind of statement can also be very hurtful to parents who have been through the roller coaster of infertility and would have loved to have more children but were unable to. It can also make parents who experienced losses feel extreme sadness at this kind of insensitive comment because their child did have a sibling.

What many only children will tell you is that they're perfectly content being onlies and that they wouldn't have it any other way. In my work as a therapist, I have seen firsthand that a sibling is not needed for a happy family. And, in fact, I have seen time and time again how a negative sibling dynamic can be the cause of long-lasting emotional pain that can last into adulthood. Children thrive when they have a loving parent or guardian and feel loved for who they are. Having a sibling is not a requirement for a happy, well-adjusted childhood. When a parent is confident with their family dynamic and content with their family size, then they can better internalize the idea that one child is the perfect family size for them, and the child will grow to feel it as well.

REFLECTION QUESTIONS

1. Think about how only children are portrayed in movies, TV
    shows, and books. Can you think of a few examples of only
    children who are portrayed negatively (spoiled, ungrateful,
    etc.), and a few examples of only children who are portrayed
    positively (helpful, kind, compassionate, etc.)?

2. Think about the types of stereotypical only child comments
    you have heard so far in your parenting journey. How have
    you responded to these? How could you have responded bet-
    ter? And how can you make it a teaching moment to educate
    those making such comments?

3. Most only children will say that they feel lonely from time
    to time. How do you feel when your child says that they're
    lonely? What are some constructive ways you can respond to
    these comments in the future?

CHAPTER 4

The Challenges of Raising an Only Child

Have you ever had another parent say to you, "You've got such an easy life because you only have one child?" Many only child parents' biggest pet peeve is when others assume that one child automatically means an easy, stress-free life.

Sometimes one child can be as challenging as having three kids combined if your child is high-energy, spirited, and keeps you busy from the time they wake up to the minute they go to sleep. Perhaps your only has some special needs that make parenting more challenging. Or your child may want to play with you all day every day, which doesn't leave much time for you to work on your own projects and get things done around the house. Everyone's parenting experience is different, and it invalidates your experience as a parent when people make uninformed judgments based solely on your family size.

While stereotypes about only children are hurtful and dismissive, there are some real challenges of raising an only child that are unique to a smaller family. I have experience with these challenges firsthand from three different perspectives: from being an only child myself, from raising one, and from my work as a therapist. For example, many people erroneously believe that "having just one" is easier than having multiple children; however, as many parents of only children know, raising an only child can actually be more difficult in several ways, as we will explore throughout this chapter. While raising an only child is an incredible experience, it is important to be prepared for the challenges as well.

In this chapter, we will discuss the top ten common challenges of raising an only child (in no particular order) and the approaches you can take to help make your life just a little bit easier.

Challenge #1: They Always Want You to Be Their Playmate

One of the biggest challenges for parents of only children is that some only children always want *you* to be their playmate, which can be draining. Because there are no other kids to play with at home, some only children view their parents as their preferred playmate. They only want to play with Mom or Dad and may refuse to play independently.

Of course, it makes sense why some only children would want their parents to play with them all the time; they may find it lonely or boring to play by themselves, just as some adults find it lonely or boring to spend time alone. Because only children are around adults so often, they might come to prefer being with them rather than the unpredictability of playing with another child their age. Kids know that playing with Mom or Dad is drama-free because adults aren't going to try to cheat during a board game or snatch a toy away, the way other kids sometimes do. But having to be the cruise director for your child can become exhausting for parents who need to work from home or have other things to take care of around the house. Most parents simply can't devote *all* their time and attention to entertaining their child.

Rashmi in Virginia said that her daughter tends to prefer playing with her to other kids. "I'm often doing things with her that she would typically do with a sibling, like painting nails. Only children tend to gravitate towards adults rather than other kids because they feel more comfortable being with another adult [because] that's what they have at home."

But when your child says, "Mom, come play with me," for the tenth time that day, it can become frustrating to parents who want to spend plenty of quality time with their child but just don't have the bandwidth to play superheroes for two hours straight, or who need some time to themselves after a long workday. While some parents of onlies enjoy hours of imaginative play with their child, others don't remember how to play imaginatively or find it dull and tedious and would rather spend quality time with their child in other ways, like reading, cooking, or playing board games or sports. But in general, many parents of only children believe that playing independently is an important life skill that their child needs to learn. They want their child to know how to entertain themselves and believe that playing independently fosters important qualities like creativity, independence, and resourcefulness.

Interestingly, there seems to be a different parenting mindset in this generation compared to past generations. Some adult only children report that their parents rarely played with them and that they spent most of their childhoods playing alone. While in contrast, many of today's parents seem to feel that keeping their child entertained 24/7 with enriching activities is one of their main jobs.

Amy Weber, LCSW, a licensed clinical social worker in New York who specializes in therapy for children and their families, has noted a change in the parenting dynamic over the past two generations. She said, "There's been a pendulum shift in our parenting dynamic; we have shifted to be more involved parents—parents who want to give their children something they were missing when they were growing up. But like all pendulum shifts, you can take it too far, and sometimes we don't give our children a chance to be bored or lonely or problem-solve. We don't want them to feel sad or angry, and we try to fix the problem."

Weber said that the implications of this are that down the line, children are dependent on their parents to get anything done. "Their parents are organizing their work for them or doing their college applications, and the kids become helpless because they're unable to get started and solve a problem . . . and then they become people who can't get started on a project at work without hand-holding or can't work as part of a team."

Regardless of your parenting style or schedule, for the sake of your child's future, only children should develop the ability to play by themselves for those times you just can't manage it. They *can* learn to play independently, even if it's challenging for them at first. The following are a few tried-and-true ways to encourage your only to play alone.

One approach is to use a timer to encourage your child to play independently for small increments of time. Many kids respond positively to a timer for a variety of non-preferred tasks (like chores or homework) because it sets a clear end point for the activity. Try a very small chunk of time at first, perhaps just five minutes, which makes it less overwhelming. Set the timer and encourage your child to play alone until the buzzer rings. Makes sure to let your child know they're doing a great job while playing, as the praise will help build their confidence. Then gradually increase the time on the timer as they master playing alone for larger increments of time.

Another approach you can try is to play with your child for a specific amount of time, say about thirty minutes, and then say something like, "I've had so much fun playing with you, but now it's time for me to take care of some other things around the house (dishes, laundry, work, etc.). You can either help me unload the dishwasher or keep playing. Which would you rather do?" Usually your child will choose to keep playing!

Another related approach is to tell your child that you have ten minutes to get them started playing and then you have other work you need to do. Most likely, your child just needs that initial encouragement to get started and then will happily keep playing while you take care of other tasks. A child may be more willing to play independently if they're already feeling content with the quality time you have just spent with them.

If part of the challenge of playing alone is that your child doesn't like to be in a separate room from you, try doing your own work while your child plays in the same room. Sometimes just being together in the same room, even if doing different things, will encourage your child to play independently. That's one reason why many parents have their child's playroom or play space on the first floor near the kitchen and family room, as opposed to an upstairs space or the basement. Kids are sometimes more willing to play by themselves when they can see or hear a parent nearby.

Challenge #2: When They Demand Constant Attention

Another challenge of raising an only child that many parents struggle with is that some only children can be demanding of their parents' attention. Some onlies demand near-constant attention, which can wear down their parents after a while. What does this look like? A child might constantly interrupt parent conversations because they have something important to tell you. Or a child might refuse to complete homework, do a puzzle, or clean up unless a parent is right there to help them. At dinner time, the child might talk non-stop and get upset if the parents try to have a conversation with each other. In the evenings, the child might insist on playing with one parent and not let the parents have time to spend together.

There can be several reasons for this kind of needy behavior. A child might behave like this because they are not getting the attention they need, and they believe that by constantly clamoring for attention, they will finally get the attention they want. Or, if there is a recent disruption in the home, like a parent's divorce or a recent move, a child might feel insecure and need more attention than usual. If you're unsure of why your child seems so needy for attention, it might be helpful to speak with a therapist who can help you explore the situation in more depth.

If your child interrupts frequently, this can be very frustrating, especially if explanations about why interrupting is rude don't seem to register or your child has difficulty remembering to wait her turn. One approach is to have them raise their hand or put their hand on your arm if they want to speak. This helps them remember to learn to wait until you're finished talking first before they can have a turn to talk. It also encourages taking turns, which is an important social skill.

In addition, you can teach them to wait until they don't hear talking anymore to start talking, like during a natural pause in the conversation. Role-play can also be helpful so that they learn when it is and is not appropriate to jump into a conversation.

Other needy behavior can include your child constantly wanting you to do everything with them or for them, as well as an unwillingness to try developmentally appropriate tasks independently. An example might be if your child will not work on a puzzle independently for a few minutes or try to solve a few homework problems alone, and instead wants your help the entire time. One suggestion to try is the timer method discussed previously. You can set a timer for a few minutes and let your child know that they first have to try working on the puzzle for five minutes or try to solve several homework problems until the timer buzzes, and after that, you will help. Gradually work up to greater amounts of time until your child feels more confident, and make sure to be generous with praise for their efforts.

If your child is demanding attention when you want to be with your spouse/partner, remind them of the recent time you spent together and then them know it's now time for Mommy and Daddy to spend time together. You can say something like, "In our family, we take turns. I spent the afternoon with you at the park, and now it's Mommy and Daddy's turn to spend time together. Why don't you play with your toys over there while I talk to Daddy for ten minutes?" This can give you a chance to have some time to talk to your spouse after a busy workday, and setting a time limit reassures your child that you will spend time with them right after. The explanation about taking turns will allow your child to feel okay about not having Mom's or and Dad's attention for a little while.

If your child monopolizes dinnertime conversation, you can also practice taking turns talking at the dinner table. Some kids don't let their parents get a word in during dinnertime conversation, preferring to constantly chatter about their own day and interests. This can be frustrating to parents because dinnertime might be one of the few opportunities to catch up with their spouse/partner. If your child tries to interrupt, remind them about the importance of taking turns. One fun approach to dinnertime conversation that ensures everyone is participating is to try conversation starter cards. I really like TableTopics cards, which have different conversation starters on them specifically for kids that can guide fun and meaningful conversations while allowing everyone a chance to speak.

Challenge #3: Under the Microscope with Constant Scrutiny

Another challenge of raising an only child is that with only one child in the home, your only might feel like they are always under the microscope. When all attention is on one child, they can feel scrutinized. This is a tough feeling for kids to deal with because being under constant scrutiny can make them feel self-conscious. They may decide that it's better to be as invisible as possible to avoid the scrutiny, which may include not sharing much about their lives with you.

With no other children to focus on, some parents notice and comment on everything about their only. If there's a stain on their child's shirt, parents will ask them about how they got it and tell them they shouldn't wear stained clothing to school. If parents think their child is not eating enough, they will comment that the child looks too thin and hound them about eating more. If the child argues with a friend and mentions that they're in a fight, parents will ask about it multiple times a day and try to resolve the situation themselves. Being an only can sometimes feel smothering when you have parents who notice and nitpick everything because they don't have other kids to focus their attention on.

One mom from Georgia, Beth, echoes this feeling. As an adult only, she said that her experience growing up was slightly different than most children of only-child families. "My parents got divorced when I was fourteen years old and I was raised by my dad. Both of my parents were overly strict. At least, I thought so at the time, and that shaped me into being an obsessive people-pleaser. My experience growing up was not a happy one because I always felt like my parents were overly focused on my every move because there were no other children in the family to focus on, and I felt like I was always being criticized and corrected."

Kids who feel that their parents are critical of them can become anxious, and this anxiety can last years. Scrutinizing your only can undermine their self-confidence, and they might become self-conscious and worry that other people are always judging their actions and appearance. It can also cause over-reliance on checking in with you for reassurance, resulting in a child who can't easily make their own decisions, lacks self-confidence, or can't problem-solve independently.

Nicole McNelis, LPC, a therapist from Pennsylvania, said that a child who feels scrutinized might also feel like they're not trusted and they can never do enough. "They can feel like if the parent is hovering, then they must be doing something wrong. What is helpful is a sense of resiliency. We have to teach our child to take healthy risks, and as parents we have to take a healthy risk; give your child some space when it feels safe, and then you build on that. It takes time and it is a process."

If you tend to lean toward this type of parenting, there are revisions you can make to give your child the very best childhood without giving up your authority to teach and provide guidance to your child as you see fit.

First, realize that living under constant scrutiny can lead your only to feel self-conscious as they try to avoid being under the microscope. They might get annoyed with constant questions and check-ins and refuse to answer questions or mumble, hoping you won't hear their responses and move on. Your child might even become distant and stop interacting with you at all. When you ask about their day, they might refuse to answer. Over time, what you perceive as helpful parenting can actually be deleterious to the parent-child relationship.

Try to limit comments that could be taken as hurtful, especially about your only's appearance. If your child's hair is a little messy or their clothes don't match, just ignore these minor problems and move on. Try to avoid micromanaging their choices in clothing, hairstyles, and appearance. Pick your battles wisely and let go of the little things that ultimately don't really matter.

Second, make sure you're spending plenty of time on your own work, hobbies, and interests so you have something else to focus on besides your child. It's important to have a life outside of your family. If you notice that you tend to scrutinize, this might be a good time to start a new project or jump into a time-consuming hobby, so you'll have something new and exciting to think about. When your only sees that you have hobbies and interests of your own, it will provide some breathing room so they won't feel like every ounce of your attention is spent on them.

Challenge #4: Helicopter Parenting

Similar to Challenge #3, another challenge of raising an only is that some parents fall into the habit of helicopter parenting. Helicopter parenting is when a parent is overprotective, always hovering over their child, making sure that everything always works out perfectly for them and that they won't fail or fall.

Helicopter parenting is not a good thing. Parents who hover and do everything for their child produce kids who don't have experience failing and trying again, thus they are less likely to develop grit and perseverance as they age. They may not understand how to cope with disappointment and frustration, which can cause them to fall apart when they encounter later life challenges. They can also be less independent and develop anxiety issues, because they don't feel confident in making their own decisions or know how to handle problems on their own. All of this inevitably leads to kids with lowered self-confidence, less ability to independently problem-solve, and possibly more difficulties taking on greater responsibilities.

Parents of onlies are especially in danger of falling into the habit of becoming helicopter parents because you only have one child and you want to do everything you can to protect them. It's natural and quite common to feel this way. You invest everything into making sure they grow up safe and healthy and to ensure they can succeed. But as a result, only children might learn to rely too much on their parents making decisions for them, not learning to do so on their own. Encouraging independent problem-solving from a young age is important now and for your child's future.

Therapist Nicole McNelis said that helicopter parenting is about control and anxiety, and when a parent is engaging in this type of parenting, it says more about the parent than about the child. "What's important to examine is why you are relating to your child like this, and what you have going on that brings on this mode of parenting. Underneath this kind of parenting behavior is usually anxiety, and that anxiety leads to a need for control."

She continued, noting that when parents notice they're engaging in this kind of behavior, they need to take a step back and recognize that it's not helpful for their parenting relationship. "Getting help with the core of that anxiety is helpful because it will change the patterns. Take notice that this behavior is hurting the relationship with your child. For a lot of parents, that might mean getting therapy, taking a class, or engaging in self-care."

If you recognize yourself as a helicopter parent, there are a few things you can do to adjust your flight pattern. First, recognize that you have a tendency to be a helicopter parent and allow your child to start having more space. Start with small steps of gradually stepping back. If you tend to hover on the playground, for instance, to make sure your child doesn't climb too high and fall, try giving your child a little more space and see how they do. If you tend to accompany your child on playdates when they're old enough to go to friends' houses on their own, try a drop-off playdate with a family you trust and see how it goes. If you help out too much with homework or even write your child's reports and papers for them, step back and let your child do their own work (with you as a supportive presence). The goal is to give your child enough space to accomplish age-appropriate tasks on their own, which builds self-esteem and self-confidence.

Next, focus on teaching your child life skills so they become more independent. Depending on their age, teach them how to prepare their own simple breakfast and lunch, how to pick out their own outfit for school, how to do chores around the house, how to mow the lawn or change a tire (if they're old enough), and even how to make basic, every-day decisions. Even very young children can help out around the house by doing simple chores, like sweeping or folding laundry. Doing chores is valuable for kids for many reasons, but one important reason is that it helps teach responsibility and helps them become more self-sufficient. Trust that your child can do some things on her own.

When things go south, focus on helping your child problem-solve, and be a supportive presence instead of solving all their problems for them. Helping your child problem-solve takes longer than just doing something for them, but ultimately will serve them much better in the long run. For example, if your child and another child get into an argument at school, instead of first calling the other child's parent to try to resolve the situation, walk through what happened with your child. Ask your child what ideas they have for resolving the issue. Role-play different things they could say to the other child next time. This will help empower your child to engage in healthy problem-solving, make their own positive decisions, and develop a healthy self-confidence.

Also make sure that when your only experiences failure, they know how to pick themselves up from it. When kids don't experience failure as children, they won't know how to deal with it as adults, when the stakes are higher. Adults who don't know how to handle disappointments and failure in an appropriate way tend to fall apart and get overwhelmed when life doesn't go their way. But if they learn the right tools as children to problem-solve and cope, they will be much better equipped to weather life's challenges. Remember that it's important to be a supportive presence, but not to solve everything for your child.

Challenge #5: A Child with Deficient Social Skills

Another challenge of raising an only is that a few don't have stellar social skills when it comes to interacting with other kids because they're used to being around adults most of the time. They might be great at talking to adults, but when it's time to interact with kids, they don't know quite what to do or what to say.

For example, they might do great with playing a board game at home with Mom or Dad, but when they're playing the same game with a friend, they get upset and frustrated with the way their friend is playing the game and refuse to keep playing. Or they may do a fantastic job building blocks with Mom at home but have difficulty sharing and taking turns when it comes to building structures with another kid. Some only children prefer being with adults because they find other kids to be unpredictable. As a result, they may choose to play alone at recess or during choice time at school.

Rashmi, a mother in Virginia, said that the biggest challenge of being an only child is missing out on the soft skills that come with growing up with a sibling. "There is just so much learning that goes on when you have siblings in the same household because every day you're problem-solving, having to share, and working things out with fighting. I have a challenge with my daughter because she doesn't like to share. That does create issues when she spends time with friends and doesn't want to share things."

Some only children are also not great at confrontation or standing up for themselves because they haven't had the rough and tumble childhood of arguing—and having to constantly work out compromises—with a sibling. They may not know how to respond to the mean things kids say at school, and be taken aback by it because they haven't had to deal with confrontation at home. Because they haven't had to tell a sibling to keep their hands off their toys or to stop going into their room, they might feel tongue-tied when confronted by bullies and not know how to stand up for themselves, which can cause them to be seen as a doormat by their peers.

One approach you can take with these issues is to find creative ways to develop your child's self-advocacy skills. You can do this by enrolling them in social extracurricular activities, like a team sport, where they will see the same kids often and learn important teamwork and cooperation concepts by participating on a team. Similarly, signing them up for a drama class or a chess club could be other good ways for them to be around other kids in a cooperative play environment.

You can also improve your child's social skills by practicing and role-playing different scenarios for the areas they have difficulty with. For instance, if your child doesn't know how to handle other kids' mean comments, you can role-play different scenarios of how they can stand up for themselves and handle confrontation. Talk through different situations and practice often. This can help your only think better on their feet.

If your child has similar-aged cousins, try to spend as much time with them as possible. Playing with cousins can be helpful for building these important social skills. Even having a pet can help your only enhance their social skills. If your dog chews up your child's toy or hogs the sofa blanket, your child will gain experience handling these situations appropriately.

If you feel your only needs additional practice, consider signing them up for a social skills class or having a therapist work with them to provide more support and guidance. As a therapist, I have run many social skills groups for kids and teens. I believe these groups are extremely beneficial for practice outside of the school setting and with a new group of peers.

Challenge #6: A Child Who Feels Different

Many children feel different because of one reason or another: a health challenge, family difference (like having divorced parents), or perhaps a physical disability. It's hard for kids and teens to feel different from their peers in any way, but feeling self-conscious seems to come with the territory at that age. One way only children might feel different is because they might be the only one of their friends without a sibling.

One of the most frequent questions that kids are asked by other kids or adults is, "Do you have any brothers or sisters?" I remember being asked that question all the time growing up. Sometimes when I answered "No," the adult asking would say something like, "You must be very lonely," or "You should tell your parents to give you a brother or sister." This made me feel awkward, inadequate, and different from all those around me at a very young age. Only children can also feel left out or different when teachers assign family projects that ask about siblings. It can be tough to see your only feeling different or self-conscious, especially if you are also struggling with feeling different due to being one and done, not by choice.

What can you do if your only feels this way because they don't have siblings? Try to emphasize that every family is different and unique, that families come in all shapes and sizes, and focus on all the positives about your family structure. Perhaps your child has involved grandparents or cousins he's close with—you can emphasize how lucky they are to have those loving relationships. Talk about how your family has fun and meaningful family traditions, or how you're always there to cheer them on at sports games because you don't have to divide your time with another child. Focusing on all the positives about your child's family situation will help your child to appreciate their only-child status and not to feel so different.

Therapist Nicole McNelis said that if your child feels different because they don't have siblings, the first thing to do is to validate those feelings. "You can say that 'there's nothing wrong with those feelings; they are understandable, and I understand why you're feeling this way, so let's talk about it more.' Then you want to support. If a child is telling you that they feel lonely or out of place, you can find connections with other families that also have only children. Then the child sees other families that also have only children and sees this community you've formed. We know logically that families come in all shapes and sizes, but when you get to see that, and experience that, it creates this feeling of belonging. Normalize the feelings, support the child, and try to find a community that is supportive and [perhaps even] looks like your family."

Another thing you can do if your child is feeling different is to emphasize all the things that your child has in common with their peers. Perhaps they have a dog, as do many of their friends, or play weekend sports, like their friends. Maybe they do many of the same extracurricular activities as the neighborhood kids. Focusing on all the similarities between your child and their peers will help them feel more of a sense of belonging and ease those self-conscious feelings about not having any siblings.

Making sure your child has a strong sense of community can also go a long way toward facilitating a sense of belonging and feeling a part of something bigger. Creating a school family, church/synagogue family, neighborhood family, or Scout family can make them feel like they belong and have other people outside of your immediate family who care about them. Many parents of only children work hard to create strong community ties so that their only child has a strong village around them.

Challenge #7: A Child Who Needs Lots of Playdates

Another challenge that parents of only children may encounter is that some only children have a strong need for companionship and don't like to be alone. These children may need many scheduled playdates, and it can be logistically difficult for parents to satisfy their child's high need for regular companionship. This can be especially challenging if your child does not have friends in the neighborhood or local cousins to get together with for spontaneous playdates and meetups.

Some kids are happy with one playdate a month, while kids with higher social needs may request playdates every day. Parents who work full-time can find it difficult to schedule all the playdates their child seems to want or need. On the one hand, you may want to do everything you can to make sure your child gets enough social time with friends; on the other, it can get frustrating or embarrassing to feel like you're begging other parents for playdates, especially if you're always the one reaching out and the invitations are not reciprocated.

Only child mom Rashmi in Virginia said that it can be more challenging to set up playdates with families who have multiple children. "For me, it's more of a priority to do playdates than it is for them. If my daughter doesn't have a playdate to go to, then she can't just go and play with a sibling. For a family with multiple children, if there's not a playdate scheduled, then they just play with their siblings. It's not as much of an impact."

If this mother's words resonate with you, and you also have difficulty finding enough families to get together with, know that there are several things you can do if you have a child who always requests playdates.

First, it helps if there are kids around your child's age in the neighborhood so that they can get together for casual playdates. If your child wants to be with friends and there are kids outside playing tag or riding bikes, you can just send your child outside to play. Many parents encourage their only to befriend neighborhood kids because it takes little to no planning to set up playdates with them, especially if kids in your neighborhood are often playing outside.

Another option for informal social time with classmates is to see if kids stay after school and play on the school playground. Or if there's another playground close by where kids from your child's school play, that can also be a good way for your child to socialize with friends. There is a playground near my son's elementary school where we would often go to after school because he knew he would see classmates there. He was able to have frequent playdates with classmates without my having to coordinate anything.

Setting up formal playdates requires a little more time and effort if your child is not friends with kids in your neighborhood, or if your neighborhood does not have kids around their age. One approach is to create a network of families from school or other activities who are also interested in frequent playdates; another approach is to sign your child up for a few structured activities so that they can get the socializing they need after school and on weekends.

It can be challenging to find other families who are also interested in frequent playdates. With many parents working full-time, kids are often in after-school programs, and then it's dinnertime, so many families have little time for after-school playdates. On weekends, many parents use this time to catch up on chores and errands, or they dedicate weekends to birthday parties, kids' sports, visiting extended family, or other activities.

And when you try to arrange playdates with families who have multiple kids, it can be even more challenging to coordinate. Many only child parents feel like they are always the ones reaching out to try to set up playdates for their child. This can lead to frustration, disappointment, and loneliness for both you and your child. You may have the most luck setting up playdates with other only-child families because they often actively look for playdates as well.

Another approach to increase social time is to add more structured social opportunities to your child's schedule. If your child is young, between the ages of two and five, and is at home with you full-time, consider part-time or full-time preschool if your child seems to need additional social time. Your local library with story time or Parent-and-Me classes that community centers or religious congregations offer can be another good option for additional social time for very young children.

If your child wants more time to socialize after school, consider signing them up for after-school extracurricular activities (like chess club or a sport) or a class (like swim class). This can help your child socialize, cultivate hobbies, and make new connections. Weekend activities can also help fill up your weekends, like Scouts, ballet class, or a team sport.

If online is easier to schedule than in person, virtual classes with Outschool (or another virtual class provider) can be another good option. Facetime or Zoom playdates can also work. They can be more convenient to schedule than in-person get-togethers, and many kids participated in virtual playdates during the COVID-19 pandemic, so they are familiar with the concept.

Research what kids' activities and classes are happening around you, and maybe even get a little bit creative, and you'll be sure to find additional opportunities for your child to play with other kids.

Challenge #8: Your Only Constantly Asks for a Sibling

Having an only child who constantly asks for a sibling can be one of the biggest challenges for parents, especially if you are one and done, not by choice. Some only children beg their parents for a sibling daily. Other only children ask question after question to ferret out why they can't have a sibling, which can get tiresome. If your child is asking about a sibling frequently, it can make you wonder if they are not content being an only. Feeling that your child is not happy can be difficult for parents and can result in feelings of anxiety and inadequacy.

Jessica from Virginia, a queer single parent by choice, said that her five-year-old daughter desperately wants a sibling. "Sometimes she asks why she doesn't have a dad. I have told her that I thought I wanted a husband, and I asked God for a husband, and he gave me a child instead. I explain that God gave me what I needed, not what I wanted, and she is very proud of that. But she also thinks that if she prays for a sister, God will give her one because that's what she thinks she needs." Jessica's daughter is now starting to realize that she is not going to get a sibling, but she has taken to calling the cat her sister.

Only children have many different reasons why they would like to have a sibling. Some only children tell their parents that they're lonely and want a sibling so they always have someone to play with. Other only children mention that they feel different because they don't have a sibling, or that it's not fair that all their friends have a sibling except them. Other onlies mention that they want to be part of a larger family because larger families seem like they have more fun. These reasons can be very difficult for parents to hear. For some kids, the wanting-a-sibling phase can last for years. What can you do if your child is always asking about a sibling?

First, it's important for you and your partner to be on the same page about what to tell your child about why they won't be getting a sibling. A child will become confused if Mom's story is that her eggs are broken and Dad's story is that they only wanted one amazing child. A lot of how you might decide to approach this issue depends on whether you are one and done by choice or not by choice. It can be tricky to decide whether you should tell your child the truth about why you are one and done, not by choice—do you really want to get into a discussion about multiple miscarriages, a traumatic birth, or infertility issues? Reflecting on your child's age and maturity level, as well as your comfort level with an honest explanation, can help guide what you should do.

Some parents tell their child that they did try to have a second child, but it didn't work out. Other parents say that Mommy's eggs are broken and that they can't make a baby anymore. Some parents provide a religious explanation. Some parents avoid answering the question and redirect their child to other topics because they don't want to provide an explanation at that time. It's all up to you how you want to answer this, but make sure to have a response ready to go by the time your child is about three—because that's when many of the questions start!

Another approach that some only child parents take is to make having a baby in the house sound extremely unappealing so that it deters your child from asking constantly for a sibling. You could tell them that a baby won't be able to play for a long time, cries a lot, and might take their toys. If there would be a large age gap, explain to your child that a younger sibling won't be into the same things as an older child, thus wouldn't be an equally matched playmate anyway. You could also let your child know that right now they have all of your time and attention, but if you had another child, things would change and you would need to spend a lot of time with a new baby. You can also explain to your child that all the things you get to do together now wouldn't be possible if they had a baby sibling.

My son started asking for a sibling a lot during pre-K, when many of his friends were getting baby siblings. I told my son that if he had a sibling, we would have to turn his playroom (which was in a spare bedroom) into a baby's room. He did not like that idea and said that he didn't want a sibling anymore. I never heard another word about it! Once kids think about the drawbacks of a sibling, many decide that the concept doesn't sound so great after all.

If your child persists in begging for a sibling, it could be a signal that they feel alone or that their emotional needs are not being met in some way. Think about what relationships might be missing from their life. Do they need more friends? Could stronger relationships with cousins substitute for the sibling bond they are seeking? Do they have enough quality time with parents, and do you spend enough family time all together? Could it be that your child doesn't feel a sense of belonging and is searching for it through an additional family connection?

Think about what a sibling represents for your child and how to compensate for that relationship in other positive ways—with friends, cousins, or even pets—that could help provide the additional companionship they are seeking. You might have to think outside the box or consider options you hadn't thought of before, like getting a pet, joining a team sport, or adding more extracurricular activities, but you can find an answer that is right for your family that will fill the needs of your child for companionship.

Finally, help your child see all the positives of being an only child. Remind them of the benefits often. Mention that siblings don't always get along and that many fight and argue regularly. Let them know all the things they're able to do because they don't have siblings, and try to make being an only child sound like the best possible structure for your family.

Challenge #9: Your Only Child Doesn't Think They Have a Real Family

One challenge that sometimes arises when raising an only child is that your child may feel like you are not a real family because of your family's smaller size. Some kids get influenced by TV commercials and movies, many of which feature families with two kids or more, and they start to believe that a "real" family only occurs when there are several children. They can internalize society's and the media's ideals so that a family with one child feels incomplete or inadequate.

Not having a brother or sister may also cause your child to feel different. They might feel different and embarrassed because they're the only one in their social circle without siblings. Your child might feel so self-conscious about their family size that they start to feel like they don't have a real, authentic family.

These are really tough feelings for a child to process. If you notice that your child feels like they don't have a real family, think about whether you are spending enough quality time with them or if you could do more in this area. Also consider re-evaluating whether your lifestyle is kid-focused enough. Do you spend weekends together as a family, doing fun activities that your child will enjoy? Or do you each do your own thing on the weekends, largely disconnected from each other? Doing more to make your family life kid-focused can help foster that family feeling your child may feel is lacking.

It's important to remind your child that families come in all shapes and sizes. If your child feels that they do not have a real family because they have no siblings, reiterate that families are about people who love and care about each other, no matter the size. You can also remind your child that they have grandparents, cousins, aunts, uncles, and pets who all love and care about them and are also part of their family.

Try to find books, movies, and TV shows that feature an only child, and mention it when you do: "Look, this movie's main character is an only child, just like you." Seeing their family structure represented in the media will help normalize the experience of being an only child. Socializing with other only children will also do the same. I think back to my classmates in school when I was growing up and many of my classmates were only children. Most of my childhood best friends were also only children. A smaller family size seemed more common back when I was growing up, so being an only seemed normal to me because I was surrounded by so many only children.

Another suggestion is to make sure to use the word "family" a lot, referring to yourselves as a family often. You can say something like, "Our family's tradition is to make pancakes on Sundays" or "Our family hosts a Halloween party every year." You can also say, "I love our family so much" often. When your child hears the word "family" being used frequently, it will help them feel that they are part of a sufficiently sized, complete family.

Also try to foster a warm family feeling in your home. Keep your house homey with lots of your child's craft projects and artwork on display on the walls, along with lots of kid-friendly furnishings and knickknacks around. A home filled only with pristine furniture that your child isn't allowed to sit on or breakables they can't touch won't do as much to foster a warm, homey feeling. You can also try creating new family traditions for holidays and have "everyday traditions" at home. Making a special effort to create wonderful family traditions (see chapter 8 for more on this) will help your only feel the specialness of each day and being a part of your family.

Challenge #10: You Worry about Your Only Being Alone as an Adult

Another challenge of raising an only child is the persistent worry many parents have about their only child feeling all alone in the world after their parents are gone, especially if they do not have strong ties with extended family. If a child has no siblings and no real relationships with aunts, uncles, or cousins, parents may worry that their child will feel utterly alone in their adult years, especially if the child doesn't end up married/partnered or when parents pass away.

Danielle from Florida is an adult only child, married to another only child, who worries about her son's future in this regard. "My only real concern about our son being an only is when my husband and I eventually pass away. I know that's a reality my husband and I will both face with our own parents, but we have each other and a couple really close friends. I truly hope my son finds people that close to him so I don't have to worry about him when we're gone."

While this is a legitimate concern, it's important to remember that your child will likely have the support of a spouse/partner when they grow up, and maybe a family of their own, so they won't feel all alone in the world, even if they don't have a lot of extended family. You can always make the decision to live near your child when they are older, or you can encourage your child to live near extended family.

Do what you can now to foster close ties now with the extended family you do have, even if they live far away or you rarely see each other. Your child and their cousins can keep in touch with video calls and emails. They can see each other when possible, even if it's only once every few years. You can also emphasize the importance of having close friends and provide your child with important friendship skills so they will be able to make friends easily at every life stage. They may be able to create a "family of choice" if they don't have relatives to provide support.

Danielle Peters, LMFT, a therapist in California specializing in emotionally supporting parents of kids who are neurodiverse and kids with special needs, said that many parents of only children who have special needs worry about their child being all alone as adults. She said that one of the most important things you can do as a parent to calm this worry is to substantially develop your support network.

"It's important to really be okay with getting help from other people and being present in other people's lives so that they can be present in yours, and they can help later on. If you're a single child with special needs and have no more remaining family, if your parents have developed a strong support network, then you will have support around you."

Peters also said that the best way for parents with only children with special needs to build this kind of strong support network is through school and activities. "The most natural way is making friends with other parents in your child's classroom and extracurricular activities. But if that doesn't seem to be working—especially when you work, it can be hard to make relationships—then I would suggest trying support groups."

There are many support groups, activity groups, and nonprofit organizations for families with special needs. Peters discussed a support group for parents who have kids with ADHD who go hiking on the weekends, saying that a lot of families she works with develop a support network through these kinds of groups because there is more opportunity to socialize. Social media is a great place to find these kinds of support and activity groups. Peters recommends looking at organizations related to your child's disability and seeing if they might offer different support and activity groups.

Parents may also worry about their only child feeling burdened and overwhelmed in the future by eldercare challenges that fall solely on them. A step you can take to make sure your child doesn't feel overwhelmed by these kinds of challenges later is to make sure you have enough money saved to cover eventual eldercare expenses, such as long-term care insurance and your retirement savings. You can meet with an eldercare attorney or geriatric care manager to discuss your options and whether or not you are saving enough to cover eventual eldercare expenses. If you've considered your eldercare needs in advance and have a plan in place, it will take a lot of the burden off of your only child.

Additional Challenges

Most of the challenges we've discussed pertain to many only children, but there can be additional challenges if you're raising a child who has special needs. Danielle Peters, LMFT, a therapist in California specializing in emotionally supporting parents of kids who are neurodiverse and kids with special needs, counsels that there can be a few challenges specific to raising an only child who has special needs. She said, "So many parents worry that their only child's disability is going to be worse because they're an only child. Without the extra social support system of additional siblings, parents might ask, 'Do I want to take energy away from the one child I have to give to another child? This child really needs my energy and might benefit less if I split my energy between several children.'"

Peters continued, "[Parents] might [also] feel that they are missing out on having a child without special needs. Depending on the special needs that [the] child has, they might feel sad about missing out on going hiking with their child, missing out on sending their child to Girl Scout camp, feeling sad about missing out on walking their child down the aisle.

"One of the things that can happen when you have an only child with special needs is that there is a grief process that happens. . . . To me, grief is about being sad that something is different than you expected it to be. It's not that you're sad that you have your child—you can be happy to have your child—but you might be sad that you're missing out on something you expected."

Boredom can be another issue that comes along with the territory of being an only child. Do you hear, "Mom, I'm so bored!" often? If so, you're not alone. Without the built-in playmates of siblings, some only children complain frequently of boredom. If their parents are not able or willing to play with them most of the time, parents can start to feel guilty and may compensate by overscheduling their child with activities or handing them a screen to keep them entertained.

Amy Weber, LCSW, a licensed clinical social worker in New York who specializes in therapy for children and their families, believes that it is important to find a good balance. "Parents feel pressure to sign their child up for everything, but kids also need downtime. They need time to come home and just hang out, have an unstructured playdate, or even be bored—it's okay to be bored."

Weber said that if your child complains of boredom, it can be a great opportunity to do some problem-solving. "When they're feeling bored, ask them why that might be, and help them brainstorm ideas of what they want to do."

She continued, "Kids want to be entertained. They're used to passive entertainment, and sometimes families feel guilty because [they're] an only child and [they're] bored. But brainstorming with your child about what they would like to do, and how they will structure that time—a lot of families have success with that."

The COVID-19 pandemic has been especially tough for families with only children. During lockdowns, quarantines, periods of distance learning, times when activities have been curtailed or canceled, and playdates occurring few and far between (and often only outdoors), many parents of only children have found it very difficult to make sure their child is getting enough social time. This has been especially challenging for families with younger children who missed out on months or years of socializing with peers and learning important social skills during early childhood.

Kristie from California believes that the pandemic has been very difficult for only children, "especially for those who took the pandemic seriously. My son was one year old when the pandemic started. None of us knew how long it was going to drag out and I was unwilling to take any risks with him. I felt terrible, but I was unwilling to take him to anything, and I think it has inhibited his speech and communication."

She continued, "Working from home during the pandemic, I didn't have time to work with him on letters and numbers, and he wasn't with peers learning how to talk or share. I feel like children who were born in the pandemic will be behind on speech, development, and social skills, and I think it's something we're going to start seeing more of moving forward."

The pandemic has been very challenging for my own family. My son was in kindergarten when the pandemic started, and his public school closed down for an entire year. During that stressful year of distance learning, I resigned from my job in March of 2020 and became my son's full-time teacher for online school. It was incredibly difficult to transition to online school for one-third of kindergarten and all of first grade, which are such important years for being around peers and learning social skills. With all his beloved extracurricular activities no longer running that year, I was worried constantly about loneliness. Luckily, my son bounced back quickly and made lots of new friends as soon as he started in-person school again in the fall of 2021.

One last challenge we'll discuss is that in raising an only child, each milestone that is the first is also the last time you see it as a parent. While parents of onlies love experiencing every part of the parenting journey with their child, this can cause many to feel sadness and regret. Some parents can feel envious and wistful of their friends who get to experience the first day of kindergarten, learning to ride a bike, or high school graduation multiple times with several children. What can you do if your child's milestones make you feel more sad and depressed than happy and proud?

Amy Weber, LCSW, a licensed clinical social worker in New York who specializes in therapy for children and their families, believes that when you feel sad about having experienced an important milestone only once, it's okay to sit in that sadness for a while. She said, "You can celebrate how far you've come and what your child has just achieved—that they're growing up—and this is the only prom and the only high school graduation that you're going to experience. It's okay to sit in that sadness and to be there. That's totally *normal.* Even for people who have multiple children. When the last child goes through milestones, there's also a sadness and a mourning."

It's important to allow ourselves to grieve. Weber also suggested doing something special to mark and celebrate these milestones. "If it's time to get rid of toys that are no longer being played with, give them to someone special or someone important, knowing that they will live on and be enjoyed again—that might help with this kind of sadness. Some families will find a family in need and donate them to a good cause, which helps them feel better about the situation."

Other ways to celebrate your only's important milestones include the following:

- Making a scrapbook for your child with photos and mementos.
- Creating a journal for your only that you both write in together.
- Creating an email account for your child and writing your child emails describing their important milestones.

CONCLUSION

We've explored many challenges of raising an only child in this chapter. Some of these challenges you may have experienced already, while others you may not have considered. Being aware of potential challenges that can arise will help prepare you for all aspects of raising an only child and will better guide your decisions on what's best for your family. Additionally, having a strong support system around you is one of the most helpful ways to weather even the most difficult parenting situations.

REFLECTION QUESTIONS

1. Think about your own childhood growing up. What were the positives and negatives of growing up in your particular family?

2. Which of the challenges discussed in this chapter are you currently dealing with? Ask your spouse/partner what they think are the biggest challenges of raising an only. Are you and your spouse/partner on the same page about how to address these challenges?

3. Do you believe that your only child feels different from other kids because they are an only? If so, how have you handled this concern?

CHAPTER 5

Coping Strategies for When Your Only *Is* Lonely

Y ou often hear the concept of the "lonely only"—that if you have just one child, they're destined for a lifetime of loneliness. The fact is that all children feel lonely from time to time, but for some reason, society has determined that only children are much more likely to be lonely than children with siblings. Many parents of only children find it ludicrous, and sometimes even offensive, that others assume that their child is chronically lonely because they are an only child.

You see this stereotype in action frequently in the media; television shows, movies, and books often feature a lonesome only child. You might even get unsolicited comments from friends and family that your child is "destined to be lonely" unless you have more children. They commonly forget, however, that not all siblings play together or even get along, which can lead to children in large families feeling lonesome too.

It is human nature that children sometimes feel lonely. In fact, all children feel lonely from time to time. People seem to harbor the negative stereotype, however, that only children are always lonelier than children with siblings, and that they are chronically lonely kids who grow up to be chronically lonely adults. People forget that most of our only children grow up surrounded by friends, classmates, and extended family, and when they're older, many have spouses/partners and families of their own. The truth is that only children will have many supportive people around them as they go through life, which helps ease feelings of loneliness.

Only children do get lonely sometimes, despite all that they might have going on in their lives with school, activities, playdates, friends, and family time. They might feel they're lacking in peer companionship and wish for more playdates or time with friends. Or they might want to be near a parent all the time at home and feel lonely when you and your partner are busy with other things. But it is a harmful misconception to say that only children are always lonelier than children who have siblings.

If your only child does feel lonely occasionally, how much do you need to worry? When you have an only child, you can't entertain them 100 percent of the time. (Well, most of us can't.) That means that some of the time, your only will be alone. If your only is generally able to keep busy, entertain themselves, play independently, make new friends, and not dwell on their loneliness, then they're able to appropriately cope with feeling alone.

On the other hand, if your child is unable to play alone for any amount of time (depending on age), frequently complains about being lonely, constantly asks for playdates, and doesn't seem to have friends, then you might want to take action, like signing them up for some structured activities, like Scouts or a weekend class, setting up more playdates, and thinking about how to add in more social time. Talking to their school counselor or a therapist might also be helpful.

Additionally, it's important to understand the difference between loneliness and solitude. Many only children do just fine with solitude, which means spending time by themselves and enjoying their own company. A child happily playing in their playroom, singing to themselves, and being imaginative and creative is enjoying their solitude. They feel content being alone because they can happily entertain themselves. Enjoying and appreciating one's own company is an important life skill, and one that only children learn to cultivate more than children who have siblings.

Loneliness, on the other hand, is usually described as a feeling of wishing you had more connection, companionship, or support than you currently do, even if you objectively do have people around you. Your child might be at home playing in their playroom with parents in the house, but feel lonely because they want to be interacting with you or their peers instead of playing alone. They might just sit in their playroom and look out the window, not knowing how to entertain themselves and wishing they were with a friend instead. Your child may also feel lonely even if they have lots of friends, because perhaps such social time isn't providing them with the specific type of emotional connection they really need.

If your child goes to school (or is homeschooled), has structure to their day, spends quality time with parents, gets to do occasional playdates, and has a few scheduled activities each week, your child will be so busy that it's less likely they will feel lonely. Beth in Georgia is an adult only child and said that she wasn't lonely growing up because of everything she was involved in. A child who has a busier schedule probably won't have much time to be lonely.

On the other hand, if your child has oodles of unstructured free time all day, spends little quality time with parents or friends, and has no weekly activities, then it's more likely your child might feel lonely.

If you think your child might be feeling lonely, don't panic! I will discuss several common causes of loneliness so you can gain more insight into your only's personal struggles. Once you've identified some of the reasons why your child might be feeling lonely, you will be better equipped to explore the many things you can do to help.

10 Reasons Why Your Only Feels Lonely (and What to Do about It)

REASON #1: NOT ENOUGH SOCIALIZATION

One reason why your only may feel lonely is because he isn't getting enough social time with friends. Some kids, especially if they're extroverts, need a lot of social time and companionship. Whether it's scheduled playdates, free play with kids in the neighborhood, or casual meetups with school friends, it's important that only children socialize with other children regularly. If your child is in full-time school, that will probably take care of some of their socialization needs; however, they may still feel lonely after school or on weekends when there's not the structure of school to keep them busy.

Some parents wonder how many playdates per week or month they need for their child to feel adequately socialized. The reality is that there is no set number of playdates that an only child needs to have in order to feel content socially. Instead, take cues from your child. If they need more socialization, they will probably let you know, whether it's vocally or by their behavior. If you are often hearing, "I'm so lonely and bored," then consider setting up additional playdates or scheduling more activities for your child until you notice a decrease in these kinds of comments.

Some more subtle behaviors to watch out for that can indicate loneliness can include always wanting the TV on as background noise, excessive napping in older kids (which can become a coping mechanism for loneliness or boredom), not wanting to play independently, restless or aimless behavior, grumpiness or sullenness, and clinginess (i.e., always wanting to be near a parent).

Danielle Peters, LMFT, a therapist in California specializing in emotionally supporting parents of kids who are neurodiverse and kids with special needs, said that there are a few signs to look out for that might indicate your child with special needs is feeling lonely. "Watch your child's moods and interactions. How are they doing in school? How do they feel about leaving social interactions? If a nonverbal child has a hard time transitioning away from interactions with other kids, this could be a sign that they want more time to socialize. Some kids with special needs might ask repeatedly for certain people, or you might feel like your child is always wanting your attention or exhibiting needy behavior. For children who cannot communicate verbally, it can also look like meltdowns or sadness."

If you notice some of the behaviors discussed and feel that they might indicate loneliness, try spending more quality time with your child and setting up more social opportunities or activities for them. If you feel you need more guidance on how to address your child's loneliness or boredom concerns, consider looking for a therapist who can help.

If you're trying to increase your child's social time with friends, consider starting with one to two playdates or meetups per month and see how that goes. If playdates are too difficult to organize, try enrolling your child in a social weekend activity, like soccer or Scouts. Providing a scheduled social activity to look forward to will free you up from having to schedule a playdate, and it provides a fun, social outlet.

But in order to set up all these playdates and meetups, you need to frequently reach out to other parents and initiate invitations often. This can be challenging for some parents, particularly if they're more introverted, work full-time, or are new to an area. Some parents of onlies feel like they're always the ones to reach out to set up playdates, and they wonder why other families don't reciprocate more.

It can feel tiresome to always be the one reaching out to other parents to schedule playdates until your child is old enough to make their own social plans. Families with more than one child might be less interested in playdates because their kids play together on their own. Or those families may be primarily looking for other families where the kids' ages match up so that none of their kids feel left out. This can be frustrating when you're looking for playdates for your child and it feels like an uphill battle to find them.

One solution might be to try to find another only-child family to meet up with frequently for playdates. Some only-child families believe that it's easier to set up playdates with other families who also have only children because they are looking to meet similar social needs. If you don't know any other only-child families, consider joining an only-child family group on Facebook or meetup.com. You can also consider starting your own local group on Facebook, meetup.com, or other social media platform.

Jennifer Sotolongo, LMHC, a maternal mental health therapist in Florida, said that parents who are one and done can be very mindful about making sure their child socializes with other children. "From a very early age, have your child explore sports, pods, extracurricular activities—activities that create community. That's the best way to give [your] child the opportunity to make friendships and create bonds so [they don't] feel alone or end up alone, which is what a parent fears."

In general, having regularly scheduled playdates is one of the best ways for onlies to not feel lonely. If they know they will have a playdate with a friend weekly or every other week, or even see the same kids at the local playground, it will be something social they can look forward to. If you can't do an in-person playdate, a virtual playdate can also be a helpful substitute. Virtual playdates can include playing a board game together online, discussing a favorite hobby (like stickers or trading cards), building with LEGOs, playing a computer or online video game together, or even making a craft or art together.

And similar to the idea of virtual playdates, keep in mind that social time doesn't always have to take place at your house. If you don't like to host, no problem! You can meet up for playdates at parks, libraries, playgrounds, or indoor play spaces. During the COVID-19 pandemic, many families got used to the idea of meeting up for playdates somewhere outside. Meeting up with another family at a local park is an easy way to get together for a playdate. Extending invitations to meet up elsewhere can take away some of the pressure to host.

If playdates don't appeal to you or your child, or are not feasible for whatever reason, then consider signing your child up for several structured after-school or weekend activities. That way, they will get the social interaction they crave, but you don't have to plan anything. You can just sign up and show up. And as a bonus, you get an hour to yourself while you're waiting for them to finish up the activity.

When you have an older only, dependence on you to ensure social needs are met will change. When you have a teen, they're the ones setting up their own get-togethers, and the parents aren't usually involved much. Most of the time, teens will text their friends to get together. But sometimes even teens have difficulty taking the initiative to set up their own friend meetups or feel too shy to reach out to others.

If your teen struggles to set up social get-togethers on their own, they may need some extra encouragement or help until they learn how to do it on their own. You can help by suggesting some ideas for ways your tween or teen can meet up with friends. Perhaps propose that they bring a friend along when you're going out to dinner or on a family outing. Or maybe you can suggest that your teen invite a friend along to an amusement park or arcade. Sometimes getting the ball rolling with ideas can provide your teen with the motivation they need to coordinate some friend meetups.

REASON #2: YOUR ONLY WANTS TO BRING A FRIEND ALONG

While only children love time with their parents, sometimes it can be lonely for them to be the only child among adults. Kids can become easily bored when they tag along to adult-oriented events, like dinner at a nice restaurant or going to an art gallery. Consider allowing your child to bring a friend to events and activities that your family plans to do. Going out to dinner? Let your only bring a friend. Going to a pumpkin patch? Bring a friend along. Going on a day trip? Let your child invite a friend to come.

Some parents don't like the idea of allowing their child to bring a friend along because it's more work for them to watch an additional child. After a busy workweek, you may not want the extra burden of keeping an eye on your child's best friend at dinner. But bringing a friend along can make such a difference for your child. If your only is saying they're lonely often, consider making the extra effort to let them bring a friend along from time to time. It might be a little more work for you, but it will make them so happy.

When your child is older, it's easier for you to allow a friend to tag along to family events because the kids are more self-sufficient. But if your child is younger than second grade, and you're letting your child bring a friend, you'll probably need to invite the friend's parent along too. Consider doing "whole family events" with another family or two, like everyone meeting up together for dinner or going to a particular event as a group.

You don't have to allow your child to invite a friend to everything. Family time is important too. But don't forget to look for occasions when it would be beneficial for your child to have some companionship during an outing.

REASON #3: NO KIDS IN THE NEIGHBORHOOD TO PLAY WITH

One advantage of living in a neighborhood with a lot of kids is that there are plenty of opportunities for your child to go out and play, often spur-of-the-moment. Whenever your child wants to play with a friend, they can go outside and find other kids to play with. You don't need to make a formal playdate because there is plenty going on outside. You might even have a neighborhood kid knocking on your door to see if your child can come out and play. Living in this kind of neighborhood is great for onlies and can definitely help with loneliness concerns.

But not everyone has the benefit of living in a social neighborhood, and some families live in a neighborhood that may have a lot of kids, but none around their child's age. What can you do if you don't live in this kind of social neighborhood but would love to find spontaneous friend meetups for your child?

One thing you can do is hang out in your community or neighborhood's common areas. Many neighborhoods have a community park, pool, tennis court, basketball area, or other common place where kids congregate. If you go at the same time every day, it's likely you'll see the same families there, over and over, which is a great opportunity for your child to make friends and have some impromptu playdates.

If your neighborhood doesn't have community amenities that can be a gathering spot, there may be a local park where your child can meet up with other kids. If you go at the same time every day, your only may make friends with other kids who keep the same schedule. We have a local playground where many of the kids from my son's school would go after school. Whenever we went, my son would play with kids from his class and I didn't have to make a scheduled playdate. Where there's a park or playground, kids will most certainly gather and be ready to play.

REASON #4: YOU DON'T HAVE PETS

Many families consider pets important for onlies because they are such great companions. If you feel your only might be lonely, consider getting a pet. A pet can be a wonderful source of companionship for an only child. Many onlies even view their pets as their furry brother or sister. Even if your child isn't playing with the pet, just having another living creature in the room can help them feel less alone. A recent survey by the Human Animal Bond Research Institute found that 80 percent of respondents said that they felt less lonely because of their pet.

Whether it's a dog, cat, or small animal (like a hamster, guinea pig, fish, or lizard), having a pet around as a constant companion can help kids feel less alone and more understood. When I was growing up as an only child, I wanted a pet more than anything. I think I asked my parents for a pet every single day. Instead, my parents' idea was to get me a robot cat named Petster. I loved that robot cat (it even meowed and purred!) and played with it every day, but it wasn't the same as a real live cat. A real pet to interact with and play with would have better helped reduce those feelings of loneliness I sometimes experienced.

Even if you never thought of yourself as a pet person, take a look into the different pet options out there. You may be surprised what pet sounds appealing and plausible for your family situation—there's a whole world of pets outside of cats and dogs. Pets are wonderful companions and help teach responsibility. If you do decide to adopt a pet, involve your child when choosing one, and be sure to talk about the responsibilities they will have for the new addition to the family. When all members of the family take an active role in choosing and caring for a pet, it's more likely that the experience of pet ownership will be a smooth and meaningful one. (See chapter 9 for a more detailed discussion of the benefits of pets for an only child.)

REASON #5: EXTENDED FAMILY ARE NOT OFTEN INVOLVED

Some only children grow up with local and involved extended family. It can be an amazing experience for an only to grow up with similar-aged cousins and see grandparents frequently. If you have local family, make sure your only gets to see their grandparents, aunts, uncles, and cousins often.

Other only children, however, see grandparents, aunts, uncles, and cousins only once in a while due to living far apart from each other. Kids who don't have much contact with their extended family, or who feel disconnected from them, can feel lonely. They know they have grandparents, aunts, uncles, and cousins, but they don't get to see them regularly, and that can be isolating. Connecting with relatives when time allows helps them feel a part of something bigger and can help them stay connected to their culture and family traditions.

If you don't have local family, don't despair! Luckily these days it's super easy to keep in touch with family who don't live nearby through email and video calls. We don't live near grandparents, but my son video chats with them multiple times per week to keep those bonds strong. He can video chat for hours—reading to them, doing art projects with them, and even playing checkers together online. We're lucky to have this kind of technology to help keep kids and extended family close and connected.

Maintaining strong family ties will ensure that your child feels a part of something bigger, and they will appreciate having those strong family connections as an adult too. (See chapter 12 for a detailed discussion of maintaining strong bonds with grandparents and extended family.)

REASON #6: TOO LITTLE QUALITY TIME WITH PARENT(S)

Some only children can feel lonely if they're not getting the attention they need at home. They may long for a certain amount of family togetherness that they aren't able to get if parents are too busy or distracted. This can occur when parents are occupied by their phones or often busy with work-related matters. It can also happen if a parent works long hours and is rarely home.

When kids aren't getting enough attention, it can lead them to become more clingy, interrupt more often, want the TV on all the time as background noise, develop an over-reliance on screens, or always insist on being in the same room with a parent. The main thing that helps is to spend as much quality time as you can with your child, but be sure you aren't distracted during that special time. Your attention should be undivided, just on them, for a portion of the day or evening when you are home together.

Jennifer Sotolongo, LMHC, has made an interesting observation in her counseling practice. She said that many only children have an especially strong interest in video games and technology, which can be a huge red flag for a child who is struggling with loneliness. An over-reliance on screens can become an issue when a parent is not very aware of the social needs of their child or may not be available to spend a lot of time with their child.

Sotolongo's advice for parents of an only child who spends too much time on screens is to first look into how many hours they are watching TV or using the iPad. "Screen time can be a problem when the child is not engaging with others at social events or gatherings; instead, the child prefers to stay home or use a device to play alone or with online friends. This can be a sign that this child may be experiencing loneliness. Sometimes, as parents, we don't have the time to spend with our child. The convenience of technology can lead to a diminished sense of engagement between parent and child, or the child and other individuals in their environment. This child then begins to prefer to play with their online community versus in-person with other children."

Sotolongo continued that if you are noticing that your child is spending too much time on technology, awareness and acceptance are important. "Awareness for the parent is important so they understand that they are in this role of their child having found comfort in technology. Then, seek community. Sign your child up for an in-person activity with other kids."

Sotolongo also advocates for the "ten-minute rule." She explains, "Use a ten-minute rule at home where you play with your child for at least ten minutes every day—read a book, play LEGOs, engage in discussion between parent and child . . . Pull them away from technology; there will be resistance at first, but a child naturally wants that in-person engagement."

If you want to go one step further, another approach to try is to declare one whole hour in the evening as "kid hour" and spend the entire hour doing whatever your child wants to do, with no distractions. That might mean playing dolls for an hour, a superhero game, or playing soccer in the backyard. Let your child take the lead on deciding how they would like to spend that special hour. It will help make that time seem extra special if you can completely unplug for that hour and not check your phone or work email.

Your child will come to relish this special time that you spend 100 percent focused on them, and it's even better if you and your spouse/partner both devote this time to your child together. You could play board games together as a family, read together, or spend time building a LEGO creation together. You may find that this routinely dedicated family time greatly decreases your child's feelings of loneliness.

If you work long hours during the week, it can help to ensure that some of the weekend is dedicated to family time. Making this time a priority will be good not only for your child, but for the family as a whole. When your child knows that Mom or Dad works during the week but looks forward to spending special time together every weekend, it will help them feel reassured and loved, as well as decrease feelings of loneliness. Spending quality time with your child when you are around can go a long way toward helping your child feel less lonely overall.

REASON #7: YOU DON'T HAVE FAMILY TRADITIONS

Strong family traditions can be some of a child's most cherished childhood memories. Kids thrive with family traditions, and some only children can feel lonely on holidays if it's just them and their parent(s) with no expected or special plans.

If family lives far away, it can be challenging to get together on holidays. For some holidays, it might just be you, your child, and/or your partner, which for some people can feel too quiet, especially if you don't make the effort to have special holiday plans. Spending time to make holidays feel festive can sometimes feel like too much work, but it's essential to make the effort! This is where family traditions come into play. If you have a few strong family traditions for each holiday, it will make holidays feel extra special for your child. On the other hand, when you don't do anything to celebrate holidays, it can lead to feelings of loneliness and missing out.

If you don't have family traditions yet, that's okay—it's never too late to start! They can easily be created. (See chapter 8 for more detailed information.) A good place to start adding some more excitement to your holidays as a family is to sit down with a piece of paper and write down some of your favorite holiday traditions growing up. What do you want to keep from your childhood and what new traditions do you want to create for your family? Try out one or two new traditions each holiday. There are also plenty of online resources that can spark ideas.

If you don't have family to get together with, consider inviting over a family friend or another only-child family to spend holidays with. For example, if you aren't able to celebrate Thanksgiving with extended family, consider inviting another family over for Thanksgiving dessert and a playdate after the meal. Or consider hosting a Friendsgiving where you invite other friends and/or families who also do not have holiday plans.

Make sure to put in the effort to make things festive. Even something as simple as a few decorations for each holiday or a special meal, your efforts can really make a difference for your child.

REASON #8: NO SENSE OF COMMUNITY

Some only children can feel lonely if they don't feel a sense of community, perhaps lacking friends at school or in the neighborhood. Some only children can pick up cues from Mom or Dad if they feel they don't have a supportive network or village. For example, kids may notice that their parents don't have any friends of their own or that they spend all holidays alone, without friends or family, and that can make an only child feel isolated.

Nicole McNelis, LPC, a mental health therapist in Pennsylvania, said that sometimes you need to find ways to expand your vision of family and community if your child needs more support. She stated, "Some of us live really far away from our families. There's the concept of building your family by choosing your family. . . . It's an idea focused on building your village and expanding the idea of what it means to be a family. Building up your support system is so critical, and you can have friends who are like family. Be intentional about that—you can expand your family in that way, and those relationships can be very meaningful."

You may not be sure how to start building community for you and your child, and it can feel overwhelming, especially if you're brand new to an area and don't know many people yet. The good news is that you can start with baby steps to start getting out there, meeting more people, and building strong connections. Getting your only more involved in local extracurricular activities or team sports, or meeting people in the neighborhood (and especially getting to know neighbors with kids your child's age) are all great ways to help your only feel more connected. A team sport or family-focused activity, like Scouts, are other helpful ways to make long-lasting connections. Consider joining a religious congregation (if that's a good fit for your belief system) and make new friends at your church or synagogue.

You can also help build a sense of community for your family by becoming involved yourself. You can volunteer at your child's school to be the room parent, chaperone field trips, volunteer on the PTA, lead a PTA committee, or volunteer in the library. All of these approaches will help you get to know other parents at your child's school and build that community for your child, and your only will love seeing you help out at school. Also consider becoming involved in your own immediate neighborhood. Participating as a member of the HOA, working on committees, planning events, and even just walking around the neighborhood and introducing yourself to people can help.

Show your only what it means to help others and build a community at the same time by doing family volunteer projects, taking up a cause, or donating money to a charity or foundation that you care about. If a friend is sick or needs help, volunteer to help out by bringing a meal or providing childcare. All of these actions will help your only feel more connected to their community.

REASON #9: NOT ENOUGH FRIENDS

Many only children have plenty of friends, some have just one or two friends, and others have no friends at all. There are many reasons why your only may be lacking in friendships. Your child may get plenty of time to socialize but still has difficulty making and keeping friends. If your child doesn't have many friends, and wishes they did, they most likely feel lonely. Does your child complain about not having enough friends? If so, don't panic. Luckily, there are many things you can do to help.

To start, consider signing your child up for a social extracurricular activity where they will see the same kids every week. A team sport or Scouts can be especially great for this because these are long-term activities where your child will get to know the other kids well, which can lead to long-lasting friendships. Try to initiate playdates as often as possible. Ask your child if they would like a friend to join you on a family activity or whether they would like a playdate with a friend. You may have to do a lot of reaching out at first, but setting up playdates for your child (or encouraging your older child to coordinate their own friend meetups) is a great way for your child to get to know other kids better and make a new friend.

Also check in with your child's teacher if it seems like they have no friends in the class. You can share your concern and see what the teacher says—the teacher may point out that your child is actually friendly with a few kids in the class, and then you can follow up with their parents and schedule playdates or meetups with those kids. Or the teacher may confirm that your child doesn't seem to have friends in the class, and she may be able to give you some ideas about why that might be. If your child needs more practice with friendship skills, you could consider signing your child up for a social skills class.

You can also start scheduling more playdates with kids your child already knows so that they can get to know them better. Or you can join parenting groups and see if you can make friends for you and your only together.

Also make sure to talk to your child about what might be going on and find out what their perspective is. Do they wish they had more friends? They might let you know that they aren't getting along with the kids in their class, that they are being bullied, or that they want to make new friends outside of the school environment. Once you know what your child views as the obstacle to making more friends, you can more effectively help. If needed, your school counselor or a therapist may be able to help your child explore these issues further.

REASON #10: WHEN IT'S JUST YOUR ONLY BY THEMSELVES MOST OF THE TIME

Sometimes your only child will have to spend a lot of time at home by themselves. Perhaps it's because you have work to do—like a huge project at work that's monopolizing all your free time—you have household chores to take care of after a long workday, or you're dealing with a family emergency, home repairs, or eldercare issues and have a lot on your plate. If this happens frequently, and your child spends a lot of time alone, your only may start to feel lonely. You might notice that they verbalize that they feel lonely, want the TV on as background noise all the time, get clingy, refuse to play independently, or always want to be in the same room as you.

If you're noticing these patterns, think about how you can spend more quality time together. Can you do your work in the same room while your only colors, draws, or reads? If you're doing chores in the kitchen, can your only be in the same room, or maybe even help you? If you need to read for work, can you both read your own books together? Think about how you and your child can be in the same room together, spending time together, even if you have to be busy doing something else. Just being present can help your only feel less lonely.

If the reason why you don't have as much time to spend with your child is because of a time-limited situation, like a big project at work or a home renovation that will eventually be completed, reassure your child that as soon as the project/situation is over, you'll be able to go back to spending more regular time with them. It can help them feel more confident about weathering more lonely times if they know that there's an end in sight.

If your only is feeling lonely, sometimes having background noise on, like music playing, can help as well because silence can feel lonely for some kids. Having photos around their room of their friends and cousins or having a pet can also be very helpful towards reducing loneliness. Making sure to schedule uninterrupted quality time with your child each day can also go a long way to reducing their loneliness.

ADDITIONAL OPTIONS TO TRY

Along with the advice mentioned previously, I've included some additional suggestions that can be helpful toward easing loneliness:

- **Join a team.** If your child craves a lot of family-like interaction, consider signing them up for a team. It doesn't even have to be a sports team. Any kind of team, like a math, chess, or dance team, also works. Teams meet regularly for practices and games/tournaments, so teammates develop close bonds as they practice and prepare, as well as meet for social events. Teams soon start to feel like a family. In addition, the structure and discipline of being on a team is helpful for many children because it teaches good executive functioning skills, like

time management. If you can coach or volunteer with your
child's team, that's an added bonus because it will
help you get to know the other parents as well.

- **Sign your child up for more activities.** If being at school isn't
  enough social interaction, your child may benefit from an
  after-school activity, especially if it's a social one (like soccer,
  theater, or chess). More solitary activities, like piano lessons or
  private swim lessons, may not be the best choice if your child
  wants to be around other kids.

- **Add weekend activities.** If your child feels lonely on weekends, consider signing them up for a weekend activity or two,
  which will give automatic structure to your weekend. This
  is especially helpful if it's challenging to schedule weekend
  playdates.

- **Structure your summer.** If it's summer and your child doesn't
  have the structure of school to rely on, consider signing them
  up for summer day camp or a week-long summer workshop
  instead of hiring a summer nanny or babysitter. This way your
  child can still be around kids and socialize regularly.

- **Keep them busy.** Adding more activities, classes, or events to
  your child's schedule can help fill their calendar and decrease
  downtime, which is when lonely feelings can surface. *A busy
  child doesn't have as much time to feel lonely!*

- **Be the fun house.** Become the go-to house in the neighborhood for fun and festivity. Create an amazing backyard setup
  with a playset, yard toys, a sprinkler, scooters, a basketball net,
  etc. You may want to keep some snacks on hand as well. If
  your house is seen as the "fun house," then kids will want to
  hang out there and your only will have more opportunities to
  have friends over.

- **Schedule more video calls.** Use technology to keep in touch
  with friends and family. Schedule a weekly video call with the

grandparents or your only's favorite cousins or closest friend. Knowing that there's a weekly call where they can catch up will help ease feelings of loneliness.

- **Connect in the neighborhood.** Get your only more involved in the neighborhood. Make sure to play in your yard often so you can wave to neighbors who walk by and get to know them. Take lots of neighborhood walks. Participate in neighborhood activities. Maybe your child can start a dog walking business or volunteer service, or help out with a neighborhood library, to build community in your neighborhood and feel more of a connection to neighbors.

- **Know your neighbors.** Make it a point to get to know neighbors better. Simply having a short chat regularly with neighbors can make your child feel more connected. You can say hi to neighbors and chat when you're out and about or outside with your child. Just knowing that you're on friendly terms with your neighbors can help your only feel part of a community.

- **Consider joining a congregation.** Whether a church, synagogue, or mosque, being part of a congregation can be another way that your child feels known and appreciated in their community. Many people find that going to services and getting involved or volunteering in their congregation can lead them to build a "congregation family." Congregations often have groups or committees to join and other ways to be social while providing a family-like atmosphere.

- **Volunteer.** There are lots of opportunities for families to volunteer, which can be great for meeting new people and giving back to the community. There are many opportunities for younger kids to volunteer with a parent—check with animal shelters especially. You might be surprised to learn that there are many virtual volunteer opportunities for kids that you can do from home. Check out volunteermatch.org and the JustServe app for a database of volunteer opportunities to explore. You'd be surprised how many options are out there, and you're sure to find one that best fits with your child's interests!

Conclusion

While having an only child who often mentions feeling lonely can be distressing to parents, keep in mind that all children feel lonely from time to time, and it's not something unique to only children. There are many steps you can take to help your child make friends, build community, and reduce feelings of loneliness. When your only has friends, stays busy with a few activities, and feels a part of their community, it's less likely that lonely feelings will have an opportunity to take hold.

REFLECTION QUESTIONS

1. Before you had an only child, what were your thoughts about the stereotype of the "lonely only?" Did you believe that only children were more likely to be lonely? How do you feel about this now, as the parent of an only child?

2. Think back to your childhood—were you lonely growing up? If so, what do you think contributed to your feeling lonely? What could your parents have done differently to help reduce your loneliness?

3. What factors have been the most helpful (playdates with friends, weekend activities) for helping your only feel connected and supported?

CHAPTER 6

Dealing with Insecurities When You Are One and Done, Not by Choice

There are two types of only-child families. Those in the first group are the families who consciously chose to have an only child. These families are usually content with their decision because they took the time to think deeply about it, weighed the pros and cons of having one child versus multiple, and concluded that having a single child was the best choice for their family. They are vocal about all the benefits of having one child. These families might refer to themselves as being one and done by choice.

The other group of only-child families is composed of those who did not choose to have an only child. They are the ones who are one and done, not by choice. Their reasons for being one and done, not by choice, are many, and each reason can be tinged with its own sadness, emotional pain, or resignation.

Perhaps they struggled with long-term secondary infertility, eventually deciding to give up on their journey to have a second child, and are struggling to accept the situation. Or they might have had a traumatic labor and delivery experience with their first child and decided not to risk any more health complications by having a second. They may have had marital issues when their child was young and decided that having a second child wouldn't be in the cards for them. Or perhaps they struggled with prior pregnancy complications, prior pregnancy losses, health issues, financial concerns, divorce, or partner refusal to have more children. These parents deal with many difficult emotions and insecurities about having just one child, especially if they are still in the thick of infertility treatments or dealing with a health condition that is prohibiting another pregnancy.

I'll take a moment to share my own story here. We are one and done, not by choice, and it took me many years to come to terms with that. We struggled with unexplained secondary infertility and were ultimately unsuccessful in having a second child. I went to every infertility clinic in my area; had all the tests; got second, third, and fourth opinions; and even had surgery. No doctor could really explain why I could not get pregnant a second time. After five years without a single positive pregnancy test, we decided to stop trying.

For several years, I was in denial about my infertility. I couldn't wrap my mind around the fact that I had a toddler at home, and got pregnant easily the first time, yet could not get pregnant again. Eventually though, as the years went by, I came to an acceptance. My son growing older, him starting elementary school, and a greater distance from the baby/toddler years helped. I started focusing on all the positives about having an only child, concentrating on the silver linings of having a small family. Although we were not successful in having a second child, eventually I was able to move past the infertility heartache and celebrate everything that's amazing about having an only-child family.

Regardless of the reasons, what most one and done, not by choice, parents have in common is that they deal with countless challenging emotions and insecurities. Often these parents feel all alone either because they're the only one in their social circle who tried to have more children and couldn't or because others don't understand their circumstances. Many feel judged by friends and family for having "just one child," while those friends and family may be completely in the dark about the struggles they have endured. While some individuals are open about their reproductive struggles, others prefer to keep them private. Many feel anger and grief at the cards they have been dealt, which can take years to process and resolve.

Along with the insecurities that accompany this kind of hardship, many of these parents also wrestle with guilt about depriving their only child of a sibling relationship. Guilt can make parents feel emotionally weighed down and keep them from seeing all the positives about having one child.

Nicole McNelis, LPC, a therapist in Pennsylvania who specializes in maternal mental health, said that it's important to allow yourself the space and time to grieve and mourn if you find yourself in this situation. "A lot of parents don't recognize that there is a grieving process involved when they imagined their family in this specific way and they're not able to achieve that. These families need to give themselves the space and time to grieve. Move through the grief, don't ignore it. Examine what lies beneath—resentment, bitterness, and pain. It's telling you something, and it's time to manage and process that pain."

Here are some common insecurities that families who are one and done, not by choice, might experience. Can you relate to any of these?

- You're not a real parent because you only have one child.
- A small family isn't as good as a big family.
- You're a bad parent because you're depriving your child of a sibling bond.

- You're heartbroken about your birth experience because it did not go the way you wanted and you won't get a second chance.
- You're disappointed about not having the opposite gender child (e.g., you really wanted a boy but got a girl).
- You started having kids too late, so it's your own fault that you only have one.
- You didn't try hard enough to have a second child; you should have tried more IUIs or IVFs.
- You should have tried everything under the sun to have a second child, including donor egg, donor sperm, donor embryo, or adoption—no matter the emotional or financial toll.
- You're not a real family because you only have one.
- You're always the odd one out. All the other families in your school, church, or social circle have multiple kids.
- You're left out of playdates and social gatherings because other families want to socialize with families who have similarly aged kids for each of their kids.
- Others devalue your family because you only have one child.
- You're not a real woman because you were only able to have one; your body doesn't work the way other women's do.
- Your partner resents you because you can't give him or her the bigger family that he or she wants.
- Your child will end up lonely and maladjusted because you only have one.

While it is common to experience some of these emotions from time to time, feeling insecure all the time can take a toll on you and wear you down mentally, emotionally, and physically. Fortunately, when you have these feelings, there are actions you can take to find peace and feel better about your situation. I will discuss a variety of coping techniques you can use when you're feeling overwhelmed with any of these challenges. But first, we will take a closer look at some of the sadness and insecurities you might be facing as a one and done, not by choice, parent so that you will better know how to help yourself with the struggles that come with this territory.

Dealing with Unsolicited Comments

It's especially challenging to be one and done, not by choice, when you have well-meaning (but annoying) family and friends who are constantly asking you nosey questions. You might find that you are on the receiving end of these kinds of unwanted comments mainly during the toddler and preschool years. (Many parents find that once their child starts elementary school, the comments decrease or stop altogether because by that point, people assume you are going to stay one and done.)

You may even get unwelcome comments from random strangers at the grocery store. You might receive unsolicited questions about why you don't have/want more children, comments about how sad it is to deprive your child of the sibling bond, or comments about how every child *needs* a sibling. You may cringe every time you are asked the dreaded question "When are you going to have a second kid?" You may feel insecure and judged because people make assumptions that you do not want any more kids, are selfish in deciding to have an only, or did not try hard enough to have a second. Most of the time it never seems to occur to these people who offer unsolicited comments that you were not *able* to have a second child. They all seem to assume that if you have one young child, you're automatically able to have another. And if they do find out that you can't have a second child, all too often you'll hear insensitive "advice" like, "Just relax and it will happen," or "Why don't you just adopt?"

These comments can sting, especially when you're in the midst of unsuccessful infertility treatments or if you've just had a pregnancy loss. You're already processing so many difficult emotions, and having others ask intrusive questions only makes you feel worse. It's no wonder that many parents who are one and done, not by choice, avoid family gatherings or social events where it's likely they will be peppered with insensitive questions. Some even avoid social events or seeing friends altogether when they're feeling especially low.

It's very possible you're feeling several conflicting emotions at once. On the one hand, you're incredibly grateful for your only child because they bring you greater joy than you ever thought possible. Your only is perfect and you love your family the way it is. On the other hand, you're grieving the family size you always dreamed of and couldn't create and feeling angry that others are able to have babies so easily while you can't. And when others ask intrusive questions, it can feel like ripping a bandage off a wound as it brings all these painful emotions to the surface once again.

Some parents who are one and done, not by choice, feel like they have to explain why they don't have more kids so that they're not judged unfairly by others. They might unintentionally overshare because they're feeling so insecure about their own situation that they feel the need to explain it away. I certainly experienced this early on in my secondary infertility journey.

Whenever anyone asked whether I had more children or when I was having a second child, I would overshare because I felt so insecure about my infertility situation. Once we decided to accept being one and done and move on, I felt more confident and no longer felt the need to offer any explanations to these frequent questions. Instead, I would simply say that we have one child and are not having more children. As you become more comfortable being one and done, not by choice, this feeling of having to overexplain will usually diminish.

There's also a distinction between questions like "Do you have other children?" and "When are you going to have a second child?/Why don't you have more children?" Most people find the first question to not be intrusive at all, but rather a neutral question. It suggests that the other person is simply trying to get to know you and wondering if you have more children. When I get asked this question, I respond with a simple "no" and move on. You don't owe the other person any sort of explanation. But the second questions have a judgmental undertone and come across as nosey and pushy.

Jennifer Sotolongo, LMHC, a maternal mental health therapist in Florida, said that friends and family might always make comments that your child needs a sibling or ask, "When will you give him a brother or sister?" And these questions can be very triggering for that mother. "It might not be healthy for a mom in this situation to try to teach these friends or family members or overexplain why she's in this situation. Seeking support—finding support groups with others going through the same thing—can be very helpful." Sotolongo said that social media does a great job with support, and someone can go onto social media and find support groups for any situation in motherhood.

But when you're in the thick of it, going about your day, and someone makes an unsolicited comment or asks a rude question about your one-and-done status, know that there are a few ways you can handle it. Some people like to turn the question back to the other person and say something like, "Why do you ask?" And then don't give them any information at all. Others want to get across how rude that kind of question is, so they may reveal a little about their situation and say something like, "After several years of unsuccessful IVFs, we decided to give up." Usually the other person stammers from embarrassment and regrets asking the question. Other one and done, not by choice, parents respond with a truthful, detailed answer because they like to be honest with people or want to educate the other person.

Still, other parents say something that shuts down the questioning, like "That was rude," or "That's something I prefer to keep private." It's helpful if you decide beforehand how you want to answer these kinds of questions so that when you're caught off guard by someone's nosey and intrusive questions, you're also not fumbling for how you want to respond. So if you're headed to a family gathering or a baby shower, and are expecting insensitive questions, it can be helpful to decide beforehand how you want to respond so you can feel confident in your answers.

Dealing with the Flood of Pregnancy Announcements

When your only child is toddler and preschool age, feeling insecure because of your one and done, not by choice, status can be especially difficult. At these ages, pregnancy announcements and baby showers are ubiquitous. It can seem like everyone you know is expecting. When you have a toddler or preschooler, many of your peers are expanding their families and having their second and third kids; however, the pregnancy announcements slow down greatly once your child gets to elementary school, which can be a huge relief.

When your child is toddler or preschool age, it can seem like every time you go on Facebook or Instagram, you're greeted with yet another pregnancy announcement, and all the while you're yearning to announce your own. You'll see pregnant moms and newborns everywhere, from the playground to indoor play spaces to preschool/daycare drop-off and pick-up. As your child gets older and the baby/toddler stage grows further away, and as the pregnancy announcements reduce to a trickle, things will improve. As you get deep into elementary school mindsets and activities, the ache for a second child will usually start to lessen. You'll get further away from the baby stage and will soon realize how wonderful it can be to have an older child who is more independent and able to do more activities. For most people, acceptance comes with time.

But even so, I still remember how challenging it was to be the only mom waiting for preschool pick-up by myself, without a baby or toddler, especially while I was in the midst of my failed infertility treatments. One by one, every mom I knew who wasn't one and done by choice started having their second and third kids while my son was in preschool. Soon I was the only mom in my social circle who had wanted more children but was unable to, and it made me feel very alone.

Rebekah from England, who is one and done, not by choice, said that "initially it was awful being around people who were pregnant. Even at the stage where I didn't really want another baby. It got to the point that I think I was hypersensitive to even the slightest idea that someone was pregnant, like I could sniff it out. And when that inevitable Facebook post of an ultrasound came, I would shout, 'Knew it!' And then cry! A lot. And then cry some more. It's been a process of challenging thoughts and accepting my feelings that has helped me get to the point that I am okay with it now. Not without pain, but I am okay [in my] acceptance of grief."

What can help with these complicated feelings? If reading others' pregnancy announcements is difficult for you, try to stay off social media as much as possible. When you do learn about a pregnancy announcement, give yourself the time and space to process your feelings; you may need to take a little breather before you're able to offer a hearty congratulations. If you're invited to baby showers or gender reveal parties and you can't bear the thought of going, send a gift and a nice note and stay home. Taking care of yourself and protecting your own heart is the most important thing when you're struggling with these difficult feelings.

Preschool drop-off/pick-up and kid-friendly social events can be an especially tough time for moms who are experiencing sadness at not being able to expand their families. If you have a hard time with preschool/daycare drop-off/pick-up or preschool social events, when other moms have newborns or younger kids in tow, consider looking for the other preschool moms who also have onlies, or bring a book or keep busy with your phone so you have something else to think about while you're waiting. If your school has a carpool line, perhaps you can do that instead.

Also, this can be a good time to focus inward and work toward living your best life in other ways. Try to put more emphasis on your own goals, talents, and interests—perhaps this is a good time to start a new business or hobby. Maybe now is the perfect time to change jobs, relocate to somewhere you've always wanted to live with your family, or write your first novel. When you have other things in your life that are new, exciting, or going really well, you're less likely to dwell on the fact that you can't have another child.

Also consider joining support groups, either online or in person. When I was going through my secondary infertility journey, I joined a number of Facebook support groups, as well as an in-person support group, that helped immensely. Just being able to talk about what I was going through with others who were going through the same thing helped me process my struggles and feel less alone. A therapist can also be helpful if you're having difficulty coping and need additional support.

Feeling Lonely and Left Out

When you're one and done, not by choice, you might feel like the odd one out if you're the only one in your social group who has one child—especially if everyone's kids are on the younger side (second grade and below). That's because when the kids are young, it's more likely that parents stay for playdates and bring the younger siblings along as well. You might also feel like your friends are getting together for playdates and meetups without you because they want to hang out with others who have similarly aged kids. In other words, they may be more likely to prefer another family that has a younger or older child so that all their kids have a playmate.

When kids are young and people are still expanding their families, talk often turns to pregnancy, the baby/toddler years, and sibling relationships. You might feel like you don't have much to talk about on those subjects if your child is older. When friends drift away and become better friends with each other because they're all having multiple kids and you cannot . . . it can be really hard to deal with.

I know that I certainly experienced being left out frequently because my friends wanted to hang out with others who had the same number of kids and similarly aged kids. I don't know if they even consciously realized they were excluding us; however, this left me feeling quite lonely and left out for a long time. Things got better when my son was old enough for drop-off playdates and when I started hanging out more with other one and done families.

Another way parents who are one and done, not by choice, might feel left out is when they see photos on Facebook or Instagram of their friends' kids and their siblings together. It's hard to not yearn for the same sibling relationship for your child, and if you're the only one in your social circle who doesn't have this, you might feel like everyone else has moved on with their lives and you're stuck in the same place. This can lead to feelings of loneliness and stagnation.

What can you do if you're feeling like you're being left out due to your one and done status? First, realize that this feeling will likely dissipate once your child is old enough for drop-off playdates. Once your child is in first or second grade, parents stop staying for playdates and tend to drop off more often. This is in contrast to the whole family playdates that tend to predominate in the younger years when parents will often bring all the siblings, especially the younger ones. So this concern should diminish with time as the focus shifts to your child and another same-aged child getting together for playdates. Then the sibling issue won't matter as much.

Therapist Jennifer Sotolongo, LMHC, said that her number one suggestion to a mom who feels left out is to find community with those in a similar situation. "It's hard to think about pulling back or drifting away from your social circle, but sometimes the immediate need is to receive support and be surrounded by others in a similar situation, who are also one and done."

If you're feeling left out and excluded, it helps to get to know more parents with only children, and then get together with them often. It can truly be freeing to meet up for playdates with other families with only children. They will likely share similar experiences and feelings as you, and you may feel like you are finally understood when you hang out with them.

If you don't know any families with only children personally, you can look for only child social groups on Facebook or meetup.com. If you aren't able to find these in your area, try posting on your local Facebook parenting group or Nextdoor page to see if any other families with only children would like to get together. You may even consider starting your own only-child family social group!

Feeling Like You're Not a Real Family

Some parents who are one and done, not by choice, may feel like they are not a "real" family because they only have one child. This is because society and the media often invalidate only-child families by showing that a family with two children is the accepted norm and the most traditional family setup. Many people seem to believe that a family with one girl and one boy is the ideal family. People may make you believe that you're "less than" because you have only one child, and as a result, parents become insecure and feel like they're not a real family.

Some moms who are one and done, not by choice, struggle with feeling like they're not a real mother because they have only one child. I have heard some people say that they will not listen to one and done moms' parenting advice "because they only have one." This can feel incredibly invalidating of your experience as a parent. Some call parents of onlies "inexperienced parents" because they don't have multiple children. When other parents think that you don't understand their experiences because you have one child, it hurts to feel like you're not sharing in a similar parenting experience.

Another way that parents who are one and done, not by choice, feel that society invalidates their family structure is on social media. On Facebook or Instagram, they may feel left out when they post a nice family photo and don't get any comments, whereas families with multiple kids often get pages of "beautiful family" comments. Experiences like these can cause the one and done family to feel like their family is "less than" or inadequate because they have a single child, which creates tough emotions to process.

Therapist Nicole McNelis, LPC, said that for only child moms who feel inadequate, "the most challenging transition [in motherhood] is from [having] zero kids to one kid—when you go from just taking care of yourself to being fully responsible for another human. . . . It doesn't matter how many children you have because there is no quantifying motherhood. Shifting [the definition of motherhood] from quantity . . . to being a mother because I have a child—own that definition of motherhood and recognize that you are mother enough [by] having one child. Own what your family unit looks like and who it consists of, and trust yourself that your family is exactly what you need it to be."

What can help with these challenging feelings is focusing on the fact that families come in all shapes and sizes, and are composed of people who love and care about each other. One parent and a child are a real family, a grandparent and a child are a real family, two same-gender parents and a child are a real family, and a mom and dad and a child are a real family. Make sure to use the word "family" often when describing your family to your child, such as "our family makes pancakes every Sunday. That's our family's tradition." Repeatedly using the word "family" will help you become more comfortable with the idea.

I also suggest reading books and watching movies/TV shows that feature families of diverse sizes and types (such as a single parent and child or grandparent and child) to show your child that all families are different.

Another idea is to find an inspirational only-child family (maybe through a blog or YouTube channel) and focus on how they espouse the concept of a fun, active, and close family with "just one child." Whenever you feel down about being one and done, not by choice, think of that particular only-child family you've read about and how much enthusiasm and joy they project. You might find them inspiring because they clearly love being together, they have amazing travels, or they are a fun-loving family who has all sorts of interesting traditions. Think about how they can inspire your family to try new things.

Coping Strategies for Feeling More at Peace with Being One and Done

We have just explored some of the insecurities that parents who are one and done, not by choice, often struggle with. Some parents get stuck on these insecurities and find it difficult to move past them until they are able to make peace with their situation. Many struggle with feelings of bitterness that they weren't able to have another child, and they might feel resentment toward those for whom pregnancy comes easily or those who have large families.

It's important to make peace with the idea that life isn't always fair and everyone struggles with their own challenges. Being one and done, not by choice, may be yours. But how do you keep these sad, painful, and resentful feelings from overtaking every minute of your day, especially when they're still raw? How can you cope with these feelings and emotions about being conflicted about your family size, while still being engaged and attentive to your child? The following are some coping strategies that may be helpful to you as you process your feelings about being OAD, not by choice.

FIND YOUR PEOPLE

One general coping strategy for making peace with being OAD, not by choice, is to find a support network of others who are experiencing the same thing. That might be an in-person support group for parents experiencing secondary infertility or for those currently undergoing infertility treatments. If you can't find something that is a good fit in person, try looking online. For example, the One and Done, Not by Choice Facebook group I joined was incredibly helpful to me to ask questions, find support, and read how others were coping with similar circumstances. Knowing there were people I could turn to who would understand exactly what I was feeling was very helpful as I worked to make peace with my situation.

Good places to find in-person support groups include the Resolve (infertility association) website, the *Psychology Today*'s Find a Therapist database (which also lists support groups on different topics), and asking your primary care doctor, OB-GYN, or therapist for recommendations.

FIND A HEALTHY OUTLET FOR YOUR ANGER

When you are one and done, not by choice, chances are that you are angry and resentful about your circumstances. Holding on to all that anger and resentment isn't good for your physical or mental health. Studies have shown that anger can negatively affect cardiovascular health and the immune system, so it's important to find positive outlets for managing these challenging feelings.

Exercise (like a good kickboxing session), running, journaling, cleaning (taking out your frustrations by scrubbing your shower), yard-work, talking to a friend or therapist, and arts and crafts (coloring can be very therapeutic) are all positive and healthy ways of coping with your anger and resentment. The important goal is to replace unhealthy coping strategies (like overeating or drinking alcohol) with healthier, more positive ones.

What you don't want to do is take these feelings of anger out on other members of your family or have the feelings negatively impact your work or friendships. Talking with a trusted therapist is another good way to process your feelings of anger and resentment in a safe and supported space.

FOCUS ON THE PRESENT

Sometimes parents are so caught up in wishing for a second child and focusing on a future pregnancy (that may or may not happen) that they are unable to fully enjoy the present moment with the child they actually have. They might spend so much time and energy thinking about a future child that they realize they missed out on many happy moments with their current child. How can you make peace with your situation, focus on the present, and love the life you have while still processing challenging emotions about not being able to expand your family?

A mindfulness practice, where you focus on the present and try to notice what you are feeling and experiencing, can be a helpful coping strategy. Just focusing on something in your current space, noticing all the sensory details (like what you can see, hear, smell, taste, and feel), while letting your feelings come and go without judging them, can go a long way toward keeping you more grounded in the present.

Other ways you can stay in the present and focus on the moment in front of you are to focus on your child's laugh or smile and how joyful that makes you feel, or to enjoy playing a board game together and cherishing that present moment with your child.

GRIEVE YOUR LOSSES

If your one and done, not by choice, journey involves loss, as many of ours do, it's important to realize that one of the emotions you are feeling may be grief. You may be familiar with Elisabeth Kubler-Ross's Five Stages of Grief concept. Her five stages of grief are denial, anger, bargaining, depression, and acceptance. You might find yourself especially identifying with one or several of them right now. For example, if you were diagnosed with secondary infertility after an easy first time around, you might find you're in the denial stage for a long time—in disbelief that you are now infertile after getting pregnant easily the first time.

This idea that there is a grief and loss response when you can't expand your family is very important to come to terms with as you process your feelings about not being able to have more children. Many of us have the experience of grieving someone or something we've lost, but we can also grieve something we want but can never have. You may grieve the life you wanted with a larger family, but at the same time, you love your only and are grateful to have her. It can be a complicated set of emotions to balance, but it is possible with introspection and time.

If you find yourself grieving the idea of the child or family you wanted to have but couldn't, one helpful approach is to find a support network of others who can relate. Perhaps that might be an in-person support group through the infertility association Resolve. (You can find a listing of support groups on their website.) Or it might be a virtual support group on Facebook for parents who are one and done, not by choice. It might also be an informal group of friends who are going through the same experience as you. But having a support network of people you can lean on and who can offer their support can be very helpful as you process your grief.

Jennifer Sotolongo, LMHC, echoes this idea when she said that if you are grieving the loss of the larger family you always dreamed of, finding a support system is crucial. "Support is so important for mothers overall. When a mother is grieving the family she expected to have, support is the number one way to process those feelings, by meeting other families who also had that same dream. It's also very dependent on time frame—how long has this mother been grieving [and] how long has she been struggling with trying to conceive? If she joins other women in the same stage of the grieving process and has one other person who can share her experience and relate to her feelings of grief, she can lean into that support."

Another approach that can be helpful is making sure you are engaging in enough self-care during this challenging time. That might look like getting enough sleep and exercise, as well as maintaining a good diet. It might also involve getting out in nature and feeling nourished by a walk in the woods or a stroll along the shore. It might involve protecting your heart by skipping emotionally triggering activities, such as baby showers, gender reveal parties, or sip n' sees. Making sure to take care of yourself, in whatever ways are most effective for you, can help you navigate this difficult time.

If you find you're unable to work through these feelings on your own, consider the invaluable expertise of a licensed therapist if you feel you need more guidance. A therapist can help you process your feelings and suggest coping strategies that will work for your specific situation.

While struggling with the challenging emotions of being one and done, not by choice, may feel insurmountable now, with time, many of these feelings lessen in intensity until you find that one day, you're able to reach an acceptance and move forward. The rest of this chapter explores helpful tips for dealing with the many challenges of being one and done, not by choice, while you strive toward reaching acceptance and making peace with your situation. Ponder which tips might work best for you and your family, and then make a commitment to implement them into your family's lifestyle.

TIP #1: FIND OTHER FAMILIES WHO ALSO HAVE AN ONLY CHILD

Being a one and done, not by choice, family in a sea of families with multiple kids can make you sometimes feel alone and isolated. It can be really hard to be the only parent at school or daycare pick-up who is not pregnant or holding a newborn, or to be constantly asked when you are having a second child by well-meaning parents of multiples. It can also be challenging to be the only mom in your circle of friends who has one child when everyone else has two or three. You might feel uncomfortable around parents who have more than one child because you feel left out of their conversations about multiple kid topics, like sibling dynamics. Or you might notice that the neighborhood moms with larger families are all getting together for playdates and not inviting you, and you wonder if it is because you just have one and have become the odd one out.

Many only-child families report that finding another only-child family with whom to be friends is the most important step that helped them move past their feelings of loneliness. Having a parent friend who is at the same life stage and similar situation as you can make all the difference between feeling isolated and alone and feeling supported and connected.

So how do you find these families? One way is to look closely at your preschool, daycare, or elementary/middle school class. Do you notice any parents without other kids in tow at drop-off/pick-up or at school events? If so, go up to them and introduce yourself! I will always remember one mom who introduced herself to me in a unique way at a pre-kindergarten class playdate. She came right up to me and said, "Hi, I'm Laura's mom, and Laura is my one and only." It seemed like she wanted to put her OAD status out there in the hopes of finding another kindred spirit. I appreciated her bravado, and we became good friends.

Another way to find other only-child families is to think about the parents at your child's extracurricular activities after school or on the weekends. Do you notice any families sitting and waiting for their child to finish soccer or swim class who do not seem to have other children with them? If so, stop by and start up a friendly conversation. You never know when it could lead to a real friendship down the road!

Other opportunities to look into are local social groups or support groups for only-child families. Check out meetup.com, a website that features local interest groups you can join for free with the goal of building more community in local areas. Meetup has tons of parenting-related groups and may have an OAD group in your area. If not, you can start one! Also look into Facebook social groups, which you can join or start for free. There might be an only child social group in your area. If not, again, you can easily start one yourself. I started an only-child family social group in my area through Facebook and members have enjoyed going to events and getting to know other nearby OAD families.

Facebook has a number of online support groups for only-child families. They are free to join and each one has thousands of members, so they can be a great way to connect with other families, ask questions, and receive support. And some members may happen to live in your local area. After joining one of these national groups, you can post something about wanting to meet other OAD families in your area. You may find some new friends by trying this approach.

Therapist Nicole McNelis, LPC, said the most important thing is to *find your people* and establish that sense of community wherever you can. "If it's hard to find someone nearby, go online and find groups. There are Facebook groups, Instagram influencers—find your community. . . . Knowing these groups exist and that there are other parents [who] also feel alone creates community."

She continued, "Find places locally that feel like home for you. For example, try out Mommy-and-Me classes, which are a wonderful way to meet . . . other parents of only children. If you're so inclined, consider starting a group. If spaces that are the right fit don't exist, don't be afraid to create them."

Also keep in mind that once your child starts elementary school, you will have a greater likelihood of finding other OAD families. In elementary school, the class sizes are larger, which means there is a higher probability of there being other one and done families in the class. There are also more opportunities in elementary school and beyond to volunteer, get involved, and meet other parents at school events and activities.

Chaperoning class field trips is a great way to get to know the other parents who also chaperone, as is volunteering to be the room parent because you get to meet many of the parents at class parties and events. I remember being delighted to learn that there were five other only children in my son's kindergarten class, and he ended up becoming good friends with several of them.

Finding that one mom friend who also has an only and who can empathize with many of your concerns can do wonders to boost your mood and mental health. She will likely understand your insecurities and may be feeling the same way, especially if she is also OAD, not by choice. Building your village with other one and done families can be the best way to find a sense of connection and belonging in a multiple child family world.

TIP #2: SKIP BABY SHOWERS, GENDER REVEAL PARTIES, AND OTHER TRIGGERING EVENTS

If your child is young, it is likely that many of your friends and peer group are in the midst of growing their families. That means that if your child is younger than kindergarten age, you probably hear a lot of pregnancy announcements. Pregnancy announcements, especially when it's for a second child, can be hard for some to handle. This can especially be the case if your friend was OAD for a long time but then became pregnant, and you were blindsided with the announcement. It can leave you feeling very alone in your struggles and like you're the only one left in your social circle who can't have more children.

Sometimes even though we want to be happy for friends who are announcing their second, third, and fourth pregnancies, it is hard to do. This is usually because we're consumed by grief, loss, and sadness at our own unsuccessful attempts at growing our family and are having difficulty with the acceptance process. We are happy for them, but at the same time, sad for us. And these feelings are all totally normal.

Certain events can be triggers for parents who are one and done, not by choice, such as baby showers, sip n' sees, or gender reveal parties. These can be hard to attend because the events are celebrating procreation and growing families, reminding you of what you can't have—another child.

Therapist Nicole McNelis, LPC, said that if there are events where you feel uncomfortable, you don't have to go; you can set boundaries.

"It's okay if certain events feel anxiety-provoking. You get to decide how you want to handle those events. Maybe you can send a card [or] a gift, but you don't have to physically or virtually go . . . and that's okay."

If you feel anxious or insecure about going, it's perfectly okay to skip these kinds of events for your own mental health. You can always send along a gift and nice note, or show support for your friend in other ways that make you feel more comfortable, like taking her out for lunch with just the two of you. Your friend will understand, especially if she knows what you're going through. It's protecting your own heart to stay away from these events and the challenging feelings surrounding them.

Some moms who are one and done, not by choice, can't handle being around pregnant women at all. It can be especially difficult if your sister, cousin, or other family member is the one who is pregnant because you can't really avoid them at family events and gatherings, and it's likely you'll be hearing about their pregnancy and birth a lot. If you haven't shared your own struggles with the pregnant mom, these situations can be hard to navigate because they won't know why you're suddenly avoiding them or changing the subject from babies to something else.

Being kind to yourself and engaging in nourishing self-care is extremely important in order to protect your own emotions when a close friend is pregnant or when you are invited to multiple baby-related events. Positive ways to engage in self-care include spending more time out in nature, exercising, spending time on your own hobbies and interests, talking with supportive friends, and nurturing new friendships that make you feel happy and content.

TIP #3: HAVE A GOOD COMEBACK READY

One of the things that parents who are one and done, not by choice, have trepidation about is having others ask them the Dreaded Questions, like "When are you going to have a second child?" or "How come you don't have more kids?" These questions are nosey, intrusive, offensive, and nobody else's business, and they bring up negative emotions for many parents who cannot have a second child.

I remember getting questions like these constantly when my son was a toddler and preschooler. It seemed like everyone in the world wanted to know why I was not already pregnant, when I was going to have a second child, and why it was taking so long. I received these questions from everyone, from moms at preschool to the cashier at the grocery store to waitresses at restaurants to well-meaning family members.

Two upsetting instances from the preschool years stand out the most in my mind. A restaurant waitress said out of the blue, right in front of my son, "Why just one? You need to have a daughter." It was so demoralizing to have a stranger make a comment like this in front of my son because I worried it would make him feel bad. I don't think he gave it a moment's thought (he was only four), but I ruminated about that comment for months.

I also remember a time at a preschool event when I was asked by a random mom why I didn't have more kids. This preschool mom I didn't know at all came up to me and, without making any preliminary small talk, asked immediately why I didn't have any other kids and when was I going to have a second. I was so taken aback by her rudeness that I didn't really know what to say.

After that negative experience, I braced myself for similarly intrusive questions any time I was at a kid-friendly event. Eventually, once my son was in kindergarten, the questions slowed down, and I was grateful when people finally stopped asking.

Mental health therapist Nicole McNelis, LPC, emphasizes that it's important to remember that you don't owe an explanation to anyone about the size of your family. And *own* that. "For so many women, we are culturally taught that we owe people an explanation. We're constantly having to explain ourselves, and it's important to own this idea that you don't have to justify your family to anyone. I use it as a mantra—**you don't have to justify anything to anyone.**

"It can be helpful to really be intentional in what you decide to communicate to other people. There's a difference between someone asking questions who you have a close relationship with and someone random at the grocery store. . . . Make sure that if you do share, it's because you're choosing to share with someone. It's a shift from 'I have to give this person information' to 'I'm choosing to share the intimate details of my life and how my family came to be.' . . . If it's someone random, you can just say, 'We're a happy family just the way we are. Families come in all sizes, and we love our family.'

"The basic idea is you don't have to justify your family, and you can be intentional on how you set boundaries . . . because it's vulnerable information. . . . One thing that can be helpful to many parents is having a comeback response ready whenever someone asks the Dreaded Question."

Having a comeback ready can make you feel more secure going into a social situation where you might be asked these Dreaded Questions. You may be able to come up with some of your own clever comebacks, but if you need help, I've included some great examples that other parents have used:

- "Why do you ask?"
- "That's a really personal question."
- "That's a really rude question, and I'm not interested in talking about my sex life."
- "What are *your* plans for more children?"
- "We're working on it, thanks for your concern."
- "We can't have any more children."
- "We wanted another, but it's just not happening for us."
- "We'd love another, but it's not up to us."

Memorize one or two comebacks that work for you and have them ready when you are asked about your childbearing plans. It will help you feel more confident going into a situation if you've thought out a few possible answers.

TIP #4: FOCUS ON THE POSITIVES OF BEING ONE AND DONE

One of the best ways to find contentment when you are one and done, not by choice, is to focus on all the positives of your situation. While it is common (and sometimes easier by default) to focus on the negatives, acknowledging that there are also many positive and wonderful things about having a single child can improve one's outlook.

There are several ways to do this. Some parents find that having a daily gratitude practice can make a big difference with their overall outlook. They either make a list or think about several things they are grateful for, every day, about their child and family. Research has shown that focusing on gratitude makes people happier and more content with what they have.

Centering your thoughts on these positives, rather than dwelling on the negatives, can better see you through your circumstances. No matter how bleak the situation, there are always silver linings. Find these silver linings and focus on them. Sometimes it helps to write them out so you can clearly see them in front of you. Let's try that now.

EXERCISE:

Take out a sheet of paper and make a list of all the positive things you can think of about having an only child. Try to come up with at least five to seven points on your list. If you are having trouble thinking of some, here are some positives to consider:

- More opportunities to focus all your time and attention on one child.
- Better balance of work, marriage, and family time.
- Easier to travel with one child.
- Less complicated to handle one child's activities.
- Financially easier with one child (because kids are expensive).
- Less worry and stress with one child to look after.
- More time to yourself for personal development/career, etc.

- Quieter, less chaotic home life.

Whenever you start to feel sadness or anxiety from being one and done, not by choice, think back to your list of positives and focus on them. Think of things that you and your child are able to do now because you only have one. This should help keep you in a positive frame of mind when doubt and insecurity creep in.

TIP #5: GET A HANDLE ON THE GUILT

Some parents with only children have a hard time letting go of guilt. Their reasons for having guilt are many and can fester and cause added stress if not dealt with. Some examples would be that they desperately wanted a sibling relationship for their child and now feel guilty that they have deprived their child of this enduring bond. Or they could not give their child a sibling and worry endlessly about their child being lonely or alone as an adult. Some parents feel guilt when their child begs for a sibling often, knowing they can't give them one.

Some moms feel guilt and shame that they couldn't give their spouse another child, worrying that they let their spouse down. They might worry that because they couldn't give their spouse/partner the family size they wanted, the spouse/partner will view them as less of a woman or harbor permanent resentment toward them for it. Some moms who are feeling especially insecure and inadequate might even suggest to their spouse that they should find a different partner to be with—one who can give them the family they want.

The best way to handle this guilt is to realize that being one and done, not by choice, is out of your control. You need to be forgiving with yourself and release the guilt. Remind yourself that you did what you could to expand your family and it didn't work out, so now you need to be gentle with yourself while you work on acceptance. If you do feel that your spouse/partner resents you for your inability to have more children, help them work through their feelings and focus on all the positives of having one child. Acceptance comes with time, and eventually your spouse/partner will reach an acceptance too.

Also remember that no situation is black and white. Even if you were able to give your child a brother or sister, there would undoubtedly be negatives to that situation, too, because maybe the siblings wouldn't get along, so they never end up playing with each other and fight all the time instead, and you'd always wonder if your firstborn would have done better as an only child. Some parents who deal with siblings fighting all day might question whether their lives would be easier and more peaceful if they had stopped at one child.

Also consider all the ways your life might be more stressful and difficult if you had been able to have more children. You might not have the amazing career you do now or the incredible relationship with your spouse if you had more children to care for. Focusing on all the benefits of being one and done can help ease this guilt.

Some parents can feel guilty when their child asks why they don't have a sibling. It can be heartbreaking to hear your child ask over and over for a sibling when you know you can't give them one and you're struggling to process your own emotions about it. It can help if you have some age-appropriate responses ready. Think about how much you want to share with your child. Maybe you went through years of IVF when trying for a sibling, or had multiple miscarriages, but don't want your child to know about these struggles. How do you want to explain to your child why they will not be getting a brother or sister?

The way I handled it with my young son when he asked why he doesn't have a sibling was that I told him, "Mommy's eggs are broken." I told him that I tried to give him a sibling but the doctor said it wouldn't happen. He only asked a few times and seemed satisfied with this explanation. I also emphasized all the positives for him of being an only child.

Think about your child's age, maturity level, and how much detail you want to share when you come up with some potential responses.

TIP #6: WORK TO MAKE YOUR LIFE AMAZING IN OTHER WAYS

It is hard for some parents to accept being one and done, not by choice. Some of them dwell on regrets and have a hard time moving forward. Some ruminate on everything that didn't go right with their journey trying to conceive baby number two and have a hard time staying in the present. If you find yourself mired in regrets about your own journey, it is important to realize that even with this disappointment, you have the power to make your life amazing in other ways! Instead of dwelling on the past, focus on the present and look ahead to the future. What are a few things you can work on now to increase your overall life satisfaction?

Having one child means you have more time and energy to improve your life in so many wonderful ways! You can write that novel you've always meant to write, start your own business, take up some new hobbies, or commit to training for a 5K race. You *can* live your best life, even if your family is smaller than you hoped. And think about it this way—it's possible you wouldn't be able to make your other hopes and dreams come true if you had been able to have a second child.

EXERCISE:

Take out a piece of paper and make a list of all the aspects of your life that are less than ideal, such as your job, house, geographical location, hobbies, marriage, etc. Under each category, start brainstorming ways that you would like things to be different or better. Think of one goal that you can start working on now and make a timeline to achieve that goal. Working toward a new goal each week or month can help invigorate and inspire you and get you out of a rut.

TIP #7: TIME USUALLY HEALS

Although it feels like it will always sting forever, eventually most parents reach an acceptance of their one and done, not by choice, status, and are able to move on. It may take years, but know that time usually heals and makes the feelings more tolerable. Those piercing feelings of anger, sadness, bitterness, and resentment usually fade with time, until one day you realize that you're content with the way things are and can more readily internalize all the benefits of being one and done. You might find that you no longer react to a pregnancy announcement with the same level of emotional pain you once did, are able to walk right by the baby clothes section of a store without feeling deep sadness, or are no longer bothered by attending a baby shower. These are some of the signs that indicate you've reached a level of acceptance and have been able to move forward.

Many parents find that they eventually stop comparing their family to others and cease yearning for something different because they have learned to love the family they already have. However, some parents still find it hard to reach an acceptance and find that the pain of being one and done, not by choice, never really resolves. If you find that your feelings of bitterness and resentment seem to be lasting a long time and aren't getting any easier to deal with, Nicole McNelis, LPC, said that the concept of radical acceptance can be helpful.

She said, "First, recognize that it's a difficult task if those feelings continue for years because those feelings are telling you that you're really struggling. The idea of radical acceptance is about saying, 'This is not okay, but I need to find a way to make peace with it.' You're the only one who can decide what peace feels like for you and what you need to do to get there. [Ask yourself,] 'How do I make peace with the fact that we couldn't have a second child so that I can move forward?' . . . If you had an idea about the family size you wanted and then you couldn't create that family, you make peace with it and find a way to move forward."

Some moms also find that as they get older and the chances of a pregnancy naturally decline, they have an easier time accepting their situation. In other words, once they start perimenopause (when the chances of a natural pregnancy are lower), they may become more accepting of being one and done, not by choice. At first it can be hard to accept when you are officially out of your childbearing years. You may find that once a natural pregnancy is no longer physically possible, you are able to move forward and embrace all the positives of being one and done.

TIP #8: FIND A THERAPIST WHO CAN HELP

There are parents who find that they still feel very bitter and resentful when they hear others' pregnancy announcements or think about their inability to have more children. When that anger and pain starts to feel chronic and negatively impacts many areas of their lives and functioning in different ways—such as avoiding friends, staying in all the time, feeling depressed often, or negatively impacting their relationship with their child—it may be time to find a supportive therapist to help work through the process.

A therapist can help you process your emotions and come to terms with being one and done, not by choice. They can also help you deal with your anger in a constructive way, process difficult emotions, create new coping strategies, and provide support. A therapist is also helpful when you cannot turn to your spouse, partner, or anyone else for the emotional support you still need.

There are several ways to find a therapist, including through a referral from your primary care doctor, infertility specialist, or OB-GYN. You can also find one on your own through a therapist directory, such as *Psychology Today*'s Find a Therapist directory. With this directory, you can input various fields (including therapy subject areas, accepted insurance, and therapist gender) and find a therapist who matches your specifications. If in-person therapy doesn't work for you, you can also find online therapy through a local counseling group or apps like Talkspace or BetterHelp.

Conclusion

Although being one and done, not by choice, can bring with it many challenging feelings as you navigate coming to terms with a smaller family size than you originally hoped for, with a toolbox of positive coping skills and lots of self-care, patience, and support, eventually you will reach an acceptance and be better able to move forward with an amazing life with your single child family.

REFLECTION QUESTIONS

1. Think about how you felt when you first learned you would be one and done, not by choice. What were your first thoughts— disbelief, anger, denial? Where are you on your journey to process these feelings and reach an acceptance?

2. Are you asked frequently by strangers, friends, and family members when you will have a second child or why you haven't had one yet? If so, how do you respond to these questions? Are you satisfied with how you have responded in the past, and if not, how can you change your responses for the future?

3. When did you feel at peace with being one and done, not by choice? Was there a particular moment in time when you realized you had reached an acceptance of the situation? How did it feel to accept and move forward?

Section III:
Raising a Happy and Thriving Only Child

CHAPTER 7

Creating the Ideal School and Home Environments for Your Only

O nly children thrive when they are in a home and school environment that is the ideal fit for them. One of the benefits of having an only child is that you have the time, financial resources, and flexibility to create the best home and school environment because there's just one child's needs to consider. This can have amazing benefits for your only child, who is lucky to have parents who put extensive thought and effort into what kind of home and school environments are the perfect fit for their unique learning styles, temperament, and interests.

For an ideal school environment, this could be a small preschool or daycare that is intellectually stimulating and where students get a lot of personal attention. Or it could be a public elementary or middle school with more resources and a larger pool of kids to socialize with. It might also be a one-on-one homeschooling environment in which a parent is the teacher. The key is to think about how your child learns and socializes best, and then find the best fit within your means.

In terms of an ideal home environment, this could be a casual, kid-friendly space where your child has plenty of room to play. It could involve creating their own playroom with lots of toys to foster their creativity and imagination. It could also involve developing your own unique family mission statement/culture where the whole family focuses time and effort on your child's specific interests, like dance, baseball, or Scouts.

Creating the ideal home and school environments for your only child are important endeavors, and many parents put a lot of thought, time, and effort into both. Read on to learn what the most important factors are for creating the best school and home environments for your only child.

Finding the Ideal School Environment

CHOOSING A SCHOOL FOR YOUR ONLY CHILD

When I was growing up, all the kids I knew either went to public school or private school. Today, however, there are many more schooling options available. Most families choose public school, but there are other options to explore, including private schools/parochial schools, charter schools, virtual public schools, and homeschooling.

One of the benefits of having a single child is that if their needs change, it is easier to change schooling options without also having to uproot a sibling. For example, if public school is not working out for your only, it's easier to make the decision to send your child to private school without feeling obligated to send other children.

Choosing a school for your child is a big decision because they will be spending a large amount of time there during their formative years.

Some families are able to choose their child's school because they are in the process of moving (and can choose a neighborhood based on the strength of the school), have the financial resources for private school, or have the ability to be their child's teacher (if they choose homeschooling options). Other families are not able to choose a school—they send their child to the public school their home is zoned for or to the daycare or preschool closest to their home. However, they can still make the most of their school experience by taking advantage of school resources and building a sense of community at the school.

If you do have the option to choose a school for your only, what factors should you consider? For some families, academic reputation is important—perhaps even the most important consideration for their ideal school. They want their child to excel at school, and an academically rigorous curriculum with access to the best teachers and resources is at the top of their list. They might pay close attention to a school's test scores or look at the percentage of graduates who go on to college before making their decision.

Others aim to find a school with great academics, but also one with the most caring and dedicated teachers. They might feel that their child will do best at a school with smaller class sizes, with teachers who focus on the unique needs of every student, and that provides a student with individualized attention.

Amanda, mom of an only child and a teacher in Pennsylvania, said that in her opinion, the best school environment for an only child is a school that has small class sizes. Amanda's family is leaning toward a private school for their son because she feels like students get more individualized attention at private schools.

When choosing a school, Amanda also believes it is important to choose a school that fits your child's personality. She said, "If they are already an outgoing child, then they may do okay in a large group setting like a public school. It's important to look at local parents' groups and ask them how their children fit into their schools, [about] the culture of the school—is there a culture of acceptance and diversity, how many kids are there of different abilities, and what kind of accommodations can be made for students with different learning needs and physical needs?"

Academics are certainly important, but only part of the picture, and they are not the only indicator of a strong school. For example, some families look for a school that places a high value on character education, which aims to shape kids into kind, caring citizens. Or they might look for a social-emotional themed curriculum that puts an emphasis on values like kindness and empathy. Others want a parochial school that intertwines a faith-based curriculum with general education.

The environment and culture of a school is fairly important, especially for those who view school as a place to build community. Many only children feel that their friends are like siblings, and school is one of the main places where children make friends, so some families decide that they prefer a school with a warm, welcoming environment where their child can easily build and find community. They want their child's teachers to really get to know them and warmly welcome them into their class. These families focus their community-building efforts on their school community and might want to find a school with lots of family social events and opportunities to volunteer.

Other families prefer a school that places an emphasis on diversity so that their child will get to know children of other cultures and ethnicities. Amanda, mom of an only child and a teacher, said that the culture of a school is the most important factor for her family. "I'd like our child to be raised in an inclusive environment, with other kids of all different abilities and ethnicities, and not stay in a small bubble at home."

Other parents look for a school that has a welcoming, active PTA where they can volunteer on committees and help plan events. For families who have lots of local family and a strong support network already, building community at school may not be as important. But for those without these local support systems, finding their sense of community at school can make a big difference.

Danielle Peters, LMFT, a therapist in California specializing in emotionally supporting parents of kids who are neurodiverse and kids with special needs, said that children with special needs do best in a school environment where they are in a mainstream classroom at least some of the time. "It's typical that a child with specials needs is with mainstream kids at recess and PE, but it's also good for them to be in the mainstream classroom during other academic times. Sometimes that works by having the child go in with an aide for social studies or art."

With so many choices to consider, the first step in deciding about schooling options for your only is to think about what kind of learner your child is. Does your child do best in a small class setting where they can get more individualized attention? Do they prefer hands-on learning projects, or do they do better with virtual learning? Consider whether your child has any learning disabilities or special needs and how these can be accommodated by a school, and whether your child would do best in a smaller or larger school environment.

Also consider an option that is often less well-known: charter schools. If your child has a particular interest in the arts or STEM, your area may have a charter school that focuses on an academic specialty along with general education. Charter schools are free (like public schools), but they are lottery-based. That means that unlike regular public school, not everyone who applies will be accepted if the school receives more applications than it has spots available. If you are contemplating this option, keep in mind that you will want to get your child's name into the lottery system as soon as you can because spots tend to fill up quickly.

In the next section, we will explore the main schooling options that are available, with special consideration to the benefits and drawbacks for an only child.

PUBLIC SCHOOL FOR YOUR ONLY CHILD

One aspect of public school that appeals to many parents of onlies is the fact that many of your child's classmates will live nearby, which can become the foundation of strong friendships. It may be an appealing idea for your child to make friends at school who live locally, which makes setting up playdates easier. Many of the kids in your neighborhood will attend the local public school, and walking to school together or waiting together at the bus stop every day can be a good opportunity for your child to get to know them and for you to get to know their parents. In this way, attending the local public school can create an even stronger connection to your neighborhood.

For many families, their current public school is the right choice for a number of reasons. Perhaps you have researched local school districts and already chose a home in a district that's known for excellent schools. If you are in the process of moving, you can also consider moving to a specific neighborhood or community that is known for its excellent public schools. If you are new to an area and don't know much about the schools, there are many ways to find out about the quality of public schools. Asking your realtor for information, talking to other parents, asking for feedback about potential schools on discussion forums or on Facebook neighborhood groups, and doing research online are all ways you can learn about different public school systems.

If you do have the ability to consider moving, think about what important indicators of a good public school are to you. Perhaps you value the larger class sizes, or the presence of a gifted and talented program appeals to you. Many public schools offer a gifted and talented program or accelerated studies program. It's an advanced track that can offer a more rigorous academic experience for your only.

For families who want public school but prefer a virtual option for various reasons, some states offer virtual public school. Virtual Virginia Academy and North Carolina Virtual Academy are two such programs that are free to participants.

CONSIDERING PRIVATE AND PAROCHIAL SCHOOLS

For some families, their local public school does not meet their needs for a variety of reasons and they want to explore other options. Perhaps you feel that public school's large class sizes might be too overwhelming for your only—some kids have a quieter personality and feel lost in a crowd. Or maybe your child would do better with smaller class sizes where they can get more personalized attention. Or perhaps you're looking for a faith-based school where your religious values are woven into the curriculum.

If any of these resonate with you, then perhaps a private school or parochial (religious-based) school might fit your needs and budget. Private schools charge tuition and offer smaller class sizes, a lower student-to-teacher ratio, and may offer more of a close-knit community feel. Private schools can be single-sex, with all-girls schools or all-boys schools, or they can be co-ed. They can be college prep schools (which focus on an advanced and rigorous curriculum); gifted and talented schools; schools focused on STEM, nature, or the arts; or schools for children with special needs.

Parochial schools traditionally refer to Catholic schools, but also include Christian schools, Jewish day schools, and other faith-based schools. And just like at secular private schools, you can usually apply for financial aid and scholarships to faith-based private schools.

Private and parochial schools have many benefits: they offer smaller class sizes, unique course offerings, sometimes a more involved parent community, and an education that incorporates religious values (parochial schools). These kinds of schools also usually place a strong emphasis on building community and creating a school family.

Many parents value private schools for the more individualized experience; smaller class sizes give teachers the ability to get know the kids better. If your child thrives in a smaller group setting, private schools may be a good choice. However, a drawback of these small class sizes is that there are fewer kids to be friends with. That might mean that your child doesn't have as much opportunity to make new friends within his class over the years.

If you live in a medium- or large-sized city, there are probably dozens of private schools to look into—from secular private schools to single-sex schools to parochial schools. There are also boarding schools (where students live on campus), which are less common.

One main drawback of private schools is the price tag. Financial aid and scholarships are often available, depending on need. Additionally, admissions to some private schools are competitive, requiring test scores, a personal interview, and recommendation letters for admission.

To find private schools in your area, first decide if you want a secular school or a parochial school. Then do some research to find schools that are near your home and what their tuition fees are. You and your spouse will also need to sit down and figure out if private school works for your budget, or if you will need financial aid to attend. You can also ask friends and neighbors for recommendations, post on social media or discussion forums, and look on websites (like greatschools.org) to read reviews. When you find some good options that you want to look more into, schedule tours at each school and see which one feels like the right fit.

HOMESCHOOLING AN ONLY CHILD

For parents who want a more personally tailored educational experience, where they choose what is taught to their child because they are the teacher, homeschooling is another option. While homeschooling used to be mainly associated with religious families teaching their kids at home so they could teach them their religious values, today many who choose homeschooling come to it with a completely secular perspective. In fact, today there are many secular homeschooling groups and secular curricula to choose from.

Homeschooling also became much more commonplace during the

COVID-19 pandemic when many families decided to withdraw from public school in order to teach their children safely at home. If you do choose to homeschool, there are plenty of religious and secular home-school groups that can provide a community and support with other homeschooling families who share your educational philosophies and perspectives.

There are many reasons why some only-child families choose to homeschool. Jill from Virginia decided to homeschool her young son because she liked the idea of customizing her son's education to meet his individual needs, as well as wanting to give him more time for free play while he's still young. "I live in a community with a lot of homes-choolers, so it felt comforting to know that we would have support from others in the same situation."

Jill continued that despite the benefits she's seen from homeschool-ing, there are some challenges when homeschooling an only child. "I'm his only playmate while we are at home during the day. In addition, many of the homeschoolers in our area have multiple kids, so he often feels left out since he doesn't have siblings like they do. He sees many of these siblings playing together and entertaining each other during outings, and he sometimes wants that too.

"However, the benefit of homeschooling an only child is that we have more time available to do fun things when our academic work is done since it takes less time to teach one child versus multiple. In addi-tion, we have more time to do activities that *he* wants to do . . . since we don't have to balance the needs of a wide range of kids with varying ages or schedule things around [sibling] nap times."

Jill's advice to others who are interested in homeschooling an only child is to first seek out fun activities and playdates that can serve as a useful social outlet for your child. "Being proactive to find meetups and interesting events is really helpful. There are many homeschool co-ops that might be useful for finding homeschool friends. It may be helpful to find others in a similar situation that also have an only child. The kids may be able to relate better on some levels, and the parents may have more time to connect too."

There are many helpful online resources on homeschooling, ranging from Facebook support groups to online discussion forums. There are even homeschooling curricula you can purchase online so that you don't have to come up with your own curriculum. Additionally, many social resources are available for today's homeschooling families, including lots of social groups and clubs just for homeschooled children.

Members of these groups get together for co-op activities and field trips. Many states' school districts offer funding so that homeschooling families can participate in activities, such as art and PE, outside of the home. Your child may be able to attend certain after-school clubs or activities at your local public school. Community centers, children's gyms, art centers, parks, and rec centers also offer science, PE, art, music, and language classes tailored toward homeschoolers so that your child can make friends, build community, and experience some new educational subjects outside the home.

PRESCHOOL AND DAYCARE

If your child is preschool age, you have many choices to consider when looking for a preschool or daycare. In fact, there are so many preschools and daycares around that it can be overwhelming to find the right fit for your family.

A first step is making a list of your top priorities for a preschool or daycare. Your priorities might include a school that's convenient to the proximity of work or home, a school that is affordable (in-home daycares are usually less expensive options), a school that offers year-round care or offers a summer camp, a school that features a specific educational philosophy (like Montessori or a forest school) versus play-based, a public preschool, or a school that is faith-based or part of a religious congregation. You can ask friends and neighbors for recommendations and post on local discussion forums or Facebook groups to get ideas.

If you're already part of a religious congregation, you might have information about your congregation's preschool. It's also important to sit down with your spouse and figure out your preschool/daycare budget and see which schools you can afford.

Once you've narrowed down your list, make appointments to check out preschools and take tours to get a feel for the differences of each school. I looked at twelve different preschools before we decided on the right one. I took my son on all the tours, and he and I both liked one in particular the best. I knew right away that this preschool was the perfect fit when he sat in on a class and didn't want to leave because he was having so much fun being with other kids. (He was two at the time.) The classrooms had bright colors and engaging décor, and an overall warm, welcoming feel. The school also offered fun specials (like yoga), and the playground was really engaging. Additionally, I liked that the preschool offered its own summer camp so my son could attend half-day camp with kids he already knew from his class. He had a wonderful three years at that preschool, and I look back at his preschool years very fondly.

You can also sign up for a Mommy-and-Me class that many pre-schools offer to see if you would like the preschool, sort of as a trial run. Mommy-and-Me classes are usually for toddler ages and meet once a week in one of the preschool classrooms. You'll get a good sense of the preschool and meet other parents and kids who would be in your child's class. It's a great way for your toddler to get used to the preschool envi-ronment and develop preschool-ready social skills, like sharing with other kids and the ability to sit in a circle and listen to stories during circle time.

BUILDING COMMUNITY AT SCHOOL

If a sense of community through your child's school is important to you, there are many ways for you to build community once your child is in school. Becoming a room parent, joining the PTA and chairing commit-tees, volunteering at the library, chaperoning field trips, and helping out informally with school events are all ways you can meet other parents and make friends.

Amanda, mom of an only child and a teacher, said that being a room parent is a great way for an only-child family to build community at school. "I got involved in the parent council and met other families. Getting involved also helps you see where the school's values lie, and if there needs to be change, you're there."

If you're at the local public school, you will also meet neighbors who have a child at the same school. Staying with your child at the bus stop and chatting with other parents is a great way to meet neighbors and build community because you'll be seeing these same people every day. Even going to drop-off and pick-up at the school and walking your child in can be a good way to meet other parents and feel connected to the school and teacher.

The biggest ways I built community at my son's schools over the years included being a room parent, joining the PTA, serving on committees, chaperoning field trips, and volunteering in the school library. Just being at the school, seeing the same people, getting to know the teachers and staff, and volunteering to help out with events helped me meet others and build that important sense of community at school for my son.

Creating the Ideal Home Environment

DESIGNING A KID-FRIENDLY SPACE

Many families with only children want to tailor their home life to fit their child's personality and interests. They also want to curate their home environments to be warm and welcoming for their only child. Some families value having a house that is "kid-friendly" with comfortable furniture and warm accents like table lamps, rugs, toss pillows, non-breakable knickknacks, and plants. They often try to go above and beyond to give their home a family-friendly feel.

Danielle from Florida said that her home has a lot of kid-friendly space. "[My son's] bedroom and our living room are 100 percent child-proof, and he's always 'helping' me in the kitchen. As he gets older, it's important to me that we keep snacks and drinks on hand so he can easily have a friend over. We also have a pool he and his friends will always be welcome to."

One adult only child remembers that her childhood home was the opposite of kid-friendly. "My parents displayed my artwork, but only in our mudroom, which was our one messy room that no one spent time in. They didn't want it cluttering up their other walls. They didn't let me store my toys or games in plain view; they wanted everything in a cabinet where it was out of sight. If you walked into my house, you would never know that a child lived there, other than for family photos."

You want your child to have positive memories of their childhood home, and that can be accomplished when there are welcoming and warm details that they will look back on fondly, like a special space to display their artwork for all to see or a fun basement with lots of games and toys.

Jill from Virginia said that creating a warm atmosphere with lots of love and supportive communication is key for a child to thrive at home. "Creating welcoming play spaces in the house is nice so that the home is inviting for lots of friends, which is helpful if there aren't siblings to play with. In addition, having a pet, even something small like a fish or hamster, may be comforting for many children, especially those [who] don't have siblings to play with."

Danielle Peters, LMFT, a therapist in California specializing in emotionally supporting parents of kids who are neurodiverse and kids with special needs, said that there a few ways to make your home environment more enriching for your only child with special needs. Having lots of sensory stimulation in the home environment is key. "If you have a child who is autistic and is sensory seeking, you could have a safe tire swing in the garage or have a miniature ball pit in the living room. This allows a child with autism to have the sensory stimulus they need. If you have a child who is in a wheelchair, make sure they have sensory toys they can play with, books they can read, and different things they can look at on each wall."

She continued that other ways to create an ideal home environment for a child with special needs include having routines in place, clear expectations, and lots of books, educational toys, and things that play to your child's strengths. It's important to tailor your home environment to your child's passions and strengths.

For example, if your child has ADHD and their passion is art and crafting, consider creating a special craft corner for your child. Expanding, Peters said, "You could have a desk that's shellacked so that your child can paint without ruining the desk, a cover on the floor so they can make a mess without ruining the floor, and all the crafting supplies right where she can access them. If your child is in a wheelchair, make sure that they can move their wheelchair on their own, and make sure the space is clear enough that they can get around. Also make sure there are spaces that are comfortable for them—for instance, that they have cushions on the floor."

There are many ways to make your home environment more kid-friendly, and most of them are quick and easy updates that anyone can do. One approach is to add some pops of color to your current décor. Have you ever noticed that when you go into a children's store or a preschool classroom that the colors are usually bright and energetic with lots of primary colors? That's because those colors are perceived as more fun, as opposed to staid neutrals or earth tones, like beiges and browns. You can easily add more color to your spaces to make them more child-friendly. The easiest way to do that is with toss pillows and colorful art. You can liven up a beige sofa by changing the entire color scheme with bright toss pillows and a cheerful throw blanket. Adding vividly colored art or knickknacks can also brighten the space.

Adding whimsical touches in each room can also make your home feel more child-friendly. In our family room, we have a plush sheep ottoman that we use as a side table. It's a fun, whimsical touch that makes for an interesting conversation piece. In another room we have a small rug shaped like a cat. My son's friends always comment on these pieces and say how much they like them.

Having your child's art proudly displayed is another easy step you can take to make your home more kid-friendly. Arranging your child's art around your home makes them feel happy that their art is good enough to be proudly displayed. You might dedicate a kitchen wall to their art and hang it from a string with clips, which adds a fun ambiance. Or you can frame it and create a gallery wall in your hallway. You can also get photo books made of your child's art and display them that way.

Other ways to create a kid-friendly home include allowing your child's toys and games to be displayed and not stored away out of sight. Having your child's toys neatly arranged in the family room or basement will help them feel like they belong in the house, as opposed to strict rules stating that toys can only be played with in their bedroom or playroom. If you treat your child's toys like clutter or an eyesore, they might subconsciously start to feel that they themselves don't belong in the home.

Your child's toys don't have to be a mess and strewn all over the place. No one likes that! Instead, attractive baskets and bins, chests, and shelves can be good ways to store toys and games in a neat, organized way. If you need some ideas for inspiration, check out Pinterest for how to organize kids' items.

A kid-friendly home might have a few breakables, but they are usually stored safely on high shelves so they won't be broken. Having a home filled with breakables on every surface might make your child feel like they need to be super careful all the time so they don't break anything. Likewise, having a room that's off limits (like a formal living room) can also make your child feel uncomfortable in your home. Many families these days have gotten rid of their formal living rooms altogether and turned that space into a playroom or media room instead.

Having spaces specifically dedicated for playtime in your home also helps it to have a kid-friendly ambience. You might have a game corner in the family room with a bookcase stacked with cards and board games for family game nights. Or you might play games at your kitchen table, so you have a special pantry space stacked with all your family's favorites.

Other families with only children focus on making their home environment conducive to academics and study with a library, dedicated study space, and lots of books around. You might want to create a reading nook with a beanbag chair, bookshelf with a variety of books, comfy toss pillows, and a reading lamp. Some families with a child who loves to build have a dedicated building corner with LEGOs, blocks, and other building toys. Others want their home to be a creative haven for their child with an art table, yoga space, or crafting spot where their child can do creative projects. Think about what your family likes to do in your free time when working to create kid-friendly spaces.

Some only-child families want to create the ideal "fun house" where their child's friends will enjoy hanging out often. They might dedicate a specific room in their home as the "hangout area," like a basement or playroom. They might add a beanbag chair, train table, Ping-Pong table, foosball table, pool table, or something similar, depending on their child's age and interests. They might make a video gaming spot with a gaming chair and game console. Or they turn their backyard into a fun outdoor hangout space with a playset, outdoor toys, a pool, a sprinkler, or a badminton net. Having a fun, kid-friendly space to gather will encourage other kids to hang out at your house, which might help your child make more friends.

If you don't have a backyard, a local park can serve as an extension of your home's green space. Midori, who lives in Japan and has a ten-year-old son, said that she always makes sure her son spends plenty of time with other kids around his age, but because they live in the city and don't have a backyard, they spend a lot of time at their local park. "I probably spent more time at the park with him than any other family in the neighborhood when he was a toddler. Even during the [COVID-19] pandemic, we have managed to have him play at the park at least a couple of hours a day, rain or shine."

If your child is older, you can ask for their input about what would make their living space more fun. Older kids can help decorate their rooms but can also give input into decorating other shared spaces, like the family room or basement. What fun features would they like to see?

Keep in mind that while you create a kid-friendly home, you do not have to sacrifice your own needs and aesthetic eye as an adult who lives there too. The key is to maintain an ideal balance between adult and child interests. In a purely adult-focused home, the child has their bedroom and maybe a playroom, and all their toys are expected to be kept in those areas and out of the shared spaces completely. If a home is too kid-focused, then toys and games overflow into all the common spaces. Have you ever been in a home where every square inch of each room is covered in toys? I sure have, and it feels chaotic and overwhelming! A happy medium is a home environment where both adults and kids feel equally welcome and comfortable.

CREATING A FAMILY CULTURE

As part of creating an ideal home environment, some families have espoused a family "culture" that focuses on one or two main interests that define their family. For example, some only-child families are "baseball families," where the child plays on baseball teams, a parent coaches the team, and their weekends revolve around travel sports and attending or volunteering at games. Other families are "dance families," where the child takes dance lessons, participates frequently in dance recitals/performances, fundraises for costumes and performance fees, and is very involved with building community at their dance studio.

Our family happens to be an "ice hockey family," where my son plays on an ice hockey team and my husband plays on his own leagues and coaches our son's team every year. As a hockey family, our weekends are frequently spent at the hockey rink for practices and scrimmages. While I don't play hockey myself, my role is to manage the avalanche of hockey gear that has overtaken our mudroom, attend games, and cheer them on. We've had some really neat experiences as a "hockey family," including my son having the opportunity to play at intermission during a Washington Capitals game when he was only five years old as part of the Mites on Ice program!

When you're very involved in your child's sport or interest, you form strong connections with other parents who are also involved because you see them frequently at classes, games, and associated social events. It's a great way to create a strong sense of community for your only child because you might stay with the same team or program for years, thus being with the same kids and their families long-term. It's this continuity that helps build community, which is especially important for only children.

Establishing a family "culture" helps create an "identity" for your family that your child relates to. This sense of identity can be especially helpful for a child who doesn't like school or has difficulty making friends at school, thus providing another opportunity outside of school for them to excel in something, as well as additional outlets for friendships and community. Having these outlets can improve a child's self-esteem and self-confidence.

Along these lines, having a family culture/identity can also be helpful for a child who struggles to find a sense of belonging within a family. Some older only children feel that they don't have much in common with their parents, and thus struggle to connect with them. They also don't have a sibling to bond with, so they can sometimes feel out of place in their family; however, having a family culture can be a way for the whole family to connect.

For example, your teen son may be quiet at home and seem uninterested in spending time with you, but the two of you are able to bond over a shared interest/activity while serving as the Boy Scout leader for his troop. Your son can develop a strong sense of pride that his parent is enthusiastic about sharing his interest in this way.

Having one or both parents involved in one particular activity, like a team sport, can be an excellent way to spend family time together, while making your child feel special that their parent is so involved. If you think about it, there are many ways to get involved in your child's activity or sport beyond coaching. You could consider volunteering to help with different things for the team, like bringing snacks to the game or helping chaperone a travel team when they go to away games. You could also teach workshops or facilitate social events for the group.

The concept of a family culture/identity is also a great way for you to create a sense of community as you connect with others who share your family's interest. This can be especially helpful for families who do not have any extended family or many friends in the area and are looking to build community with others.

Nicole McNelis, LPC, a therapist from Pennsylvania, said that family is so much more than the people you're related to—it's also about where you belong in the larger community. She explained, "Creating communities where we want to belong, where we enjoy the activities that are taking place and the relationships cultivated in those settings, is very important. We create these larger communities and surround ourselves with them. For most of us, belonging is a primal human instinct. It's important to look at your family, what types of things you enjoy doing together, who you enjoy being around, and how you want to engage in the community. You can be really intentional about it, and say, 'We're choosing to do this because we're seeing this as something that's valuable to our family.'"

For example, if you're a soccer family, you might find your sense of community at the soccer field—volunteering at games, carpooling to games, and inviting soccer friends to your house for end-of-season get-togethers. If you're a Cub Scouts family, you might find your sense of community going to pack meetings, attending pack events, and volunteering to help out with the pack in any way needed. Or maybe you're a beach family who spends every weekend at the beach, has beach-themed décor in your home, and loves everything about the beach!

You can even decorate your house to reflect your interests. For example, if you're a hockey family and you have a basement or playroom, you can decorate the walls with hockey sticks, hockey jerseys, hockey pucks, and photos of your favorite teams. If you're a nature family and spend every weekend hiking different trails, you could frame photos of beautiful vistas you've seen together or make collages of nature items, like pretty leaves and pinecones you've found on your walks.

Whatever shape it takes, having a family culture can provide a strong emotional foundation of belonging, tradition, and togetherness for your child.

CREATING A FAMILY MISSION STATEMENT

Along with creating a family culture, some families also decide to create a family mission statement. Think of the company or nonprofit where you work—do they have a mission statement? Most businesses and nonprofits do because it helps the entity narrow their focus and figure out what values they believe in that tie into the work they do.

A family mission statement can help your family discover what's most meaningful and then build a lifestyle around it. For instance, if your family values building community and giving back to others, you could create a family mission statement around these values and spend your free time volunteering for different causes. If your family values travel, you could create a family mission statement focused on exploring the world around you and spend much of your free time traveling.

Amy Weber, LCSW, a licensed clinical social worker in New York who specializes in therapy for children and their families, believes that family mission statements are helpful because they make future decisions and boundaries a little easier. She said, "If you are a family that values generosity, then hoarding Halloween candy is not in your value system. You can always go back to your family mission statement and remind the adults, too, that this is a decision you're making in line with what your values are."

You can involve your child in helping create your family mission statement. This might be a document you write out, or it could be more of a visual representation with a collage made on poster board or other special display on a wall in the family room. The important thing to remember is to make it fun and involve everyone in the family to write it up and decide how to display it.

Conclusion

This chapter covered all the different ways that you can generate the ideal home and school environments for your only child. Your goal in building these ideal environments might be to create a variety of educational, community, and family experiences that are the ideal fit for your child's personality and interests. Your only child is lucky to have attentive parents who can focus all their time, resources, and creativity to ensure that they have the most wonderful and meaningful childhood possible.

REFLECTION QUESTIONS

1. Think about your own school experience growing up. What did you like and dislike about your own school experience? Do you want the same school experience as you had for your own child, or something different?

2. When you think back to the home environment you grew up in, what stands out to you the most? What did you like about

your home environment, and what do you wish could have been different?

3. Do you consider your house to be a "fun house"? Is this a priority for you? What else could you do to make your home more of a fun hangout spot?

4. Do you have a family mission statement? If not, what are some options for your own family mission statement?

CHAPTER 8

Developing New and Exciting Traditions for Your Family

Family traditions are the ways that people celebrate and mark important holidays, milestones, and events within a family. Traditions are also a great way to make cherished memories. While decorating for the holidays and doing holiday-related festivities are some of the common traditions that many families enjoy, keep in mind that you can also create memorable and amazing everyday traditions for your own family. Strong and enduring family traditions throughout the year become many only children's favorite memories from childhood.

When people think of family traditions, they usually think of Thanksgiving or Christmas customs, like a classic Thanksgiving turkey dinner or putting up a Christmas tree and holiday lights. For holidays, some families might set out cookies and milk for Santa, host a special

New Year's Eve dinner, or invite friends and family for a Passover Seder. But there are many other family traditions you can create for the major holidays, and new ones you can establish for a variety of holidays and milestones too.

For example, you could plan a Friendsgiving meal around Thanksgiving every year, celebrate Groundhog Day by going on a nature walk and looking for groundhogs, or honor a half-birthday with half a birthday cake. The possibilities are endless, and family traditions are a great way to let your creativity shine! But the key is to do the same thing every year so that your child will come to look forward to it. If every year you do something completely different for each holiday, that's perfectly fine too, but you likely won't build the foundation of enduring family traditions.

The best part about creating your own family traditions is that you have free rein to come up with any traditions you want. Even if you didn't have any traditions growing up, and it's something you feel regretful about, you can create as many as you'd like for your own family. In this chapter, I first discuss the value of family traditions and then explore some suggestions and tips for creating your own.

The Value of Family Traditions

When you look back on your own childhood, chances are some of the memories that stand out the most involve family traditions. Whether it's remembering big family Thanksgivings at your grandparents' house, your family's annual Halloween party, your yearly fall trip to a pumpkin patch, or an annual Fourth of July BBQ with family and friends, it's family traditions that endure through the decades and create fond memories for your only.

Jill from Virginia said that her family strives to create family traditions so that they can create good memories for the future to look back on. "We have some seasonal traditions, including going apple picking every fall. We make a fun day out of it, get yummy treats after picking, and then we go home and bake something with the apples together. Also, at the end of the year, we create a family photo album that we get printed and delivered. We review the album together in early January and reminisce on the previous year's adventures. Since we homeschool, we have flexibility to do road trips during less busy times. We usually do a mini-getaway close by for a night or two in May before the tourist season hits. We try to visit a kids' museum or science center. We hope these traditions, and others, will continue."

Family traditions also let only children feel a part of something bigger, beyond their immediate family. Whether it's a brisket recipe that's been passed down for generations in your family, a Diwali celebration with extended family, or a Christmas Eve tradition at church that your family has always participated in, traditions help kids feel more connected to their extended family, religion, and culture. It can be very special to see the youngest generation participating in the same family traditions you enjoyed when you were their age.

Some people have the mindset that if they have a small family, they don't need to bother with celebrating holidays in a big way. Let's face it—it can be a lot of work to cook a full Thanksgiving dinner with all the trimmings, go all out decorating your house for Christmas, or plan a big holiday celebration. But it's *so* important that you make the effort! Kids feel special when they see their parents putting in so much work to make holidays festive. They will notice the small details. Kids really do appreciate the effort and will remember the work you put into it. They also look forward to family traditions, and it's comforting when they know to expect the same customs year after year.

Family traditions can also help your child bond with extended family. If your traditions involve grandparents and extended family, they may help enhance your child's special connection with these relatives. Your child will love baking hamantaschen every Purim with their grandmother or eating Aunt Mary's special pumpkin pie every Thanksgiving.

They might look forward to their grandparents' Christmas party or a Fourth of July BBQ with extended family.

Traditions with extended family help a child feel part of something bigger and create warm feelings of family connection that your child will always value. When grandparents or other extended family share cherished family traditions with your child, it helps them learn more about the unique traditions and cultural practices passed down through the generations within their own family.

Additionally, family traditions help kids stay enthusiastic about spending time together as a family. Especially when they reach the teen years, many kids are no longer as excited about spending time with their parents, or feel they that they don't have much to say to their parents anymore. But fun family traditions can keep their interest in spending quality family time alive, and they may be more willing to participate in the activity "because it's a tradition."

Creating family traditions takes some effort, but it's time well spent. I would argue that it's even more important for families with only children to make the effort to create strong, dependable family traditions. Some only children can feel like they're missing out around the holidays when they see media images of large families all having fun together at a huge Thanksgiving table, or the boisterous fun of opening gifts with siblings on Christmas morning. They might feel badly that they don't have siblings to share in these holiday experiences with, and their quiet holidays might not feel as festive and fun if it's just them and their parents. This can especially be the case for only children who do not have local family and who don't celebrate holidays with extended family due to distance.

Nicole McNelis, LPC, a therapist from Pennsylvania, said, "If it feels like something is missing, there might be an underlying need that is not being addressed. Perhaps that underlying need is that you want to be around more people for the holidays. If you don't have local family, or if getting together with family doesn't make sense, do you have friends that you're close to that you want to have a celebration with? Or is there another family who is also in a similar situation? If so, perhaps getting some friends together for a Friendsgiving, or another celebration on a different day, could be a helpful solution. Create a larger celebration with your chosen family."

If you prefer to celebrate with just your immediate family for holidays, you can still make it special and festive. McNelis continued, "So often we feel these cultural pressures, [like] Thanksgiving [must be] a big, chaotic meal with twenty people. But what if it could also be three people having a quiet dinner or going on a mini-vacation and enjoying each other's company somewhere beautiful? What's important for children is creating traditions and creating community, regardless of what those look like. Think about: What does your family need regardless of family or societal pressures? What would be most meaningful? And who do we want to spend that time with?"

If your only child is bothered by the fact that he doesn't have siblings, perhaps feeling like he is missing out on that kind of experience (especially around the holidays), family traditions can help him feel like he has a strong foundation of family togetherness. He'll know that he still gets to do the same things as other kids by having fun family traditions. And you can even include your child's friends in some of your family traditions, like baking holiday cookies together or decorating pumpkins. Your child will really love including his friends to share in your cherished family traditions.

Families Who Have No Family Traditions

Some families don't do any kind of family traditions at all. If this describes your family, you may want to explore further why you haven't set up any family traditions. Is it because you don't have time? Because it seems too overwhelming? Because you think your child is too young to appreciate them?

You might want to reconsider not having any family traditions, because creating them doesn't have to take much effort. Some adult only children have negative memories from childhood, in part because their parents did not create any family traditions or celebrate holidays in a meaningful way. But adding even one or two beloved family traditions can make all the difference to your child in terms of fostering a positive childhood experience.

Nicole McNelis, LPC, believes that it's important to reframe your thoughts if you feel that it's too much effort to prepare a traditional holiday meal for a small family. "I think about a cookbook I once read about cooking for one person. Even if your family is two or three people, you deserve to have beautiful, nutritious meals prepared with love—you are deserving of that. If you believe that it's not worth it to put in all of this effort, this can feel really dismissive of your family unit. We want to reframe that to 'Our family is three people [and] fully deserving of the most amazing Thanksgiving meal we could think of.' It is a beautiful idea steeped in this larger idea that we are deserving just as we are."

Sometimes families are in the tough situation of not having any extended family nearby to spend holidays with. This can feel lonely for both you and your only child, and it can feel like you're missing out. You might feel envious of friends who post social media photos of their huge extended family holiday celebrations, where everyone seems to be having tons of fun and enjoying each other's company. If it bothers you to see others' huge Thanksgiving gatherings or holiday dinners with big, loving families when you never have holiday plans with relatives, think about ways you can change things up this year, and how you can make holidays more special for the three (or two) of you.

One idea for making holidays more special in this circumstance is to consider traveling somewhere fun to spend the holiday. If you find that some holidays can feel depressing without a large extended family celebration, doing some holiday travel can make the holidays feel more festive.

One year for Thanksgiving we didn't have any plans, so we decided to travel somewhere fun and spent the holiday in Hershey, Pennsylvania. We had a lovely Thanksgiving dinner at the hotel and spent the day at Hershey Park because it was open. We had a great time on all the rides and swimming in the hotel's amazing pool, and my son still talks about that fun and memorable Thanksgiving.

If you don't have any holiday plans and aren't able to travel, you could also consider spending holidays with family friends. This is a great idea in theory, but can be challenging in practice because so many people have their own plans with family around holiday time. But if there is another family you know of who also has no holiday plans, invite them to spend it with you. You could plan and host a Friendsgiving at your house or invite friends to join you for your Passover Seder. If you don't want to invite them for the actual holiday meal, there are other ways to include friends in your holiday celebrations. One idea is to invite them for dessert after Thanksgiving dinner or invite them for a holiday cookie-decorating get-together around Christmas. It might be the start of a beautiful yearly tradition for both your families.

How to Develop New Family Traditions

Creating new family traditions sounds like a great idea, but it can feel overwhelming, especially if you work full-time and don't have a lot of free time for extra projects. It might feel like one more thing on your plate that you have to deal with, or you may think it's a great idea but have been putting it off. If you don't have any family traditions yet, don't worry! You can easily create them, and it's not too late to start.

The best way to begin developing new traditions for your family is to start small. Choose one or two holidays to add a tradition to this year and see how it goes. Next year you can add a few more.

To get started, first choose a holiday to introduce a new tradition. Let's say you choose the next one coming up, perhaps Halloween. Think about what you already do to celebrate Halloween and whether you think it's worth keeping or not. Then think about some new things you could add to make the holiday more fun and special—maybe even do an online search for some ideas.

For instance, if you already do trick-or-treating and decorate the outside of your house, and are happy with the effort you put into this, think about another tradition you could add. Could you create a yearly pumpkin-decorating contest and invite your child's friends to join you? You could provide a pumpkin for each child, along with decorating supplies like markers, paint, stickers, and ribbon. After some fun time spent together decorating, you could hand out prizes for the pumpkin that is the "scariest," "cutest," and "most original." You could serve Halloween treats and make it a fun pumpkin-decorating party. If you host this every year, it will become a cherished Halloween memory for your child.

Another idea for a new Halloween tradition is that you could plan an October outing to a pumpkin patch and invite another family or your child's friend along. Taking a hayride out to a pumpkin patch and picking out the perfect pumpkin can become a fun fall family tradition. Another idea to try is a yearly Halloween party in your backyard, basement, community clubhouse, or at a nearby park. Asking kids to come in costume, providing some snacks, and letting them run around (or even coming up with some Halloween-themed games) can make it a fun time. The important thing is whatever tradition you decide, make sure to do it every year so that it becomes a family tradition your child will look forward to!

If you're finding it hard to get started, you can get lots of inspiration for family traditions online! Check out blogs that focus on holidays or family traditions. You can also join a Facebook group focused on family traditions, search online for inspiration, browse through Pinterest, or talk to your friends about what they do.

Kristie from California said that she decorates for almost every season and holiday. "I change the house over for the seasons. My son really likes to get involved in that; he likes to rearrange things." Kristie also has a special Christmas tradition that she wants to keep going in her family. "I [put] silly string at the bottom of everyone's stockings. After the stress of opening all the gifts and getting rid of wrapping paper, we all go out and unleash our stress with a silly string fight, and I want to continue carrying on that tradition."

Danielle from Florida, who is an adult only child, said that she didn't really have a lot of traditions growing up. "I think with splitting time between my divorced parents, it made it hard since I switched holidays a lot." However, she is creating new traditions for her family. "We're starting traditions of our own now though, with holidays being my favorite. We'll do Elf on the Shelf, celebrate Twelve Days of Christmas with a different movie every night, milk and cookies for Santa, Christmas pajamas, and a book on Christmas Eve. Our son is still so young, so I'd love to start more traditions as he grows up."

Besides the major holidays, you can create special traditions for family birthdays as well. Chances are you probably already have a birthday party every year for your child. What else could you do to make their birthday special that could become a cherished family tradition? What about writing a special birthday letter to your child every year and saving them all in a folder to give to them on their eighteenth birthday? Or what about making a special birthday dinner where all the food is their choice? Or doing a "yes day" for their birthday, where they get to choose what to do all day?

Important milestones can also be ideal for creating family traditions, such as the first and last day of school, or when your child loses a tooth. On the first day of school, could you incorporate some new

Examples of Everyday Traditions to Try

» Special weekend pancake breakfasts, and let your child choose the toppings!

» Friday night game/movie night, where your child chooses the movie and game.

» Sunday night potluck dinners with friends.

» First day of school special photos with homemade "Back to School" signs.

» Last day of school special photos with homemade "Last Day of School" signs.

» Unique gift from the tooth fairy for each tooth lost.

» Monthly sightseeing activity in your area.

» Fall nature hikes to look at the changing leaves.

» Annual snowman building contest.

» Spring flower planting. Help your only pick which seeds to plant in the garden and prepare the area together.

» Read a bedtime story together every night.

» Create a family journal, and every week make sure to write in it.

» Try a new sport/activity together each month.

» Monthly family book club, where your child chooses the book.

» Monthly international cuisine night. Let your child choose a country and then help you cook a traditional meal.

and exciting traditions that they will always remember? Like taking a first day of school photo each year in the same spot in your house (perhaps in front of a bookcase) so you can see how big they've grown. You could also have a special "tooth fairy" tradition, where you do something unique for each tooth lost.

Also consider everyday family traditions you can create to keep the magic alive throughout the year, such as cooking a special pancake breakfast on the weekends, doing a Friday night pizza and game night, or having a weekly Sunday night potluck dinner with family friends. You could also do a monthly family sightseeing activity where you go to a new place in your community that you've never been to. Family volunteer days are another great tradition you can create for your family. You can decide on a nonprofit or charity together, and then decide how you will volunteer together. There are many volunteer opportunities you can do with kids, and there are even plenty of virtual volunteer opportunities your family can participate in. Look at volunteermatch.org or the JustServe app to get some ideas.

Don't be afraid to get creative and create new family traditions that are silly and fun. Also try not to let the tradition discourage you either because it's too complicated or overwhelming. Make sure it's something you *all* can look forward to doing each year. You can always try a new tradition out this year and see how it goes. If it goes well, decide to make it a yearly family tradition.

Conclusion

Creating a few cherished family traditions is a wonderful way to make great childhood memories for your only, as well as for your whole family. As we've seen in this chapter, your traditions don't need to be time-consuming or elaborate, but you should try to continue them every year so they become something your child looks forward to. When your only looks back on their childhood, having a few fun, silly, or meaningful family traditions may become some of their most cherished childhood memories.

REFLECTION QUESTIONS

1. Looking back on your own childhood, did your family have any family traditions? If yes, what are some of your favorite family tradition memories? What traditions did you grow up with that you would like to keep for your family?

2. Take out a piece of paper and write down a list of all the holidays (both major and minor) that your family celebrates. What traditions for these holidays do you currently have, and what new traditions can you add? By doing this, you can

make a year-round calendar of family traditions. When you list them all on one sheet of paper, you will see how many new and fun family traditions you can try for the coming year.

3. What are some everyday traditions that you could add to make things more special for your only? For instance, are there any weekend traditions your family can start? Is there a fun way you could celebrate the first and last days of school, losing a tooth, or getting a good report card?

CHAPTER 9

The Value of Pets for an Only Child

Many only-child families believe that there is incredible value in having a family pet because of its many benefits, including teaching responsibility and providing love and companionship for your only. Many only children come to view their cat or dog as their furry brother or sister and treasure them as an important member of the family.

You may be considering getting your first pet or adding an additional pet to your family. If so, you could be wondering how getting a pet will impact your only child. Let's discuss the benefits of owning a family pet, what to consider if you're having reservations about it, and how to choose the pet that's right for your family.

What Are the Benefits of Pets for Only Children?

As a society, we love our dogs, cats, and smaller pets like fish or hamsters, but there are also many nontraditional pets out there that you could consider adding to your family, like bearded dragons, hermit crabs, or ferrets. Over eighty-five million households in the United States have a pet, so clearly many people find pets to be an important addition to the family.

Statistically, most people in the US are dog owners (sixty-three million households), with cats coming in second (forty-two million households). Pets are well known to reduce stress (petting a cat can lower your heart rate), increase physical fitness (like the extra exercise you get when you walk your dog), and provide much-needed companionship. Pets can even help people with physical and emotional disabilities and special needs, like guide dogs and emotional support animals.

For children who have special needs, having a therapy animal can be a helpful source of support and companionship as well. A child with autism or anxiety, for example, might have a trained support dog who helps them regulate their emotions. The dog can help a child calm down when they're upset, increase self-confidence, and decrease anxiety so they feel more comfortable in stressful situations.

Danielle Peters, LMFT, a therapist in California specializing in emotionally supporting parents of kids who are neurodiverse and kids with special needs, said that pets are fantastic for children with special needs because often these children have a strong affinity for animals. Pets can provide companionship, help with loneliness, and, most importantly, provide social feedback that is so important for kids with special needs.

Some pets are specific service animals; usually dogs are trained as guide dogs for the blind, but others can provide anxiety relief, calm an upset child, or be trained for detecting blood sugar changes or seizures. Peters said that it can be hard to find a dog trained for your child's specific needs, but she recommends contacting organizations for the specific disability your child has. For example, if your child is blind, contact organizations for the blind that may have resources and contacts specifically for trainers who work with that disability.

Peters continued, "You may have a child who really struggles with being gentle, or struggles with the physical aspect of relationships, and pets do really well with providing feedback around that. If you have the right animal, it can be really helpful." She further explained that if your child is learning to be gentle and you have the right dog, when they're too rough with the dog, the dog will get up and leave. "Then the child no longer gets to interact with the dog and they learn that 'If I want to love on the dog, I have to do it gently.'

"There's [also] something about having an animal in the house that provides an extra level of stimulation. If there's one mom and one child, the house can be really quiet. But adding an animal in adds that extra level of stimulation."

Pets are such wonderful members of the family, and they have many benefits specifically for only children. First, pets provide a source of companionship for onlies that can be helpful whenever Mom or Dad can't interact with them. Always having a loving pet around can keep them company because your child can play with the pet whenever lonely feelings creep in. Even just being in the house together can be a source of comfort and companionship. Having a cat or dog keep your child company while they play makes them feel like they're not alone and makes it more likely that they are willing to play independently.

Pets can also be a constant presence that your child can rely on. It can be comforting for your child to know that a pet will be waiting for them when they come home from daycare or school. Many children love to burst through the door and see their cat or dog waiting patiently for them, or appreciate when their dog accompanies their parent to pick them up at the bus stop. They may also eagerly look forward to seeing their pet after a trip away from home.

Many onlies also sleep with their pet because they like the feeling of security from having an animal in their room at night—especially for kids who are scared of the dark or have difficulty going to sleep. My son sleeps with our cat and feels special that the cat chooses to snuggle with him every night. They both curl up together while he is reading books, and then when he turns out his light, the cat goes to sleep at the foot of his bed.

A pet is a built-in friend and family member who is always there for your child, and only children bond strongly with pets. Your only might watch movies with the family pet, play dress up, or play fetch in the backyard with them. This is especially true for dogs who can go places with your child and play together outside, so it's like being with a friend. When they're at the park or hiking around a lake, bringing the dog along can make family outings more fun for only children.

Kristie from California said that they have a German shepherd who was a rescue dog, and their dog was with them for three years before they had their son. At first, they were concerned because the dog was their one and only and all the attention was his, but when their son was born, the dog took on the role of being a big brother. "He is protective over our son and very gentle with him. They actually play together; they play chase, they run around the house, they both get their zoomies at the same time. It's really important for my son to have someone else other than Mom or Dad [who] he can play with."

If your only feels lonely because they don't have a brother or sister, a pet can fill this void. Some only children feel different because they are the only one in their class or social circle who doesn't have a sibling. It's tough to feel different from everyone else, and it's a feeling that many onlies struggle with. Having a pet is one way that can help onlies feel like they fit in with everyone else because many kids also have pets. If your only often talks about feeling different from other kids, focus on the many ways that she is similar to other kids, including the bond and adventures that she has with her pet.

A pet can also help your child grow and mature because it teaches responsibility and empathy to a young pet owner. Your only will become more responsible from taking care of a pet. Research shows that having a pet can increase a child's self-esteem and foster improved social skills. A child gains empathy from reading an animal's body language and thinking about how their pet feels in different situations, which can be especially helpful for children who have difficulty with social skills.

There are many pet care–related tasks that your only can help with, from feeding, watering, walking, and playing. Even young children can help pour food or water into a bowl and feel proud that they are helping, which will enhance their self-esteem and self-confidence. When my son was little, one of his chores was feeding our cats. I poured their cat food into a pitcher, and then he could easily use the pitcher to pour the food into their bowls. He was very proud to help take care of his pets in this way.

Kids can also help take care of small animals. Jill from Virginia said, "Our son helps take care of our pets by playing with them and assisting with weekly cage cleanings. He gives them treats, and . . . loves to find fun toys for them to play with when we visit pet stores."

A pet can also help your only be more social. If your only wishes they had more friends, a pet might be able to help. A dog can lead to greater opportunities for socializing and making new friends. When your only helps walk the dog, you can more easily meet and talk to neighbors because a dog is an instant conversation starter. Or if you take your dog to a dog park, you can chat with other families there. You can also join dog or cat meetup groups and connect with others who have similar pets.

A pet can also inspire an interest in helping animals. If your only is older, they can start volunteering with animal rescue groups or at an animal shelter. You can also get your dog or cat certified as a therapy animal and have your child accompany you when your therapy pet does meet and greets at retirement communities or hospitals.

Another value of having a pet for only children is that a pet lends itself to lots of whole-family togetherness, like walking the dog together, playing with the cat together, watching fish swim around, or playing with a hamster by setting up obstacle courses for it. A pet can bring your family closer because caring for them is something that all of you can do together. Jill from Virginia said, "Adding pets to our household has made our home feel a little more alive. It's nice to have other living creatures to nurture and care for together as a family."

Pets can add much love and companionship to your home. They can enrich your child's life, and your child will enhance their social skills and sense of responsibility by helping to take care of your pets.

When Your Only Wants a Pet . . . but You Don't

Does your only really want a pet but you truly don't? You might not be able to have a pet at home for allergy reasons, or you might work full-time and don't have the time or energy to take care of a pet. Perhaps you might not have room for a pet due to limited living space or have the proper budget for one (because some pets, like dogs, are especially expensive to maintain). Or you might live in an apartment or condo that doesn't allow pets. Or you simply might not be a "pet person."

Despite any or all of these reasons, your only may be begging you for a pet every day, trying to wear you down. But still, you are wary of or completely against the idea. What can you do to compromise or let your child know that while you understand their perspective, a pet is not in the cards right now?

When I was growing up, I wanted a pet more than anything. I begged my parents for a pet pretty much every day, but they didn't want one. Instead, they got me Petster, a robot cat from the '80s. It was sort of like a Roomba with fur, and it had a robotic meow and purr. It was a sad substitute for a real cat, but despite this, I loved Petster and played with that robot cat for years.

That childhood yearning for a pet never went away, and when I was in my early twenties, I adopted two cats. We've had cats ever since, and I've raised several kittens. Having a pet when you didn't grow up with animals is an adjustment at first, but I can't imagine not having our two wonderful cats.

If your only wants a pet and you don't, consider a compromise. If your only wants a cat or a dog but these are too much maintenance for your liking, could you consider an easier pet to take care of? Like a small tank with a few fish, or a hermit crab, hamster, gerbil, lizard, or turtle. A smaller pet that doesn't require as much space or time could be a good option for everyone. Compromising may help your child see that you are taking their interests under consideration but are just unable or unwilling to get the exact pet they want right now.

Jill from Virginia wanted to start with a small pet. She said, "We aren't big pet people in general, but we thought it would be nice to add a new animal member to the family. We started off with a fish since we wanted something low maintenance. Our son seemed to enjoy having a pet fish, and when others talked about how many siblings they had, he would tell them he has a pet fish (instead of a brother or sister). We later upgraded to a pet hamster, which we got for his birthday since it would still be a mostly low-maintenance pet. We hope to upgrade again to pet guinea pigs in the future."

If you have allergies, you could consider looking into hypoallergenic breeds of the pet your only is interested in. If you have a cat allergy, a hairless sphynx cat might be one breed that could work for people who are allergic to cats. If you're allergic to dogs, a goldendoodle may be another good choice. Reptiles, hermit crabs, and fish might also work well for those who have allergies. There are several options out there of different hypoallergenic breeds, sizes, and temperaments. Just be sure to do the research to find out which animal is right for your family.

If you are unable to have a pet due to difficult circumstances, there are also other meaningful ways for your only to interact with animals, such as volunteering at an animal shelter, watching live tours at aquariums online, or participating in a summer camp at the local zoo. You could also adopt an animal at an animal sanctuary and visit that animal on a regular basis.

There are many volunteer opportunities that kids can participate in to be around animals, and some are even virtual. You don't need to have a pet to be an animal advocate. Virtual volunteer opportunities can give your child the opportunity to interact with animals, help them in unique ways, and give back to their community. Check out volunteer-match.org or your local animal shelter or rescue groups to get started looking for in-person or virtual volunteer opportunities.

While it can be a challenging situation if your child really wants a pet and you feel differently, it is likely you can find a compromise that makes all members of the family happy. With a little research, you can find meaningful opportunities outside the home to interact with animals or find a special pet you might not have considered at first that will delight all members of your family for years to come.

Choosing the Right Pet for Your Family

Choosing the right pet for your family is an important decision with many variables to consider. It is important to think about the age of your only and how much he can participate in pet care and interact with the pet when making this choice.

The first decision you need to make is what species of pet you want to have and whether it's compatible with your only's age. If you have a baby or toddler and adopt a puppy, you may have your hands too full because puppies are a lot of work. If you have a four-year-old and get an aquarium full of fish, they may not be that interested in watching fish and instead want something they can play with. Likewise, an older child might do better with a more interactive pet, like a cat or dog. You also want to make sure that the pet's temperament and care needs are a good fit for your family. Talking to a veterinarian and other pet owners can be helpful in making this decision.

Once you've decided on the type of animal and species you want, do internet research to learn more about what specific breed would work best. Ask friends and family for their thoughts and advice. If you've decided on a dog, do online research and talk to others about what dog breed would best fit your family, as well as what taking care of a dog is really like. If you know you won't be able to walk a dog more than once or twice a day, research what breeds have lower exercise requirements. If you aren't home much and won't be able to play often with an energetic kitten, consider getting two kittens to entertain each other or adopting a calm older cat. Discussion forums about pets can be a really helpful place to ask questions and learn more.

An important factor to keep in mind is that there will be an adjustment period for everyone in the family once you bring your new pet home. It may take your child some time to get used to your new pet and the new pet care routine, especially if you have adopted a dog who needs multiple walks a day. Your child might even be a bit jealous of the time and attention you're giving to the new pet. It may take a while to find your groove. Be patient and give it time. Soon it will feel like your pet has always been with you.

Once you've welcomed your new pet into your home, let your only participate in coming up with the pet's name. If you don't want to give your child full power in picking the name, I suggest narrowing down the options to a few that you like and then letting your only decide on the final name. Or you could have everyone write down their first choice of name on a piece of paper, assign a number to each name, roll a dice, and go with that name. Your only will love being a part of the name-choosing process, and the pet's name will always be really special for her.

Conclusion

In this chapter, we've explored the value of pets for an only-child family and how pets are a great choice for companionship. Besides being lovable companions, pets can enhance your entire family's well-being and quality of life. With some introspection about your family's needs and some research on the animal that will be the best fit, you will be well on your way to finding the perfect pet that will enrich all of your lives.

REFLECTION QUESTIONS

1. Did you have a pet when you were a child? If so, how did you feel about your pet(s)? If you were not allowed to have a pet growing up, how did you feel about that? Were you able to connect with animals in another way?

2. Why do you think that pets are important for only children? What do you think are the most important benefits of having a pet for onlies?

3. If you don't have a pet now, but would like to adopt one, what characteristics and qualities would your ideal pet have?

Not-So-Typical Pet Ideas for Your Only

If you're looking for an animal companion that's more unique than a cat or dog, consider some of these interesting pets:

» bearded dragon
» ferret
» chinchilla
» hermit crab
» chicken
» hedgehog
» turtle
» lizard
» snake
» gecko
» iguana
» tarantula

CHAPTER 10

Planning Meaningful Trips and Vacations for Your Only Child

Many families with only children love vacations and travel. Whether it's a day trip to an amusement park, a long weekend in an exciting new city, or a week at the beach, there are many different types of vacations that appeal to only children of all ages. For some families, travel is a passion and their goal is to take as many trips as possible. In fact, the ability to travel more often and more easily is one reason why some families decide to have an only child.

Do you like to travel? Or do you want to travel more? How can you ensure that your only child will enjoy vacations without siblings to entertain them? How can you cope if your only becomes bored on trips? In this chapter, we will explore the benefits of traveling with only one child, the types of trips that appeal to onlies, how to manage potential vacation pitfalls, and the various ways you can make new memories as a family as you enjoy traveling together.

The Benefits of Traveling with One Child

As everyone knows, travel is expensive. Plane tickets, hotel rooms, dining out, rental cars, and sights/attractions/admission tickets all quickly add up. Travel is less expensive, however, with a single child versus multiple children. Many families with more than one kid cannot afford to travel as often as they would like because of the costs and challenging logistics involved when planning a trip. Because of this, one of the reasons why some families decide to have an only child is to be able to travel more.

Nikki from Minnesota sees many benefits to traveling with an only child. She said, "I think traveling with an only is one of the greatest blessings for our family. We are not only able to afford to travel more often, but we are able to focus on what each of us wants to accomplish on our trips better. Thus far, we have only seen positives to this arrangement. I am also able to travel alone with my daughter without feeling overwhelmed or outnumbered."

Kristie from California said that she hasn't taken her three-year-old son on any trips yet because of the COVID-19 pandemic, but she feels like they would be able to afford more trips and take their son to more places because they have an only child. "We will be able to afford better family vacations with having one child, and entertaining one child versus multiples on a trip sounds way less stressful. We are currently talking about a Disneyland trip and being able to spend extra money and giving him an extra experience because it's just him."

Traveling is also easier with an only because you only have to pack for one child, entertain one child, and plan activities around one child's interests. It makes the logistics of travel planning much easier, especially when you don't have to factor in different activities to suit multiple ages, juggle sleep schedule changes for multiple kids, or plan around different nap times. Some families with multiple children feel that their vacations are not restful or relaxing, but rather very similar to their day-to-day activities at home, just in a different location. Families with multiple kids can often return home from a trip feeling more exhausted than when they left. In these instances, they decide that travel with young kids just isn't worth the hassle and expense.

In contrast, travel can be more relaxing and meaningful with one child. When you have one child, you can tailor the trip specifically to your child's interests so you don't have the stress of juggling multiple activities for different ages. Additionally, your trip can feel more like a vacation because one parent can spend time with the child while the other does their own activity, like go to the spa, take a walk on the beach alone, or go to an art museum. Each parent is also more likely to get some relaxing alone time on vacation when you have a single child, which can be more of a challenge when you have multiple children.

Danielle from Florida said, "As my son gets older and more independent, I imagine it'll be so much easier to pack and go somewhere. Once he can pack for himself and get himself ready, it will be such a time saver. . . . It's also that much sooner we get to go on big trips!"

Danielle believes that only having to keep track of one child on trips sounds less stressful too. "I do eventually plan on letting him invite a friend, but probably not until the teenage years when they can kind of go off on their own for short amounts of time."

Many people like to travel because it's a break from the slog of their daily routine. When you travel with just one child, it's more likely that both parents will feel refreshed at the end of their vacation, instead of feeling drained and like they need a vacation to recover from their vacation.

Types of Trips that Appeal to Only Children

Family trips work best when you tailor your vacation plans to your child's age and interests. If you have a younger child, easy trips centered around one location with built-in entertainment can work well, such as the beach, Disney World, and camping. For instance, a trip to the beach is ideal for young kids because they can entertain themselves all day by playing in the sand. If you have an older child who would appreciate culture, history, or art, a city vacation touring museums and cultural sights can be a good choice. Older kids also may enjoy national parks, historical sites, amusement parks, or adventure trips and tours.

If your child has a particular interest, such as American history or trains, see if you can incorporate these into your trip. A child with an interest in American history might love a vacation in Washington, DC, or Colonial Williamsburg. A child with an interest in trains might love taking a train trip or going to a train museum. If your child is interested in nature and the outdoors, the US National Park Service has Junior Ranger programs that many kids enjoy. You can also combine different activities into one vacation so everyone gets to do something they like. For example, you could combine a busy city vacation touring museums and taking tours with a restful few days at a nearby beach area.

It's important that all members of the family have a good time on vacation. Nikki from Minnesota said that her family has taken many different kinds of trips. "We have done Disney, Florida beaches, many Southern states to get away from the brutal Minnesota winters, camping, and resorts. Even when we go to destinations that are more adult-friendly, I take the time to research what there may be nearby that my daughter would enjoy. When we have traveled to destination weddings that may not be in a location where we would have chosen to vacation, I also try to find some local historical sites for us to learn about and visit."

Some only children feel lonely or bored on vacations without other kids around to play and interact with. While some only children are able to go up to other kids on vacation and ask them to play, other only children are shy and don't want to put themselves out there. Some ways around this problem are to plan a vacation with another family (or two); organize a vacation with extended family so your child has cousins to play with; plan a child-friendly trip with built-in entertainment, such as the beach, Disney World, or an amusement park; or go to a place that has a kids' club (like a cruise or all-inclusive resort).

Nikki from Minnesota, who is an only raising an only, explained that her daughter does not get bored on trips. "I am a planner and make sure that we have plenty of options for things to do. Once she is older, we will absolutely allow her to bring a friend on trips though. Some of my favorite memories are of vacations with my parents and a close friend."

A vacation with other family members, such as grandparents and cousins, gives your child more people to bond with. Special vacations with cousins can be extra fun for an only child and provide lots of opportunities to make wonderful memories. When vacationing with family, many families choose easy trips that appeal to multiple generations, such as renting a beach house together or going on a cruise. We have taken several trips with my son's grandparents, including a cruise and a trip to Disney World, and my son has loved the extra special time with his grandparents. Getting a vacation rental can be a great way for the entire family to stay together without the expense of having to rent multiple hotel rooms.

Nikki from Minnesota said that her family often travels with others. "We often travel with my parents, which is wonderful. We have also done camping and resort experiences with our close friends and their children, and those have also been fantastic. I think the key, at least for us, is being flexible about as much as you can, while having firm boundaries about the things that you need for a successful trip. For example, when you have a child who naps, planning activities around that is vital to everyone's enjoyment. We are so excited to continue traveling with our village, and for our daughter to experience traveling with her cousins."

You might also consider all-inclusive family resorts, cruises, and family camps that are great for all ages, where your child will have an opportunity to meet other kids and make friends. These can also be great options if you're planning a multi-generational vacation because everyone can choose different activities during the day, if desired, and reconvene for meals. These types of vacations are also a good opportunity for your child to meet other kids. The friendships made on vacations can last for a long time. Growing up as an only child, I often made friends on my vacations, especially beach trips, and I even ended up being pen pals with some of these kids for years.

Some parents prefer to have time to themselves on vacation, so they choose to go where there is a kids' club. This allows their child to hang out with peers and stay busy for a few hours while parents do their own vacation activities. If you're considering a kids' club, make sure your child would be okay being dropped off in a new setting with a bunch of kids they don't know. Some kids wouldn't do well-being dropped off at a playroom where they don't know anyone; others would do fine with it. Cruises, all-inclusive resorts, and some hotels have kids' and teens' clubs.

If you need some ideas to plan your trip, check out travel discussion forums, family travel blogs, or browse the travel section at your local bookstore or library. There are even a few Facebook groups just for only-child family travel where you can get additional inspiration. It can also be fun for you and your child to check out children's books for locations you're interested in and learn about new travel possibilities.

Find New Vacation Spots or Return to Old Ones?

Should you return to the same vacation spots every year or try out new ones? Some kids respond to the familiarity and nostalgia of returning to the same vacation spot year after year, while others like to try new places each time. Which would your only child prefer? Both approaches can lead to fun times and fond memories. Another way you can think about it is by asking: Does your family like to stick with what's worked in the past, or does your family prefer to experience new adventures?

New adventures each year can be exciting, and trying out a novel vacation spot every time can give you something fresh and exciting to look forward to. Perhaps you try out different locations each year or different types of vacations for variety: camping one year, a cruise the next, and a city vacation after that.

One positive about returning to the same vacation spot year after year is that it can become a cherished family tradition. When I was growing up as an only child, my family vacationed in Marco Island, Florida, every winter break. I loved that trip because the familiarity of it was comforting and I knew exactly what to expect. We always went at the same time of year, stayed at the same wonderful hotel, went to the same beaches, swam in the same pools, ate at the same restaurants, and took the same day trips. Going there always felt magical to me, and I remember those trips vividly.

If you have the luxury of being able to take several vacations in a single year, you could do a half-and-half approach. For example, in the summer, you could return to the same beach spot every year, and then for your other vacation week, try a different type of trip, like a city vacation or camping trip. This allows you to look forward to one vacation that's a nostalgic family tradition and then enjoy another that is completely new and exciting—the best of both worlds!

Let Your Child Participate in the Trip Planning

If your child is old enough to voice an opinion about what kind of trips they would like to do, consider their input as you plan your vacation. You can give your child a choice between two or three trip options (such as Disney, camping, or the beach) and see what they choose and why.

Keep in mind that it's important to balance the needs of all family members on vacation. Young children may be bored if the trip involves a lot of adult-interest sightseeing, like art and history museums or guided tours of cities. Try to find a compromise so that your vacation offers something for all members of your family. A mistake some parents of onlies make is to plan family vacations that they want to go on, without regard for whether their child will find it fun and interesting. This is a recipe for a bored and complaining child.

If you can, try to involve your child in the actual vacation planning; it'll help build enthusiasm for the upcoming trip. If your child is old enough, perhaps call a family meeting so your child can provide input into your destination choices and maybe even help plan the trip. When your child has a say in where you will go and what you will do, they will likely be more enthusiastic about the vacation. Make sure to plan several vacation activities that your child will love, like visiting a local zoo, going to an amusement park, or a day at a beach.

Danielle from Florida said, "I always do my best to include [my son] on vacation plans. I ask him about places he wants to visit, [then] research them with him ahead of time so he can pick some activities he'd like to try. Instead of only doing what me and my husband want, we really ensure he's involved in the planning and making sure we do at least a few activities he wants to do."

The best way to plan a kid-approved trip is to find kids' books about the places you're going (a book about the beach or a travel guidebook with lots of photos). You can check out some books from the library on each destination or watch some YouTube videos. Ask your child what they would like to see and do on your vacation. You can even look online together and find activities you could do, then get their opinion about which ones they would like best.

If your child is older, they can help you read guidebooks and do research online to decide what to see and do on your trip. If your child has some control over the activities or sightseeing you will do, they're more likely to be invested in the trip and have a more positive attitude about traveling. Some kids can get ornery and cranky on vacations because their usual routines are off, they're not around their friends, and they may have little say in what activities the family does on vacation. Some may even complain that they're bored on trips. If your child helps plan the trip and feels invested in it, it's more likely you can avoid the vacation crankies.

Should You Let Your Child Bring a Friend Along on Trips?

Some families allow their only to bring a friend along on vacations. Your child will probably be extremely enthusiastic about this idea, but before you say yes, consider whether or not it will make your vacation more stressful to watch another child. Parents who allow their child to bring a friend along on trips feel that it will make the trip more fun because their child might otherwise be bored without another kid around. On the other hand, parents who don't allow this usually don't want to watch another person's child on their vacation because it's supposed to be a relaxing getaway, not a babysitting trip.

Usually, parents wait until their child is in upper elementary or middle school to let them bring a friend on vacation so that the additional child is able to take care of themselves. If you do want to try having your only bring along a friend, make sure the friend is well-behaved and listens to you. You might want to try a day trip or a short overnight trip to see how it goes with bringing along a friend before considering a longer trip.

Here are some important things to consider when you allow your only child to bring a friend along on your vacation: Do you pay for everything for the other child, or should the child's parents provide them with spending money? How will you handle it if the other child doesn't listen to you? If the friend has food allergies, are you able to manage those? How will lodging work? Perhaps a vacation rental would be logistically easier? It's important to think through all the possible issues that can occur before allowing your child to bring a friend along to ensure that it's a positive experience for everyone. Good communication with the other child's parents is also key.

Vacations as Family Reunions

Many only-child families enjoy vacationing with extended family. It can be a convenient way to spend time with family if they live far away, while enjoying a pleasant vacation at the same time. It's also a great way for aunts, uncles, and cousins to all come together from different parts of the country for a reunion. Vacationing together can be a fun way for your child to bond with cousins they don't see very often.

There are many positives to vacationing with family, but it can be a challenge if you are all sharing the same vacation rental because everyone's ideas about daily schedules, meal prep, sleep schedules, noise levels, and cleaning could be different. One option for a stress-free family vacation/reunion is to do something where everyone has their own space, like camping, a cruise, or an all-inclusive resort, so you can get together for meals and a few activities without having to spend the entire day together or share the same living quarters.

Should You Vacation with Another Family?

Vacationing with others can be a fun and enjoyable experience, and going on a trip with another family or two with whom you're friends can be the best of both worlds—your child gets to vacation with a friend and you don't have to take care of another child because their family will be there. Additionally, you get to socialize with your own friends too. And a big bonus is that the kids entertain each other so the adults can get some time to read or hang out, thus a more relaxing vacation experience for everyone.

The only caveat is that it can be hard to agree on a location that suits everyone. What can sometimes work better is to choose the vacation spot yourself and then invite a few friends to join you, whether it's a vacation rental that you chose or a city trip, and everyone stays at their own preferred lodging.

Some families who want to vacation together plan a trip to the beach because the beach is an easy vacation logistically—it can keep kids happily entertained for days without having to plan many other activities. Many families will rent a beach house together and take turns cooking and cleaning. Camping can be a similarly easy trip to plan.

There are plenty of other kinds of vacations that can also be wonderful if you're traveling with others. Some families go on a cruise together, where each family can do their own thing and meet up for meals or shore excursions. Others might do a city trip together, and each get their own hotel rooms and meet up for some sightseeing. Others do a weekend trip to an amusement park.

Many families who vacation with another family do so with their longtime friends because planning a vacation with another family is a big commitment. You want to make sure that the kids get along and will have fun, but you also want to make sure that the adults' personalities are compatible and that you and the other family have similar expectations, schedules, and ideas of what constitutes a fun vacation.

There can be a few tricky issues that come up when you're vacationing with another family: Who chooses the vacation spot or lodging? Will you split the cost of the lodging or get your own hotel rooms? Who decides the schedules? How do you deal with others' differing parenting styles? What happens if you find out on the trip that you're really not compatible?

One way you can see if you and the other family are compatible vacation companions is to try a day trip or an overnight trip first and see how that goes. You'll soon find out if the other family has punctuality issues, doesn't pay their fair share, procrastinates, has completely different schedules from you, or is annoying to be around. After you've discovered this, you can decide if you're compatible enough for a longer trip.

Conclusion

Traveling with your only child can lead to many wonderful experiences and lifelong memories of quality time spent together. By involving your child in the trip planning, you can make sure to create a meaningful and fun vacation that suits all members of your family.

REFLECTION QUESTIONS

1. Think back to vacations you took as a child. Which ones were your favorites? Which ones did you not like and why?
2. Were you allowed to bring a friend on trips when you were growing up? Why or why not? If you were allowed to bring a friend, was it a positive experience? How do you feel about your only child bringing a friend on trips?
3. Does your only child get bored on trips? If so, how have you addressed this? What steps can you take in the future to encourage your child to be more engaged in your family's travel?

Section IV: Building a Strong Sense of Community for Your Only

CHAPTER 11

The Importance of Strong Friendships

How to be a good friend and how to make new friends are some of the most important social skills concepts that parents can teach their only children. Making friends is a lifelong skill that is especially important to develop in the early years, and friends your child makes when they are young may become an enduring support system throughout their life.

You may have heard the concept that friends can become your chosen family. If your only complains about not having siblings but has several close friends, they can become as close as siblings and your only will feel that strong, family-like bond. But if your child doesn't have close friends, or perhaps even struggles with friendships, it may be comforting to know that friendship skills can be learned and practiced. This chapter focuses on the importance of strong friendships, as well as tips and suggestions for improving your only child's social skills to help them make new friends.

This chapter also discusses the importance of friendships for you, as the parent of an only child, and how you can have more fulfilling friendships and a stronger, more supportive social circle around you.

All parents need a village to help raise their child. This is especially important for parents of only children, and specifically for those who don't have a support network or local family around to help.

The Importance of Good Friends

Friends are one of the joys of life. Most of us remember our earliest friendships from childhood with great fondness. Some especially strong childhood friendships can end up lasting decades. Your childhood best friends may have remained by your side through to adulthood. They could have been your roommates in your first apartment, bridesmaids or groomsmen in your wedding, or even become your child's godparents. It can be comforting to stay friends with the people who "knew you way back when" because there's so much history to those friendships.

Many only children end up making a best friend or two who become like a sibling—someone to do things with, laugh with, confide in, and go through childhood together. Nurturing this kind of friendship for your only will help them have a strong connection to someone their own age with whom they have things in common. If you put an emphasis on the importance of developing strong friendships, it will help your child understand the value of good friends and give them the courage to seek them out.

Improve Your Child's Social Skills

Does your child struggle with making new friends? It can be heartbreaking if your only child doesn't have any friends at school or complains that they always play alone at recess. One way to help your child find and develop friendships more easily is to help them improve their social skills.

Think about some of the challenges your child has with friendships: Do they have difficulty making new friends? Do their conversation skills need improvement? Are they unable to read subtle social cues? Or do they have difficulty keeping friends because they don't know how to sustain a friendship? Once you've diagnosed where the problem may be, try to work on improving your child's social skills in those areas. There are several ways to do this.

The first is to role-play social skills with them in the areas where they are having the most challenges. If your child has difficulty making new friends, you can practice the skills of introductory greetings, making small talk, and conversation starters. You can also role-play different social situations that cause anxiety for your child and give them the tools they need to work through them. For example, if your child freezes up when meeting someone new because they don't know what to say or what questions to ask, role-play different situations with you being the potential new friend until your child feels more comfortable.

Also ask your child to focus on making connections with other children—what do they have in common? For example, if your child overhears another child talking about their favorite board game, and your child also likes that board game, that's a connection! Or if your child notices another child playing with the same toy they have at home, that's a connection! Your child can use that piece of information to begin a conversation and maybe even suggest playing together! Practice having your child find connections with other children wherever they can, and focus on how they can find things in common with peers. You can practice these kinds of conversation skills until your child feels confident introducing themselves, asking someone else questions to show interest in them, and keeping a conversation going.

If your child has difficulty keeping friends, try to figure out why. Is your child bossy? Does your child always have to be right? Does your child have poor sportsmanship skills? Does your child gossip or say mean things to others? If so, these issues could be getting in the way of lasting friendships. Does your child talk only about themselves without letting their friends get a word in? Does your child consider the opinions and needs of others? Or perhaps your child is possessive about friendships and doesn't want their friend to have any other friends.

Once you've determined what the problem might be, ask them to role-play some situations that might be challenging for them, such as taking turns or resolving a conflict with a friend. If you find that these friendship concerns are too challenging for you to deal with, or that you could benefit from another perspective, consider working with a therapist or finding a social skills group to further explore these issues.

Other ways to work on your child's social skills include getting a social skills workbook designed for their age level and working through the activities together. There are many wonderful social skills workbooks that feature exercises designed to help your child build stronger social skills. One that I really like and use a lot is called *Social Skills Activities for Kids: 50 Fun Exercises for Making Friends, Talking and Listening, and Understanding Social Rules* by Natasha Daniels. Your school's guidance counselor might also have some social skills workbook suggestions and might offer a social skills group or lunch bunch group that your child could join to get more social skills practice at school.

Also consider signing your child up for a social extracurricular activity with the goal of making new friends. If kids have an activity in common (like a passion for art or a love for soccer), and see each other weekly, it might be easier for them to make new friends and have something to talk about. A long-term extracurricular activity, like the Cub Scouts or a team sport, may be the best choice so that friendships have a chance to flourish over many months.

If you think your child needs more practice or guidance, you could consider enrolling them in a social skills class. Many therapist offices or counseling centers offer these, and there are even social skills camps in the summer. Check with your school's guidance counselor, therapist, or your pediatrician for recommendations. You can also find social skills groups on your own by doing a Google search for "social skills groups" in your area, or going on the *Psychology Today*'s Find a Therapist directory and looking under the "support groups" tab.

Social skills classes are usually based on age or grade level and focus on specific social skills topics, including making and keeping friends, conversation skills, conflict resolution, and more.

Encourage Playdates and Friend Meetups

Another way to help your child make strong friendships is to encourage playdates and friend meetups. Having school friends is great, but it can be helpful for your child to spend time with their friends outside of school too. Encourage your child to invite friends over often and, hopefully, your child will be invited to others' homes as well. If you don't like hosting playdates at your house, you can still host in other ways by choosing places like parks, indoor play spaces, or art centers to meet and play at.

The Playdate Dilemma

Some only-child families feel that it's challenging to find other families who are as interested in playdates as they are. Your only child may ask often for playdates, but you might struggle to follow through because everyone else seems too "crazy busy" to commit. You also might feel like you are the one who is constantly reaching out and doing all the inviting and your invitations are rarely reciprocated. Or worse yet, other parents ignore your playdate invitations altogether and don't even respond. You might feel taken advantage of if other parents are constantly asking you for favors but they don't also seem interested in getting together. All this can leave parents of only children feeling lonely, frustrated, and bewildered about how to get more social time for their child. They might feel rejected if they're the ones always reaching out and there's no reciprocation. Can you relate?

There may be several explanations for this frustrating phenomenon that many parents of only children have experienced. Although it's hard, try not to take it personally. First, it's important to realize that many families with two working parents use weekends as a catch-up time, to get chores, errands, and cleaning done that they don't have time for during the week. These families may also want to have family time on the weekends if they work all week, or they may earmark that time to see very close friends or extended family. All of that takes up a lot of their free time on the weekends, so they don't have much discretionary time left over to fit in a playdate. It's not that they're rejecting you and your family, it's that they don't have the bandwidth to add in a playdate with all the other things they're trying to fit into their limited weekend free time.

Add in multiple kids with sports, birthday parties, and extracurricular activities and it's easy to see how some families' free time is extremely limited on the weekends for playdates. These families may decline playdates not because they don't want to spend time with you but because they're so busy with these other activities.

Other reasons why people don't reciprocate or reach out about playdate invitations include that they feel like their kids see other kids at school every day, so there's no need for spending additional weekend hours on playdates; they view weekends as family time and only want to spend that time together; or they just don't like playdates, and so they have decided not to do any. All of these reasons can leave only-child families, who tend to be the most interested in pursuing playdate opportunities, in a bind.

What can you do if you want to set up playdates for your child but have mainly been unsuccessful? If you live in a social neighborhood with lots of same-aged kids, this can be a way to solve the playdate dilemma because you can just send your child out to play with other kids outside and you don't have to formally coordinate anything. It can be nice for your child to decide spur-of-the-moment that they want to play with neighbors, walk out the door, and find a group of kids to play with. However, some people don't have kids in their neighborhood who are a similar age to their only child. If you don't have a social neighborhood, consider enrolling your child in multiple weekend activities. This way they can still socialize on the weekends with other kids and look forward to the same fun activity every week. Other options to try include a weekend playgroup or meetup group that meets weekly, a social weekend activity like Girl/Boy Scouts, or going to playgrounds where your child can informally play with other kids.

When setting up formal playdates with other families, you'll be more successful if you make them as easy as possible for the other family. Some families are so busy that they won't say yes to a playdate unless it's incredibly easy for them to manage. Meeting up at a playground or park can be a good first playdate activity so that no one has to host at their house, which some families can find burdensome. Some people don't like to host playdates or are too busy to make sure their house is in tip-top, playdate shape. And some are turned off by overly formal playdates, like meeting up at your house for a nice meal, because they feel that they can't reciprocate and so will decline altogether.

Try inviting another family over for a very low-key playdate, like an afternoon playdate with cookies and juice or playing in your backyard. They will be more likely to reciprocate an invitation for a playdate like this because the bar was set lower. If your house isn't perfectly put together and spotless, that can also make you seem more relatable and may make it more likely that the other family will eventually reciprocate. Weekend playdates in the late afternoon can be a good time for a casual playdate because many kids have sports on weekend mornings. I've found that 1–3 p.m. or 2–4 p.m. are good times for weekend afternoon playdates or friend meetups for older kids who aren't limited by nap schedules.

While your goal in setting up playdates should be to create a fun experience for your child and additional opportunities to get to know friends, remember that a reciprocated playdate invitation should not be something you should always expect when you invite for a playdate. It's important to host playdates because you enjoy them and because they benefit your child, not because you're expecting a return invitation. It's a nice gesture when the other family does reciprocate and invites your child over, but it's not something you should automatically expect.

Something else to keep in mind is that while your child is still young, you will be the one in charge of setting up and arranging playdates. This can be challenging when your child is in public school in a large class and you don't know any of the families yet. How do you even start setting up a playdate when you've never met the other family?

Start by asking your child who they seem to get along with best, then ask the teacher for that parent's email address (or there may be a class directory), and email them to see if it would be possible to set up a playdate. I've done this many times with parents I don't know. Usually when I don't know the parents, I suggest a very easy, casual playdate at a playground or park. It can be a little awkward to reach out to someone you don't know to set up a playdate, but it usually ends with the kids having a great time, and your child will be so happy to meet up with a school friend outside of school.

If the kids are young, you will be staying for the entire playdate, so keep some conversation topics in mind so you and the other parent are not standing around in awkward silence. It can be challenging to make small talk with someone you don't know for one or two hours, but the kids always end up having a lot of fun, so it's totally worth it!

Also know that the nature of playdates changes as your child grows. When your child is still young, playdates will be the kind where the parent stays. These days most parents tend to stay for playdates through kindergarten or first grade. A generation ago, playdates were drop-off much sooner. I remember having drop-off playdates in preschool when I was growing up! When playdates are not yet drop-off and the parent stays, it adds another dimension because you're going to be socializing with the other parent for around two hours. Some parents think this is fun and engaging, especially those who are looking to make new friends, while other parents find it exhausting and tiresome. If you're the type who dislikes non-drop-off playdates, keep in mind that playdates will soon become drop-off as your child gets older.

If you have a tween or teen, you won't be arranging playdates for them anymore; instead, your child will probably use text to invite friends to meet up. Encourage your child to invite friends over or to meet up with friends regularly so they can get to know classmates outside of school. Also consider allowing them to invite a friend along when you go out for dinner or on a family outing.

If you have an older child, you won't have as much opportunity to meet your child's friends' parents as you once did when they were younger, but you can still accompany your teen and meet the friend's parents the first time they go over to someone's house. It's helpful to meet your child's friend's parents at least once, at their home, so that you have a sense of whether they seem like responsible adults and whether their home appears safe. Get to know them a little before you drop off your child. If they don't seem responsible, or if you see something in their home that concerns you (e.g., aggressive dog in the home, prescription medication sitting out in the living room, beer bottles lying around, etc.), you don't necessarily need to have your child end the friendship; instead, you might consider having your child invite the friend over to your house for their get-togethers.

Make Your House the Fun House

Another way to encourage your child to make friends is to make your house the neighborhood "fun house." If kids have fun at your house, they're more likely to want to hang out there again, and it might be easier for your child to make friends.

You can designate one room or area as the fun area. For instance, if you want to make your basement the hangout spot for your child and their friends, consider putting in an air hockey table, foosball table,

Ping-Pong table, train table, or whatever fun thing your child's age group would be interested in. Likewise, you can make your backyard the fun spot and have a playset, soccer net and balls, and outdoor toys. If your child is into video games, creating a gaming room with comfy chairs, a large-screen TV, and a spot for snacks will ensure that your child's friends will be interested in hanging out there.

Other ways to make your house the "fun house" is to entertain often and to host yearly parties. Hosting a casual neighborhood backyard playdate, a yearly Halloween party, a yearly Fourth of July BBQ, or even an informal monthly potluck with friends are all ways you can create a fun atmosphere that's conducive to strengthening friendships and building community for both you and your only child.

The Importance of Building Community through Family Friends

Beyond having their own friends, it's also wonderful for an only child to have family friends. Family friends are friends of Mom or Dad who have a special bond with your child. It provides a sense of comfort and caring when an only child has family friends who care about them, ask about them, and remember their birthdays and graduations.

Family friends might be Mom or Dad's childhood or college friends, previous and current neighbors, or co-workers. It's memorable and special for a child when they join Mom and her best friend for ice cream or when Dad's friend from college sends a graduation card or asks how they're doing in school. It can be really nice for your only child to have their "special aunt" (who is your college roommate) attend their birthday party or middle school graduation. It's lovely when this kind of special person takes an interest in your child and remembers important events in their life.

Only children benefit when they feel a strong sense of community around them. Having a special bond with friends of the family can help only children feel a greater sense of community and belonging.

Modeling Good Friendship Skills for Your Child

Being an only child means that a child doesn't have a sibling who can help them better understand how to be a good friend; instead, they look to their parents to learn about friendship. An only child who grows up never seeing their parents with friends of their own is likely to be at a disadvantage socially and may have diminished friendship-making skills. They won't know how to place an emphasis on developing friendships if they don't see their parents having any. They also won't know how to nurture friendships if they don't see this behavior modeled at home. Some kids can figure it out on their own, but others can't.

An only child without a good role model for friendship skills might also not realize how important it is to have friends and might grow up devaluing friendships. In other words, if Mom doesn't have any friends herself, the child may believe that it's fine not to invest in their own friendships. So if you don't have any friends, it may be a good idea to think more about how your own challenges with friendships may be contributing to your child's social skills development and attitude about friendships.

Today there are so many ways for adults to meet new people and make friends, from meeting new friends at work to joining groups, classes, or clubs to making friends through online groups, in the neighborhood, or through volunteering. One of the best ways to help your child learn how to be a good friend is to model good friendship skills yourself. So if you don't have any friends, now's the time to go out and make one!

In Australia, Keren's family focuses on the value of friendships. She said, "My husband and I each have . . . friendships that are very strong, so much so that we consider them family. Because we feel this way about our closest friends, we understand the importance of strong friendships for our daughter. She is a somewhat shy child, so we have made a great deal of effort to ensure she develops the skills necessary to build positive, lasting friendships. . . . We take our daughter regularly to playgroups, swimming lessons, [and] mother's group playdates, and we socialize often with our friends and their children, even going on vacation with these families."

There are several ways that modeling positive friendship skills can help your only child with their own friendships. The first is that when they observe you with your own friends, it shows your child what it means to be a good friend. When they see you making the time to talk to your friends on the phone, keep in touch with them regularly, and make the time to meet up with them, it will help your child understand the value of friendship. When your child sees that you value friendships, they will learn how to value and keep friends as well.

Some kids have difficulty knowing how to get a conversation started or how to get a friend's attention in a positive way. If your child sees how you greet your own friends and how you start conversations with them, it will help them develop their own conversation skills.

Allow your child to observe how you take care of friends. This will show them how to be a kind, nurturing friend who shows their own friends that they care about them. If a friend is sick or just had a baby, do you bring them a meal or drop off a care package? If so, let your child help out when preparing the meal or creating the care package. They can help pick flowers in your yard to make a bouquet or help you bake a dessert for your friend; they can also help you deliver them. Showing friends kindness and empathy will help your child build these skills themselves and teach them how to nurture their own friendships.

I try to model good friendship skills for my son whenever I can. He sees me make the time to talk to friends on the phone or go for walks with friends. We host playdates often and entertain regularly so that he understands the importance of good hospitality. When we visit someone's home, I review the most important points of being a good guest, such as saying "please" and "thank you," addressing hosts properly, having good sharing skills, helping to clean up after the playdate, and thanking the hosts for inviting us at the end of the playdate.

Learning friendship skills is one of the most important concepts you can teach your only child. Through modeling these skills at home, and teaching the importance of good friendships at every age, you can set the stage for your only to have strong friendship skills of their own.

The Importance of Creating Strong Friendships for YOU

Some parents of only children feel lonely and wish they had more friends. The parenting journey can be isolating without good friends to go through it with. That's why having Mom or Dad friends, and especially parent friends who are at the same life stage as you, with similarly aged kids can be incredibly helpful. When you have a friend who is going through similar milestones and issues as you, it can help you feel supported and less alone. It can be especially invaluable to find a friend who also has an only child.

It would be great if it were easy to make friends, but as an adult, it's actually quite hard. It's not as easy as when you were in school/college and had lots of opportunities and time to meet new people and get together with friends. Now, as adults, people are busy with family, jobs, eldercare commitments, hobbies, and household responsibilities. When all that is on your plate, there isn't much time left over to nurture new friendships. Sometimes it takes years of joining groups, reaching out to others, extending invitations, and trying to be a good friend for a new friendship to take root. This can feel frustrating to some parents who are eager to make a good friend now.

Ask yourself the following questions to gauge where you are with your current friendships:

- How often do you feel lonely?
- Do you have a close friend or two to confide in?
- Do you have a close friend who shows up for you when you need them to?

- Do you have friends you can ask parenting questions to or share resources with (such as best summer camps in the area, what supplies you need for kindergarten, etc.)?
- Do you have friends that are activity partners (take walks together, go running together, etc.)?
- Do you have friends you can get together with, both with and without the kids?

After taking a look at your social circle, do you feel content with the number of friends you already have? If not, are there acquaintances in your circle that you could potentially turn into closer friends? It's always easier to start with the friendships you already have, rather than making brand new friends from scratch.

If you want more friends but don't have them yet, what can you do? The first step is to get out there, join groups, and participate in new activities. Joining groups, volunteering, and trying new activities can all help you meet new people and make new friends. Here are some examples of different groups you could join:

- moms' or dads' groups
- only child family social groups
- book clubs
- running/walking groups
- neighborhood groups/HOA committees
- room parent/PTA at your child's school
- church or synagogue groups
- volunteering for a local charity
- pet groups
- cooking clubs
- adult recreational sports or dance groups

Once you've joined a group or activity, give it a real chance to work (with time and commitment). If you join a group, get impatient, and decide to quit after one meeting because you haven't met anyone, it will be tough to make new friends. Try three to four meetings or classes before you make a decision on whether a new group is worth your time or not. Also look for groups or classes that meet weekly instead of monthly—seeing the same people often is one of the most important ingredients for making new friends. If you join a group that just meets monthly (or even less frequently), it will be harder for new friendships to grow.

If you can't find the right group for you—start one! It's relatively easy to start your own social group these days. Meetup.com or Facebook are both great ways to start your own group. All you need to do is think of a good group name and concept, plan a few initial activities, get the word out, and you're all set!

When my son was an infant, I started a local moms' group on meetup.com. We did park playdates, lunches out, playground get-to-gethers, and moms' night out events. It soon grew to over three hundred members, and I made many long-lasting friendships through that group. Then I started an only-child family social group on Facebook because I couldn't find an in-person group for only-child families in my area. That was also successful, and we did park, playground, and other fun meetups. I highly encourage forming your own group if you're not finding groups in your area that meet your needs.

If you're wondering what else you can do to meet new people, consider these additional tips for making new friends:

- **Start local.** To make new parent friends, you could send out a message on your neighborhood listserv, Nextdoor site, local Facebook parenting groups, or your personal social media page. Mention that you're looking to make new friends. See what putting yourself out there does—perhaps you'll get many offers to meet up!
- **Growing relationships with acquaintances.** Think about acquaintances you have who you would like to get to know better. Take the initiative and reach out. Invite them for a walk

or for coffee, sticking with something low-key to start. If it goes well, you might want to keep meeting up and eventually make a new friend.

- **Take a class.** There are so many adult education classes out there, both in person and online. To find them, check to see if your county or town has an adult education program. There are also art centers that offer art classes, music centers that offer music classes, dance studios that teach a variety of dance styles or fitness classes, craft stores that offer arts and craft classes, and plenty of other online classes to explore. Not only will you learn a new skill or gain a new hobby, but you'll meet new people who could turn into great friends!

- **Support groups.** Support groups are another great way to meet new people because participants are going through the same experiences or dealing with similar problems. A search online may bring up support groups in your area of interest or need, many of which are hosted through nonprofit organizations. For example, if your child has ADHD and you are looking for support around this issue, consider looking into the organization CHADD (Children and Adults with Attention-Deficit/Hyperactivity Disorder), where you can find a local chapter that might offer a support group. Or if you're struggling with infertility, RESOLVE: The National Infertility Association offers many different in-person and online support groups. Your doctor, therapist, or medical specialist may be able to recommend other support groups for you to look into. You can also find support groups on *Psychology Today*'s Find a Therapist directory; just click on "support groups" at the top and search in your area. Some support groups are virtual, which makes it convenient to attend.

- **Volunteering at school.** Consider getting involved in your child's school to meet new people. There are many ways to help out and meet other parents, including volunteering on the PTA, being a room parent, chaperoning field trips, or helping out on different committees or with activities (like school talent night or school fundraisers). Being a room parent can be helpful for meeting others because you send out many emails, organize class parties, and coordinate volunteers. It's also a good way to start conversations with other parents in the class. You might even be able to arrange some all-class playdates as the room parent.

- **Mommy-and-Me activities.** If your child is young, think about joining a Mommy-and-Me class. It's a great way to meet other moms because a Mommy-and-Me class is where the parent participates with the child, who is usually in the zero-to-three age range. You can find Mommy-and-Me music, Mommy-and-Me gymnastics, Mommy-and-Me swimming, or a preschool-based Mommy-and-Me class. There are also some moms' exercise classes you can join that are specifically about bringing your child to the class so that you don't need to find childcare. They meet frequently, and you will most likely see the same moms attending each time, so there's a good chance you will make friends.

- **Hang out a little longer.** Whether your child is in preschool, elementary school, middle school, or an extracurricular activity, plan to hang out a little longer after drop-off or pick-up and see if you can chat and get to know other parents. When my son was in preschool, there was a carpool line where parents would wait in the car for drop-off and pick-up, but there was also the option to park and walk in. I always parked and walked in for drop-off and pick-up because it was a good way to chat with other parents and provided an opportunity to socialize.

- **Socialize during your child's sports/activities.** When your child is involved in a sport or other type of extracurricular activity, many parents stand around and chat with each other while they wait. Take this opportunity to talk and get to know those waiting alongside you. If you're not sure how to strike up a conversation with someone you don't know, you could say something like, "Wow, your son is really great at hockey! Has he taken this class before?" Using the activity as a starting point can be a good way to open the conversation. If your child is older, parents tend to drop-off at the activity and come back when it's over, but you can still hang out a little longer during drop-off and pick-up to socialize.

- **Join a religious congregation.** Connecting with others who share your faith is a good way to meet new people who have things in common. You will start seeing the same people when you go to weekly services and other congregation activities and events. After you have joined a congregation, joining committees and volunteering can get you out and about, meeting new people and making new friends.

Decide What Kind of Friendship You're Looking For

What kind of friendship are you looking for? Are you interested in a friendship where you just get together with the kids for playdates, or are you interested in getting together with friends for adult conversation without the kids? Or perhaps even a mix of both?

It's important to figure out what kind of friendships you're seeking because some friendships are more based on getting together with the kids and others are focused more on the parents' interests. Some parents with busy work schedules only have the time and bandwidth to get together with the kids. Others want to have their own friends and make time for parents' night out events. Make sure to figure out what kind of friendship you're looking for so that you can be ready when the opportunity presents itself.

Dealing with Rejection

Some parents are hesitant to put themselves out there because they're afraid of being rejected. Rejection can sting and can lead some people to feel hesitant about reaching out or trying to make more connections in the future. But in order to make friends, you do have to reach out, and sometimes you're the only one reaching out for a while. Keep in mind that everyone experiences rejection from time to time. Just keep trying to meet new people and make new friends, and your efforts will pay off as you eventually find what you're looking for.

Building Your Village

You've probably heard the concept that "it takes a village to raise a child." But what exactly is a village? Some people consider a village to be their safety net, consisting of people they trust, who can serve as an emergency backup if they need help. For example, if you are unable to pick up your child from school due to an emergency or need someone to deliver groceries if you're sick, you could call someone from your village to help. Others consider their village to be more of a source of social support and caring—people you can lean on as confidantes and those who will show up for you. So if you had surgery, you could count on the people in your village to offer help or set up a meal train. Your village might consist of your friends, family, and paid professionals, like a housekeeper or nanny. For those parents who don't have any local family, having a strong village becomes especially important.

Making new friends and creating a strong village are similar concepts but can be slightly different. Having friends and having a village are both important, but your village members don't necessarily need to be good friends, and your friends don't necessarily need to be members of your village, though many times they are. It would be ideal to have a social circle of friends *and* a supportive village. Some lucky parents have both!

Some parents of only children have a strong, supportive village, while other parents have almost no village. Which group are you in? It can be very challenging and also quite stressful to raise a family when you do not have a supportive village around as your safety net. When you have no one to list as an emergency contact on school forms, no one to be a backup if you have a crisis, and no one to call on if your spouse isn't around and something stressful happens, it can be very scary and difficult. For those who don't have a village yet, you may need to hire people (like a babysitter, housekeeper, or nanny) to serve as your village.

If you aren't sure about the strength of your village, here are some questions to ask yourself as you evaluate:

- If you have a personal emergency and your spouse isn't available or is out of town, is there someone you could call to help you, who you know could be right over?
- If you had to have a medical procedure and wanted your spouse to be with you, is there someone who could babysit your child?
- If you have an important parenting question that you can't find answers to online, is there a trusted person you could ask, whose advice you trust?
- If you can't pick up your child at school because you have to stay late at work last minute or are stuck in terrible traffic, is there someone you could call to pick up your child if your spouse is unavailable?
- Do you have a few people to list on school emergency contact forms?
- If you and your spouse are both sick, is there someone you could call to bring you groceries or medicine, or even help out with your child?
- If you had to have surgery, is there someone who could help out around the house or set up a meal train for you while you get back on your feet?

Building a strong, supportive village is a high priority for many parents. But it can be hard to know where to start and what to do to create that village.

The first step in creating your village is to take a good look at your current social circle. Who do you already know who could become a part of your village? While some people you know may already have a full village (perhaps they have lots of local family in the area or grew up locally and have lots of connections), others may be searching for a village just like you. Focus on those friends and acquaintances who are in a similar situation. Is there anyone you know who is new to the area, has no local family, or is a single parent who might be interested in having you as a part of their village? What about the other only-child families you know—could they use an additional village member? They might love to have you as part of their village! Also consider people with whom your friendship has grown strong enough that you feel comfortable asking for help if needed.

Start with the people who might be most receptive first. Once you've identified a few people who potentially could be in your village, start reaching out. Be helpful to them, support them, and show that you're thinking about them. Be proactive about ways you can help them out. Perhaps you could offer to drive their child home from an activity to save them a trip, or maybe you could bring them a meal if you hear they just had surgery. If you offer to help them, chances are they will be receptive to helping you when you need it.

While you're working on building your village (which can be a slow process), if you feel that you need some village members right away, what can you do? If you don't already have a babysitter, look for a trusted one by asking around and getting recommendations. Having a trusted babysitter as a backup person can help you feel like you have the start of a village. A babysitter will allow you and your spouse to have a date night once in a while, and knowing there's one other person you can count on in a pinch can go a long way toward making you feel more comfortable in your parenting journey.

Finally, keep in mind that it can take years to build a supportive village. These trusting friendships don't happen overnight. With some patience and the confidence to put yourself out there, you will be able to build a village of supportive people who will be there for you throughout your parenting journey.

Conclusion

As an only-child family, friendships for both you and your child may be one of your top priorities. When your child is happy socially and has several close friends, it can make such a difference to their overall well-being. And when you feel content in your friendships, it will increase your overall quality of life as well. While it can take some time for both you and your child to make new friends, it is something that's well worth working towards.

REFLECTION QUESTIONS

1. When you were growing up, how did your family value friendships? Did your parents have friends of their own? Were your parents good friendship role models for you?
2. Did you have difficulty making friends as a child? If so, what do you think was the main friendship challenge you struggled with?
3. Do you think being an only child makes it harder or easier to make friends?
4. Do you struggle with making new friends as an adult? What do you think has made it difficult for you to make new friends?
5. Are you happy with your parenting village? If not, what steps can you take now to help build your village and support network?

CHAPTER 12

Maintaining and Nurturing Ties with Grandparents and Extended Family

Only children, like all children, love spending time with their grandparents and extended family. Maintaining strong ties with grandparents, aunts, uncles, and cousins gives only children an enduring sense of family, belonging, and community. Spending time together also gives only children an appreciation of their family history, culture, and traditions. And giving your only the opportunity to grow up experiencing a close cousin bond or strong connection to older generations is invaluable.

Some only children come from big families, with lots of cousins, aunts, and uncles. Others come from very small families, with just one or two cousins (if any) and maybe just one aunt or uncle. Your child might have grandparents who live locally, or grandparents who live thousands of miles away. Both large families and small families, living close or far away, have their own blessings and challenges.

Danielle from Florida is an adult only child, married to another only child, who loves her small extended family. She said, "My husband and I really only see our parents often. We both have some aunts and uncles and cousins, but we really only see them for big family events, like weddings. Even holidays are typically only spent with our parents. I honestly love it. I'm not always trying to make time for a ton of other people, and our son gets so spoiled by his grandparents since he's the only child. It works great for us!"

On the other hand, Sarah from England, who is an adult only child herself, said that she never minded having a small family growing up, but she ended up marrying a man with a large family, so her daughter has lots of local cousins. "My husband has two siblings, plus three cousins with whom he is very close, and they and their families (plus his aunts, uncles, and grandparents) all live within a mile of us. My daughter has six cousins, two of whom are the same age as her, and all of them attend the same school and spend time together regularly. I am glad of this. . . . Even though I didn't mind being an only child, that stereotype still exists, and having so much family around her of a similar age stops any 'only child' comments from my in-laws."

If you don't live near extended family and wish you did, you might feel some sadness if you don't get to see them very often. This can feel like a void, especially during holidays with all the media images in movies and commercials of large, loving extended families getting together and having a great time. You might feel like you're missing out on a big family experience, especially when you have a small family of your own.

This can be distressing, especially if you don't have a strong support network of local friends who can be like your family. While it can be difficult to cope if you don't have a loving, supportive extended family, you can still value and celebrate the long-distance family relationships you *do* have. And this is possible, even if you don't get to see each other very often.

Maintaining strong ties with extended family is usually easier to do if the family lives nearby, compared to those grandparents and extended family who are a plane ride away. But in this day and age, with the modern technology of video calls, maintaining strong family ties with long-distance family can be done more easily. Your only will still feel connected to family who lives far away if you work hard to maintain those long-distance ties by keeping in touch frequently.

The Challenges of Having No Local Family

Some only-child families live in the same city as their grandparents and extended family, which can be great for support, emergency backup help, and creating strong family bonds. Although some local grandparents are not very involved, many are. Some only-child families even have grandparents living with them in a multi-generational household. It's wonderful when kids can get to know their grandparents by either living with them or getting together often and having them share in family milestones and important events. When grandparents can attend your child's sports games, be at every birthday party and graduation, and spend time with your child on the weekends, it can create a strong bond between the generations. If this is your situation, consider yourself very lucky!

But some only-child families live far away from grandparents and extended family, with no local family at all. If this is your situation, it can be especially challenging to raise a child without a family village. Imagine having no family around to help if something goes wrong, or if you need a medical procedure or surgery and have no one to watch your child. What would happen if you and your spouse both got sick at the same time? Would you be able to ask a friend to help out in these situations? These kinds of dilemmas can create a lot of stress for only-child families who live far away from family and is a reason why some only-child families decide to be one and done. They simply feel that one child is all they can handle with no family support.

The following are some of the unique challenges you might face if you don't have any family who live close to you:

- You feel like you have no emergency backup to help out if there is a problem.
- You struggle to find people to list on the "emergency contact" section on school forms.
- You feel sadness about spending many holidays and milestone events without family, and it can feel like there's a void when family can't be at your celebrations.
- You envy your friends who have active and involved grandparents who help out with raising their grandkids.
- You feel a general lack of support from family in your parenting journey.
- You feel alone without having an experienced grandparent to lean on for day-to-day parenting advice.
- You feel exhausted because the only way you can get a date night or a break is to hire a babysitter, which can be too expensive, logistically difficult, or uncomfortable to leave your child with someone you don't know very well.
- You worry that your only is missing out on important, quality grandparent time/relationships.
- You don't have local cousins for your only to have weekend sleepovers and spontaneously hang out with, and you worry that your only won't develop strong bonds with his cousins.
- There isn't enough opportunity to create new family traditions with grandparents, aunts, uncles, and cousins whom you only see once every few years.
- You feel sad that you have very few photos of the grandparents with their grandchild because they only see each other once a year.

- You feel envious of friends with local grandparents who are able to babysit for them whenever they want or even provide full-time childcare.
- You resent the added expense of traveling to see family and/or spending all of your vacation weeks and money visiting far-flung family instead of having your own vacations.
- You're not able to easily go away with your spouse for a weekend because there's no local grandparent or family member to watch your child.
- You feel completely on your own without a family support network.
- Your weekends might feel empty; when others are getting together with grandparents and local family, you struggle to fill your weekends.
- You and your parents disagree about how often visits should occur, which can be stressful.
- You feel like the odd one out, perhaps as the only family whose child doesn't have a grandparent coming for Grandparents' Day at school or attending their birthday party or graduation.
- You and your parents argue about who should be the one to move closer to family. Your parents may believe that you should uproot your family and move out closer to them, or vice versa.
- You feel disappointment that your child is missing out on these important intergenerational relationships, especially if you grew up with local family and wanted the same experience for your child.

As you can see, having no local family can be challenging for only-child families in many different ways. You might feel a variety of emotions, including sadness, disappointment, resentment, bitterness, and inadequacy, especially if you grew up with local family and know how enriching it can be to have those close bonds.

You might feel disappointed that your child won't have those same experiences, like weekly sleepovers with cousins or going to Grandma's for a weekly Sunday dinner. It can feel disappointing to not have family attend when there are special events like Grandparents' Day at school or when your child has a milestone event, like a birthday party, special performance, team event, or big school event like graduation. Occasionally long-distance grandparents can fly or drive in for events like these; however, many families feel that it would be better and more convenient if grandparents lived closer and could easily attend every important event to be more involved in their child's daily life.

Additionally, you might feel disappointed about how much of your only's childhood the grandparents are missing out on and wish that they could be geographically closer. You might worry that your only and their grandparents won't make many memories together if they're seeing each other once in a blue moon. Your only might remember FaceTiming with their grandparents a lot, but it's different from spending quality, in-person time with an extended family member who is physically present in your child's day-to-day life.

If you feel dejected about not having local family, you're not alone. Families who have involved local grandparents or other extended family are very lucky. But it's important to focus on what you *do* have instead of dwelling on what you don't (which is a recipe for getting stuck in a bitter rut). If you do find yourself feeling down about this issue often, it can be helpful to cultivate a gratitude practice, where you focus on what you *are* grateful for regarding your extended family.

Do you have four healthy grandparents, even if they live far away? Not everyone does, and that's something to be grateful for! Are you able to meet up with extended family at least once a year, even if you don't get to see them as often as you'd like? Not everyone can, and that's something to be celebrated! There are always silver linings to be found for every challenge, so it's important to focus on those when you're feeling unhappy.

Even though most only-child families would prefer if they did have involved, local family, not having local family does have a few upsides that are important to note. When you have no local family, there can be more freedom to make your own life choices without feeling judged. Sometimes having local family who you see often means that everyone is always "up in your business," maybe even questioning your life decisions or judgments frequently. They might ask to be privy to everything that's going on in your life, or nitpick your life choices, which can feel smothering. They might also expect you to share in their particular opinions or perspectives about certain issues, like politics or religion, and then become upset when you don't. When your family is far away, they're less aware of your day-to-day life, so that mental distance means you can be freer to make your own decisions and have your own perspectives.

Another upside of not having local family is that there is also more distance from family drama and dysfunction, such as a grandparent who is estranged or family members who frequently engage in unhealthy behaviors. When it does occur, you're far enough away that you're removed from the situation and won't have to be as involved as you would if you lived closer. You might get multiple phone calls or emails about the family drama, but at least you can screen your calls and ignore emails if you don't want to deal with it at that time.

There is also less pressure to attend family events when family is out of town. Some local extended families like to get together for weekly events, which can soon start to feel like too much time spent together. You might feel obligated to attend all of these events, and they can monopolize your free time. When you don't have local family, you don't feel as pressured to attend events you're not interested in. There is also more freedom to do your own thing for holidays because you're not tied to family get-togethers. You have more freedom to decide how you want to celebrate and with whom.

How to Nurture Family Ties When You're Far Apart

It can be challenging to maintain strong ties and a close relationship with extended family when you live far apart. You've got phone and video calls, but you may wonder if those can really be as fulfilling and meaningful as spending time together and making memories. Your child may feel like they don't really know their grandparents, aunts, uncles, and cousins if they only see them once or twice a year in person and the rest of the time on video calls. And if your child doesn't get to know them growing up, there may be no real relationship with these family members when your child is an adult. Because they didn't live near each other or have enough opportunities to foster strong family bonds, no real emotional closeness may develop over the years. And as a result, there is a possibility that your only will feel like they don't have many meaningful extended family connections as an adult.

The good news is that there are many different ways you can nurture strong ties with grandparents and extended family, even when you live far apart. And today's technology makes it easier than ever to do so.

One way to do this is to video chat frequently. The nice thing about video chatting (versus long-distance phone calls of the past) is that it's free, so you can video chat whenever you want. During the COVID-19 pandemic, when we didn't see my parents for a long time, we kept in touch by video chatting almost every day. My son developed a very close relationship with his grandparents through this arrangement. He would be on the call for hours, reading to them, playing games together, and drawing together. Cousins can also video chat and do playdates over video in order to nurture that important cousin bond. You can get creative with video calls and do family projects together, like baking, creating an art project, performing in music recitals, or writing a story together.

Alejandra from France said that her daughter has only met her parents in person once. Instead, they rely on video calls, photos, and storytelling to keep the connection strong, despite the great distance. She said, "My parents live in Mexico, and we video call them every day. They came to visit a few months ago for the first time. And what's amazing is that when they came here, they had a very strong relationship with their granddaughter, even though they had never met her. Since my daughter was a baby, I have showed her photos of all the family. I always talk about them and tell stories about my parents when they were kids. I told her stories about them and how important they are to me. I think that's why she has that strong connection with them, despite the distance. On video calls, her grandmother tries to play with her through the screen, tells her stories, and sings her songs; her grandfather shows her his collections. . . . All these kinds of connections, a child can feel through a screen."

Video calls are a very helpful way to stay in touch with grandparents and extended family who live far away, but your only child may develop "Zoom fatigue," where they grow tired of the same old video calls. Of course, in person would be better, but if video calls are what you have to work with to connect with grandparents and extended family, here are some ways to jazz up your video calls:

- **Try a virtual family book club.** Everyone reads the same book and then discusses. This could be a kids' book that the grandparents choose and send to your child.
- **Family quizzes.** There are lots of quizzes that you can do with your family to help everyone get to know each other better. You could ask questions like, "Who in our family is the oldest?" and "Who in our family is the best cook?" Questions like these can start lots of interesting family conversations and help your child get to know their grandparents better.
- **Share stories.** Have grandparents share important family stories with your only, and tell these stories again often. Your only will come to love hearing them, whether they are about their own parents or other family members.

- **Do a family art project together.** You can send grandparents
  an art kit and have the same one for your child. Everyone
  works on the art kit together at the same time while you chat,
  then you can have fun showing off your finished artwork.

Outside of frequent video calls, another step you can take to maintain
strong family ties with faraway family is to vacation together, perhaps
by meeting in the middle of your two locations. For instance, if you live
on the East Coast and grandparents live on the West Coast, and it's an
ordeal to travel such a long distance (especially with a young child),
consider meeting in the middle somewhere that would be convenient
for both. You could do a camping trip, find an all-inclusive resort, or
rent a nice vacation property halfway. That way neither party feels over-
burdened by always having to be the one to travel long distances. These
vacations can strengthen relationships and provide amazing memories
for your only.

When you don't have local family, holidays especially can feel
lonely. It might seem like you're the only ones you know who don't
have extended family to celebrate holidays with. You might envy your
friends who celebrate holidays with huge, fun family celebrations with
lots of aunts, uncles, and cousins. In comparison, you might feel like
your party of two or three is too quiet or inadequate in some way. If you
can't celebrate holidays in person with your extended family, what else
can you do?

During the COVID-19 pandemic, many of us did Zoom holidays
(spending time together over video conference apps like Zoom). While
in person is ideal, Zoom holidays can be the next best thing! Getting
together in this format is something that never occurred to me to try
before the pandemic, but we did a few Zoom holidays and it worked
out great! We continue to do them when we can in order to connect
with extended family who live far away. If your family is too far away
to get together for in-person holidays, consider having your holiday at
home and Zooming them in. You can do the same for birthdays, family
reunions, and other milestone events.

One benefit from this method is that you can spend holidays with extended family that you rarely get to see. During the pandemic we did our son's birthday party virtually, making it extra special by Zooming in extended family that we generally only see once every few years. My son loved having some of his cousins join him for his party, and that really made it memorable.

You can also go old school and keep in touch with extended family by emails, texts, phone calls, and letters. When I was a girl, I spent hours every weekend on the phone with my grandparents, who lived very far away. I looked forward to those weekly long-distance calls all week. And despite the distance, I was able to maintain a wonderful relationship with my grandparents, who I only saw in person once a year. Your child will also enjoy texting photos to Grandma and creating cards and letters to send. Sending photos and letters often helps keep relatives in the loop with what you're up to. You can text them or put them on a photo-sharing account, like Shutterfly or Dropbox, so that grandparents can easily see them.

When possible, try to attend extended family's birthday celebrations and important milestones in person to help make the day extra special and to show your child the importance of keeping those connections strong and celebrating meaningful events with family. Your extended family members will appreciate you making the effort to travel to them for their important milestones.

To keep grandparents in the loop about school events, let them know when your child has something important coming up, like a Grandparents' Day, ballet recital, or soccer tournament. Maybe they can visit and be there in person. But if not, perhaps you can make a video at the event so the grandparents can also feel a part of your child's special moment.

The following are some additional tips for nurturing ties with relatives who live far away:

- **Try to visit at least once a year.** This can take different forms—one year you travel out to them and the next year they can travel to you. Spend time prior to the visit talking up how much fun you're going to have visiting and all the exciting things you plan to do.

- **Try to attend milestones and big events for your extended family.** If it's your child's cousin's Bar Mitzvah, try to attend. If your only's aunt is getting married, try to attend. You'll get to see lots of extended family at these occasions, which will make them even more special. Attending big events and milestone events in the family may lead to many happy memories and enhanced family closeness.

- **Consider trying out a family journal.** This is a book with writing prompts where you take turns answering the prompts and writing in different responses. This could be an activity for your child and grandparents to do over video calls, or something your child and a cousin could do together. You can keep these as wonderful family history notebooks.

- **Encourage grandparents to share their advice.** What advice can they offer, either about a specific situation or general advice? Your family will create stronger connections together as you listen to each other, either over a video call or by phone.

- **Share interests and cultural traditions.** Help grandparents brainstorm ways they can do this. Grandparents can cook on video calls, share their favorite family recipes, teach your child about their religious traditions, or learn about family history together. Also ask your only to share their interests with the grandparents. My son was really into dragons during the COVID-19 pandemic and did video calls with his grandparents almost every day; over video chats, he got Grandma and Grandpa into learning all about dragons. They would even make dragon art projects together.

- **Consider doing occasional family reunions with the whole extended family.** Think about unique ideas for a family reunion—perhaps a cruise, all-inclusive resort, family camping trip, or even a BBQ in a park. Any of these would be fun and memorable and will provide amazing memories for your only! Find a location that's convenient for everyone and try to plan the reunion at least six months in advance so that family members have the opportunity to request time off work and plan around school commitments.
- **Have your only make birthday and holiday cards** for grandparents and extended family, and handwrite thank you notes to send to those who celebrated special events with your family in any way.
- **Consider becoming old-school pen pals with cousins.** They can write actual letters (or send drawings) to each other. Writing back and forth can help them get to know each other, and it is always fun and special for kids to get a card or letter in the mail addressed just to them!

How to Nurture Family Ties with Local Family

Some only-child families are lucky to have grandparents and extended family close by. While many families in this situation are satisfied with the time they spend with their local family, others struggle with issues like boundaries, frequency of visits, and differing expectations. Some even wonder why their local grandparents aren't as involved as they would like them to be.

Picture this scenario: Your parents live just ten minutes away, but despite their close proximity, you barely see them. They still work, have an active social life, volunteer, travel, and seem to spend lots of time with their own friends, but whenever you ask about spending time together, they say they're too busy. For whatever reason, they are not making it a priority to see you and your family. You're happy that your parents have such full lives, but disappointed and resentful that they don't make time to see you more often.

What can you do if this describes your relationship with local family? It may be time to have a gentle discussion with them about what obstacles are getting in the way of more frequent get-togethers. Do they feel unwelcome in your home for some reason? Do you think some aspect of your parenting choices is off-putting to them? Do the times you suggest to get together just not work for them? If you can find out what's standing in the way of more frequent visits and a closer relationship, you can work on resolving the issue together.

On the flip side, you might have local family who want to spend every waking minute with you. Your family may be ultra-enthusiastic about visiting and want to monopolize all your free time, leaving little time for you to spend with friends or take care of your own chores and errands. In this case, you may need to set boundaries about how often the grandparents can visit. For some families, seeing grandparents and extended family once a week is plenty. For others, seeing them once a month is a better fit. It's up to you how often you want to see extended family. Figure out how many times a month would work for visits, then explain that they need to stay within those boundaries.

To decide what works for you, think about whether getting together with family is enjoyable or stressful. If stressful, you may want to decrease the frequency of your visits. Also think about how you want to juggle family events with your other responsibilities. If you work full-time, and weekends are your only time to get things done, you may not want to spend every weekend going to a different family event when grocery shopping and errands are also on the schedule.

Some only children live in a multigenerational household, with grandparents or extended family all living under the same roof. If your child has this living arrangement, there can be many wonderful benefits. Rashmi is a single mother living in Virginia who is raising her daughter in a multigenerational household. She believes that multigenerational households have many benefits for only children, saying, "My parents live with us and [have] known my daughter her entire life, and they took care of her until she went to daycare. They're very bonded. They're very nurturing with her; they play with her, they provide comfort and support, and they watch her sometimes, which is a huge help to me if she has to stay home from school."

Rashmi continued, "It's been a good support to have them because they can also share things about their culture. . . . I think that's another huge advantage. They can share their experiences. . . . Now my daughter wants to go to India, and she wants to learn our language, Punjabi."

Like all situations, a multigenerational living situation isn't perfect, and some challenges can arise. Rashmi has learned that amidst the benefits, she has had to figure out how to handle the unique family dynamic. She said, "They [do] spoil her, which can be a bit challenging. It can also be challenging from a discipline perspective because being from an older generation, they have different ideas of discipline."

When living this close with extended family, it's helpful to set clear boundaries so that the benefits outweigh any negatives that arise.

If your child has local cousins, take advantage of this good fortune! It can be so special for an only child to grow up near similar-aged cousins. Getting the cousins together monthly for a playdate or meetup can keep their relationship going strong.

Rashmi said that for her daughter, growing up with similarly aged local cousins has created a special bond. "My sister lives just a few miles away, and we try to do a lot of things with her family so that my daughter doesn't feel alone as an only child. My daughter and her cousins are almost like siblings, they are so close in age, [so] they fill that role for my daughter. She has to share and problem-solve and do all of those things when they're interacting together.

"When there isn't anyone to play with, like her other friends, we can sometimes do an impromptu playdate with her cousins. . . . They do a lot together—go to the pool, go fruit picking together, snuggle puppies who are too young to be adopted. My daughter doesn't feel like she needs another sibling because she gets that kind of interaction from her cousins. When they get tired of each other, then we go home."

Kristie from California said that her son is lucky to grow up with local cousins. "My niece, who is five, loves being around my son. They're best friends. They love being with each other, and I think it's so important. She has been such a source of play for him, running his energy out, helping him with his toys. It's been wonderful." Kristie hopes they maintain this strong connection over the years. She said, "I hope they have each other—as a parent you don't want to leave your child alone with no one. All he has are these cousins, and I plan on doing my best to keep them close."

Attending each other's important events is a great way to nurture the cousin relationship. Many cousins even do sleepovers, which can be a wonderful way to strengthen the cousin bond. Having local cousins nearby can provide a wonderful sibling-like relationship for your only child.

When Grandparents Aren't Interested or Involved

If grandparents (or other extended family) aren't that interested in a close relationship for one reason or another, it can be disappointing. Some only-child families have the experience where one set of grandparents are local and involved and the other set lives far away and is less involved.

Kristie from California has experience with both involved grandparents and those who are not as present. Kristie's parents live close by and are very involved; they are her son's caregivers when she and her husband are working full-time. But her husband's parents live far away, and distance keeps both sides of his family from being more involved in their daily lives.

Kristie tries to keep her husband's parents in the loop, and she sends them photos two to three times per week. She also has tried Facebook Portal and FaceTime so they can talk with their grandson and watch him grow. But "they have difficulties with technology, which makes keeping in touch with video calls difficult. I don't know if or how often they will ever be able to come out this way because of the distance and difficulty with travel, but we hope that if they don't, that we can travel to them at some point.

"I'm trying my best to keep that connection with them because I feel it's incredibly important, but on the other hand, my child is really lucky that he has my parents so close and all the things they do for us."

Getting together with grandparents can be difficult for several reasons. Some grandparents live thousands of miles away and are content with a yearly visit. Other grandparents live locally and could theoretically spend every weekend with their grandchild but are too busy with other things and don't make much effort to visit. Others are not involved because they don't approve of how their adult children choose to parent or the other life choices they've made, and so have decided to distance themselves. Some grandparents are estranged from their adult children and have never met their grandchild.

Other times it's the adult children who are keeping their parents at a distance because they feel that they will not be a positive influence on their child. This can include grandparents who are estranged from the family and have little or no communication with their adult children, or grandparents who engage in unhealthy behaviors, like drug and alcohol addiction. There can be a variety of reasons why grandparents are not a part of your or your child's life right now.

You will also find grandparents who just aren't interested in being traditionally involved grandparents. They may be busy working, traveling, or dealing with their own health issues and don't have the time or inclination to spend time with their grandchild. They may prefer to be grandparents "on paper" rather than involved in person. Or sometimes they just aren't available to get together for family events like holidays and milestones.

This can be very hurtful and hard to understand for many adult children, but it's important to keep in mind that we can't control others' behavior—we can only control our own reactions to it.

While it's understandable to be disappointed in grandparents who aren't interested in traditional warm, loving, and involved grandparenting roles, you can either choose to be perpetually disappointed by their shortcomings or to accept the way things are and try to make the best of it. Everyone has their own ideas of what it means to be a grandparent, and there's probably not much you can do to convince them to be what *you* wish them to be. It can be very difficult to let go of your expectations for how you wanted the grandparent relationship to be.

If you had a vision that your parents would be the ideal doting, involved grandparents—and they are not—it's natural to feel let down, disappointed, and resentful. This may be something that you grieve for a while as you let go of the ideal grandparent vision and work to process this loss and disappointment. But if you feel stuck and struggle with chronic feelings of resentment and bitterness, a therapist can be beneficial in helping you process your emotions, handle feelings of rejection, and help you grieve what you longed for so deeply.

Nicole McNelis, LPC, a therapist in Pennsylvania, said that if you have grandparents who are not involved, think about what need you are looking to fill. "Are you looking to spend time with extended family and build those bonds? And if so, where else can you get that need met? If you're looking for your child to get experience being around people who are older, can you volunteer at an assisted living or help serve lunches to seniors as other ways to [get] those needs met?

"It's okay to feel hurt if your parents don't want to be involved in the way you wanted them to be. And it's okay to feel grief because of it. When we think of grief, we often think of losing someone or something, but that doesn't always have to be the case. Grief can also occur if the thing we wanted didn't turn out the way we wanted it to. In managing that grief, it is not a thing to be 'gotten over.' Instead, you work to find a healthy way to manage that grief . . . and then move forward with it. You figure out a new plan.

"You might ask, 'How can we compensate for lack of grandparent involvement in our child's life? What would make sense here?' Getting support, finding other individuals who are in a similar situation, therapy, and coming to that grief from a place of understanding can all make a significant difference."

Building a Family of Choice

When grandparents and extended family don't live locally—or if any of the previous sections about disinterested or aloof grandparents describes your child's grandparents or other family members—and it's important for you to have a strong, family-like support network nearby, it is upsetting . . . but don't despair! There are things you can do. One approach is to build your own "family of choice" with other special people in your life. A family of choice can consist of friends who value you, support you, and are there for you, just the way traditional family members are.

When you invest in strong friendships, they can become something similar to family. While it does take a lot of time and effort to make friends who are like family, they can be there for you and support you the way that family members do. You can invite friends to spend holidays and milestone events with you, and they can even be godparents for your child. Strive to make good friends, offer to help them out whenever you can, show up for them, and it is likely the friendship will grow close over the years to where you have the family-like support you're seeking.

Amy Weber, LCSW, a licensed clinical social worker in New York who specializes in therapy for children and their families, believes that creating a family of choice is critical. "People are not living so close to their extended family anymore, so it's really important to have social supports and a network of people who feel like they could be family. If you're not finding this in your neighborhood, look at school and teams and the playground—strike up a conversation with people. It's not going to happen overnight, but be bold and ask for their phone number . . . and [get together] for coffee. It's very important to have in-person friends and social supports who can be there for you if you have an emergency."

Consider finding an "honorary" or "surrogate" grandparent who can be a part of your child's life when grandparents cannot or don't want to be there. An honorary/surrogate grandparent might be someone who doesn't have grandchildren but would love to be a grandparent—maybe a neighbor, religious congregation member, or someone in your book club. It could even be a resident at a retirement community who you get to know through volunteer work. There are many older adults who have so much love to give and would jump at the chance to have a "special" grandchild and get to know your family. These honorary grandparents can come to Grandparents' Day at school, bake holiday cookies with your child, spend time with your child telling stories, and attend their birthday parties.

How would you find out if someone is interested in taking on an honorary grandparent role? Spend time with them and see if they seem interested in getting to know your family better. Perhaps they make comments about wishing they had a grandchild or express regret that their own grandchildren don't live closer. Help them out when they need help; maybe they need someone to deliver groceries to them or water their plants while they are on vacation. As you get to know each other over time, you can see how the relationship develops and find out if they might be interested in an honorary grandparent role.

Another approach is to see if there is another extended family member who might take on a more involved role when grandparents cannot. Even if you don't have involved grandparents, perhaps you have just one family member, like an aunt or uncle, who can help your child connect with the family and feel supported. An extended family member taking an interest in your child—celebrating his birthday, asking about school, showing up at team games and recitals—can make a big difference.

If you can't find an honorary grandparent and there aren't any family members interested in a closer relationship with your family, that can be a tough situation to deal with. But what you can do is work toward building a family of choice by focusing on making friends who are like family. A family of choice can be there for each other and support each other just like blood relatives do.

Jessica, a queer single parent by choice from Virginia, said that her five-year-old daughter loves her "cousins," who are actually Jessica's best friends' kids and part of their chosen family. "We have a memory book with pictures of everyone and she will say, 'Look at all my cousins.' She's branched out on what her definition is of 'sister' to include our cat and her cousins, and she seems okay with that."

Her daughter's actual cousins live far away, and Jessica's daughter doesn't understand the distinction between blood relative cousins and family friend cousins. And in addition to their chosen family cousins, her daughter also has five godparents. "One of them is my cousin, the others are my friends. We don't make the distinction of blood relatives versus not. . . . Where I grew up, we didn't have blood family anywhere near us, but my mom had a vast network of Filipino women who were present in my life. I have tried to do the same. I chose people to be godparents who know our story. I want my daughter to be able to talk to her godmother and ask questions about her story. I wanted the godparents to be people who could be resources about our family's narrative and who are supportive of my journey."

Nikki from Minnesota, who is an only raising an only, also has a chosen family. She said, "I was blessed with a chosen family growing up, courtesy of my parents, and have always seen the significant value in it. My village consists of my best friend from childhood and her family, along with my other friends I have made over the years. I am also still close to all of my parents' friends and their children. While my village looks a bit different than most (my friends are not close with one another, so they aren't directly part of one another's villages), I truly feel as though I have a far better support system than most people, including those with siblings. When building a village/chosen family, it is important to remember that you get what you give. You need to truly invest in people and love them well in order for them to become more than just friends or acquaintances."

You might have someone in your life who could be part of your family of choice, like a best friend or neighbor. But if you don't have someone like this in your life already, how exactly do you connect with others who might be looking to make friends who can be like family?

Start by getting to know people who recently moved to your area (transplants) and/or those who also have no local family. People who recently moved to your area may not know many people yet and are eager to make friends. They may also have the time and space in their life to make new friends. And those who have no local family may be looking to meet others who also want to get together for holidays or vacations.

Hobby/interest groups, like a walking group or book club; meetup groups; classes; and other parents you meet through your child's school or activities can all be opportunities to find others who are also looking for similar connections. Try to get to know the parents in your child's class or extracurricular activity who may have just moved from out of state or who don't have any local family. Start small with a simple walk, coffee, or park playdate to see if you're mutually compatible as family friends. If you see each other frequently and have things in common, it's likely that a friendship will form. Offer to help them out and show up for them. Over time, this individual might evolve into the type of friend who can be an essential part of your chosen family.

Conclusion

As we have explored in this chapter, relationships with grandparents and extended family are wonderful and beneficial for only children and should be nurtured whenever possible; however, not every only-child family has interested and involved grandparents and extended family. Finding honorary grandparents or building a family of choice with like-minded friends can be a healthy and meaningful alternative.

REFLECTION QUESTIONS

1. Think about your relationships with grandparents and extended family when you were growing up. If you had family locally, what was that experience like for you? If you did not have local family, did you find that difficult or lonely?

2. Before you had a child, what did you hope your parents would be like as grandparents? Have they met that ideal or do you wish they could grandparent in a different way?

3. Have you tried to build a family of choice and find friends who are like family? If so, were you successful? How did the experience go for you?

CHAPTER 13

Choosing the Ideal Home and Neighborhood for Your Family

When you have an only child, choosing the ideal neighborhood for your family becomes extra important. Beyond the usual considerations of a good school district, safe neighborhood, and convenient location to jobs, finding a family-friendly neighborhood with lots of kids and many opportunities to socialize is often valued by families with only children. If you're house hunting or thinking about selling your current home, this chapter is for you! We will explore how to evaluate a potential home and neighborhood that will be perfect for an only-child family and discuss all of the different factors to consider as you start to house hunt.

It can feel like a tall order to find everything on your wish list: a great home with all your must-haves; a family-friendly neighborhood with lots of kids; many neighborhood social opportunities; an active and involved HOA; amenities like a neighborhood park, pool, or club-house; or a nearby public school within walking distance. Even though you might not find a neighborhood or home that has everything you're looking for, it's likely you can find one that meets most of your needs.

What Do Only-child families Look For in a Neighborhood?

When you're house hunting, the quality of the house, location of the neighborhood, and proximity to work are all important factors, but so is the social character of the neighborhood. Many only-child families look for a neighborhood that has a friendly, social atmosphere where they can easily meet other neighbors, make friends, and build community. A social neighborhood offers opportunities to bond with neighbors, such as game nights, book clubs, walking groups, holiday parades, driveway meetups, backyard playdates, and neighborhood parties.

One mom of an only, who lives in Washington, DC, had two very different neighborhood experiences with her only child, who is now a teen. She said that her first neighborhood was fantastic because it was a townhouse community with a number of block parties and everyone hung out outside. She had a large community of friends and included them in their celebrations. But, little by little, everyone moved on to single-family homes and, eventually, the group disbanded.

This mom and her daughter also moved eventually, and they did not have success in their new single-family home neighborhood, where social life revolved around the swim team. They tried the swim team and joined initially, but her daughter didn't take to it, nor could she relate well or connect with the other athletic kids in the neighborhood.

It can be disappointing when you don't connect well to your new neighbors or community. But if your neighborhood has a lot of kids, it's more likely your child will be able to find a few they connect with.

Often high on many only-child families' priority lists is find-ing a neighborhood that has a lot of families so that there is a greater likelihood of their only child making neighborhood friends. It's much easier to meet other neighbors and make new friends in a social neighborhood that has a lot of kids, rather than one that doesn't offer any opportunities to gather and get to know neighbors. Many families find their closest friends in their neighborhood because they see them so often.

When you see neighbors often, like when you're watering your plants or raking leaves in the yard, you're more likely to become friendly. All those casual opportunities to get to know each other and chat when you're outside often add up to a close friendship. Additionally, when kids play in the neighborhood outside after school and on weekends, there's lots of time and opportunities for them to get to know neighborhood kids and become friends.

So before you start house hunting, it's important to think beyond the house and consider your ideal neighborhood. What do you imagine your ideal neighborhood to be like? Some families feel that an active HOA or a neighborhood with many social groups are on their "must haves" list. They want an engaged community where neighbors know each other and are friendly and where there are lots of events and activities hosted by the neighborhood. Some families look for a neighborhood with amenities, like a community pool or clubhouse, where they can gather and meet other neighbors. Other families prefer their peace and quiet and are interested in a neighborhood where people keep to themselves; they might want to find their social life elsewhere, like through their religious congregation or extracurricular activities.

But for many families, finding a social, family-friendly neighborhood is key. If you don't have any local family, you might hope that your new neighborhood can provide a vibrant social life and sense of community. But how can you tell when you're house hunting whether a neighborhood will work for your family? The following are some things to look for:

- Try to find out if most kids in the neighborhood go to the local public school or if they drive farther to private schools or charters. It might be harder for your child to make friends in the neighborhood if they go to public school and the other kids go to another school, or vice versa. There won't be the same opportunities to hang out at the bus stop or walk to school together.

- Does your neighborhood offer groups like a social committee, parents' group, walking group, neighborhood book club, or other neighborhood groups and committees? Is there a neighborhood newsletter or events calendar? If so, take this as a very good sign that it's an active and social neighborhood. If not, and a social neighborhood is a priority for you, you might want to give buying a house in this neighborhood a little more thought.

- How friendly does the neighborhood seem? It might be easiest to look at the Nextdoor site or the neighborhood's social media page to try to gauge this. If there is a social media page, how active is it? Do people post often about getting together or planning events? Or do you only see mundane posts every few months about topics like garbage pick-up or snow removal? Also see if you can walk around and talk to neighbors. Are they friendly? Some people value a friendly community where neighbors are eager to help and want to get together often. For others, this is not a priority, and it doesn't bother them if they only see their neighbors once or twice a year.

- Do you know anyone who lives in the neighborhood who can serve as a "reference" for the neighborhood? Speaking to someone who actually lives in the neighborhood you're interested in can help you better understand the pros and cons of the neighborhood. Ask your realtor if he or she knows anyone who lives in the neighborhood who you could speak with. If not, see if you can find the HOA email address on the neighborhood website or social media page and email an HOA member to find out more about the neighborhood.

- Use local Facebook parenting groups to do research on potential neighborhoods, including to help gauge their family-friendliness. You can post something like, "Hi, I'm doing research on a couple of neighborhoods we're considering moving to: Elmwood and Chestnut Hill. Can anyone share insight about these neighborhoods and whether they're family friendly? Thanks!" Or you could post, "Hi, I'm looking for a few options of family-friendly neighborhoods in Wilmington. If you love your neighborhood, can you share where it is and what you like about it? Thanks!" If you post something along these lines, you will likely get a lot of helpful responses and insight.

Many only-child families also consider neighborhood demographics when searching for a home. Many prefer a neighborhood where there are mainly families with kids, especially those around their child's age. Some neighborhoods have mainly older adults and empty nesters, while others have more young families. If the neighborhood you're interested in has a lot of kids but they're nowhere near your child's age, you might think twice about buying a house there if having close friends in the neighborhood is something you'd like for your child. For example, if you have a third grader and the neighborhood mainly has babies and high school kids, it is less likely your child will find other kids in the neighborhood to be friends with.

Your only may prefer a neighborhood where there are kids around their age that they can run around with outside and hang out at each other's houses. The nice thing about having neighbors to play with is that playdates don't have to be scheduled; instead, they can be more spontaneous! If your child having friends around their age in the neighborhood is a priority for you, you might want to find out the ages of the kids in the neighborhood you are considering. Your realtor can be helpful with this, as can local parenting groups on Facebook or other discussion boards. If there is an HOA, you could also try to talk with an HOA member to learn more about this.

Along with a family-friendly and social neighborhood, many only-child families also focus on the strength of local schools when they are searching for a new home. They might look for a home that's zoned for a top-rated public school. Or, if they are doing private school, they might look for a house near the school. One plus about attending public school is that your child will make friends at school who usually live very close by, which makes things easier when setting up playdates.

Some only-child families specifically look for a neighborhood with an elementary school within walking distance because they value having a school nearby. It's also a nice way to build community when kids walk together every day to and from school. But if your neighborhood does not have a school within walking distance, know that kids can also build community when they wait for the school bus together at the bus stop or when they ride the same bus together.

Other only-child families look for a neighborhood that offers great amenities, like a community swimming pool, swim team, tennis courts, clubhouse, or neighborhood park, because these can also be great ways to meet neighbors and build community. If your neighborhood has a community pool, this is a huge benefit because a pool is a great spot to meet up with neighbors during the summer and get to know them better. A neighborhood pool might also offer a neighborhood swim team, which is another way for your child to make friends if they like to swim.

A neighborhood pool can also be an ideal meeting spot for neighborhood social events, like summer BBQs, movie nights, parties, and other fun events. My friends with neighborhood pools are so lucky! I think it would be so wonderful to have a great community pool within walking distance to hang out at during the summer, and it's such a great place to build community and make new friends for your only. A community clubhouse, tennis courts, or neighborhood park can similarly offer great spots for neighbors to gather, thus more opportunities to socialize with neighbors.

One important factor that many only-child family house hunters don't consider is the relationship between yard size and neighborhood congeniality. While many people value large yards for the space and privacy, what they don't realize is that in many cases larger yards lead to less social neighborhoods. Sometimes neighborhoods with smaller yards and more density make for a more congenial neighborhood experience that only-child families are looking for. If you're in a townhouse or condo community where you see your neighbors often, and kids play outdoors in their driveways or shared common spaces, it's more likely you'll get to know your neighbors well and make friends. If, on the other hand, you live in a neighborhood with large yards and houses that are far apart from each other and no communal play space, it's less likely you'll get to know your neighbors because kids will more likely play in their own fenced backyards.

Think carefully about what kind of neighborhood experience you would prefer. There are trade-offs with both smaller and larger yards, but this may be an important factor to consider if you are house hunting and value a social neighborhood.

You will also need to consider how much yard or outdoor space you would like for your family's outdoor preferences. Some only-child families who like to spend time outdoors want a large yard with an area for a playset, room to run around, space to entertain, or maybe even their own pool. Other families are content with a small yard, or no outdoor space at all, and prefer to utilize parks as their outside time. Others want a house right on a beach or lake where they have water access, and others prefer a house with many acres of land or a farm. It's important to clarify what type of outdoor space you prefer when embarking on your housing search. The age of your child and how your family prefers to spend its time are important factors to consider when thinking about your new home's outdoor spaces.

Also consider what kind of neighborhood setup you prefer and what would be most conducive to your only child meeting new friends. Would you rather be in a more traditional neighborhood, where there are houses or townhomes on a residential street, or a condo in a building with multiple floors? Do you prefer a more rural area, where you get a lot of land but the houses may be spread far apart and your closest neighbor may not be within walking distance?

For Alejandra in France, living in an isolated area is the biggest challenge for her with raising an only child. She said, "I live in the forest, and my next neighbor is five kilometers (3.1 miles) away. It can become difficult for my daughter to have friends over . . . We try to see [school] friends once or twice a week, but they live fifteen minutes away, and there aren't other kids who live nearby. I also don't have a drivers' license, so I have to rely on my husband to take us to play-dates. Sometimes we don't see people for a whole week."

When considering buying a property, think carefully about what makes the most sense for your family and how your choice may affect your only child's abilities to build community with neighbors.

Where to Find Other Only-child families

It's common for only-child families to want to find a neighborhood that also has lots of other only-child families. But where can you find them? It can be difficult to figure out whether or not your neighborhood meets this criterion before you buy, unless you already know someone who lives in the neighborhood and can give you the scoop. You can also ask your realtor, who may have some insight.

From my own observations, and from talking with other only-child families, it generally seems that if a neighborhood has larger houses and larger yards, it is less likely to have many only-child families. In other words, if you're looking at neighborhoods with five-bedroom single family houses, it's more likely that you'll find families with three to five children living there because they need all that extra space. While some only-child families do decide to move into a larger house, many seek smaller homes because they don't necessarily need several extra bedrooms. If you do move into a neighborhood with huge houses, it can be hard not to feel like the odd one out if you're the lone only-child family in a neighborhood surrounded by dozens of large families.

It might also be harder to make friends in this kind of neighborhood because larger families often look for other large families to be friends with so that all the kids have someone to play with. Unfortunately, it's less likely (but not impossible) that a family with five kids is going to want to be friends with a family with an only child.

So where can you find neighborhoods with a larger number of only-child families, if that is a priority for you? To start, look for neighborhoods with smaller single-family homes, townhouses, or condos/apartments. Only-child families are more likely to prefer a smaller home because it's more cost-effective when you don't need all the extra bedrooms. Many only-child families live in a home with two or three bedrooms—one for the parents, one for the child, and (if there's an extra bedroom) a guest room or office.

It's also more likely to find only-child families in the city or close to a city. Many young couples start out living in a city and then move out to the suburbs once they have children, when city life gets too expensive, or when they want a larger place. City life is usually expensive, with high real estate prices for urban living with all its amenities. Many families end up moving out to the suburbs for a lower cost of living and more space. However, many only-child families keep living in the city or move to the closer inner suburbs because they value the cultural experiences and amenities gained from living in a city. The reason for this is because with just one child, they can afford to stay in the city and rent or buy a two- or three-bedroom apartment, condo, or townhouse.

When you're evaluating a potential neighborhood for its only child friendliness characteristics, talk to prospective neighbors, talk to your realtor, stroll around the neighborhood and note the size of the families you see playing outside or walking in the neighborhood, and observe the ages of the kids to see if they're around your child's age.

Also keep in mind that neighborhoods do turn over every few years. If a neighborhood you're considering has mainly high school kids, in a few years these families may move out and more families with young kids could move in.

Jessica from Virginia said that her neighborhood has had a lot of turnover and families with two kids have moved out to the suburbs. That leaves her daughter with no friends in their condo community, which borders a community courtyard area. "The community courtyard, which was full of kids, is now down to my daughter. We've talked about [it], and she has figured out that people will move out when they have another baby—apparently that's how it is." For now, Jessica and her daughter get together with school friends instead. "We have playdates on playgrounds with kids from school who live a few blocks away."

Jessica's solution might work for you. But if you're looking to make new friends in the community right now, having families with kids of similar ages or many only-child families in the neighborhood may be an important consideration.

What Kind of House Do You Want?

Some only-child families prefer an urban neighborhood with older homes and a charming feel. Others want a one- to two-bedroom condo or apartment in an urban area that is within walking distance to shops, restaurants, and points of interest in the city. A number of families want a large house and yard in the suburbs where they have lots of space, tranquility, and peace and quiet. And still, other families prefer a rural location where they own many acres for a farm. Locations and characteristics of a place vary so widely that you're bound to find what best fits your family.

Jessica from Virginia, who is a single parent by choice, loves her home, which she describes as a tiny two-bedroom rowhouse. It has a large master bedroom and a small additional bedroom, which works for them. She said, "There are a lot of aspects I really love. My daughter also agrees that our house is perfect for us.

"When I was pregnant, I decided that I would move into the small room and my daughter would get the big room. She has this giant room with all of her stuff, and she gets to organize it. It's her space. All I need is a bed and a night table in this little guest room. She loves the fact that she has a big room with a big, full-sized bed. Also, we have a pretty nice backyard. In the summer, we put a giant inflatable pool back there and it's an oasis. My daughter really enjoys splash parties out there." Jessica also appreciates her neighborhood's communal, outdoor space. "We have a beautiful, grassy courtyard/common space. It's like we live on a park. It's wonderful!"

In terms of the actual house, think about the feelings you want your house to exude. Do you want a warm, homey surrounding? Or more of a sophisticated, modern vibe? Or perhaps a casual, laid-back atmosphere fits your style best? What about a one level house or a two-story? Consider how your only child might feel about growing up in the home you choose. Think about any special features of the home that will make for special childhood memories.

Perhaps the home has a lovely screened-in porch where you can host parties and gatherings, or maybe it has a big yard and playset that your child will love to play on. Perhaps it has a treehouse that will make a fun outdoor play space for your child and her friends. Maybe there's a nice big wall in the kitchen where you could post your child's artwork, or a fun loft space that would make a great play area. Perhaps the room that will become your child's room has a lot of natural light or a lovely view of the backyard. A rooftop deck can be a great play space that your child will love, or a basement rec room can be a fun spot to host friends.

A home your child can cherish as much as you do is an important factor when buying a house. Think about the overall feeling you experience when you walk into the home and try to imagine what it would be like for your child to grow up there.

How to Make Your Home the Ideal Hangout House

Some families want to make their house the ideal hangout spot, where all the neighborhood kids or their child's friends will want to gather. They might choose a house with a large basement and furnish it with a Ping-Pong table, pool table, foosball table, or a sofa and big-screen TV, or they might choose a house or apartment building with a pool so that their child's friends can swim there. They might pick a house with a good-sized backyard for a playset, outdoor toys, and plenty of space to entertain, or they might choose a house with an extra guest bedroom that can be turned into a playroom.

If being the hangout house is important to you, think about what kind of spaces you might need in order to make this goal a reality, and factor that into your preferences as you search for houses.

When You Have Buyer's Remorse

What can you do if you've already bought a house and you're stuck in a neighborhood that is less than family-friendly or, at worst, downright cold and aloof? Maybe you misjudged the neighborhood, thinking it would be social, and it turns out you've lived there for years and you've never even met your next-door neighbors? Perhaps it's the house itself that turned out to be a disappointment or an unexpected money pit?

The unpleasant truth is that buyer's remorse happens. When you're house hunting, sometimes you don't realize how family-friendly a neighborhood may or may not be just from going to the open house or seeing the neighborhood a few times. Or you might overlook flaws in a house that only make themselves known once you've lived there a few months. While it's not pleasant to feel like you made a mistake with your home purchase, don't despair! All hope is not lost.

If it's a neighborhood mismatch, there are some things you can try. If you've tried to reach out and haven't made any connections with neighbors, see if you can get involved in the neighborhood in some way. Consider joining your HOA or condo board, and see if there are some committees you can join to meet neighbors. Better yet, if there is a social committee, consider joining it—people on the social committee are usually a fun bunch who like meeting new people.

If you do decide to join your HOA/condo board, it comes with several benefits: you can get to know your neighbors, get the inside scoop on the neighborhood (including neighborhood gossip), and implement some positive changes to your neighborhood. Maybe you'll be the one to start up a social committee if your neighborhood doesn't have one or you'll be the one to plan a family-friendly neighborhood event (like a Halloween parade). Start small and try out one idea at a time to see how it's received. If your neighborhood doesn't have a listserv or Facebook page, maybe you could start one.

If you do end up starting a social committee or joining an existing one, you might come to realize that your neighborhood isn't as aloof as it seemed and there *are* some neighbors who are interested in being neighborly. Chances are if you think your neighborhood is unfriendly, others do too, and you could be just the person to make some positive changes.

Nicole McNelis, LPC, a therapist in Pennsylvania, said that it's valid to feel rejected if you bought a house thinking it was going to be a good fit and then turns out not to be. "It's disappointing when new neighbors are dismissive and not welcoming. What you can do is validate the feeling, figure out what is missing, and look for the need behind this feeling. Then find a community outside of the neighborhood that embraces your family and where you can find that community and welcoming feel and where your family is accepted for who they are."

Another thing you can try, especially if your neighborhood doesn't have an HOA to join or you don't know many people in your neighborhood, is to get out there and make the effort on your own to meet neighbors. If you and your child can make one or two friends in the neighborhood, it can make all the difference to feeling like your neighborhood is a friendly, welcoming place. Here are some suggestions to try:

- **Take walks.** Make an extra effort to take neighborhood walks (easy to do if you have a dog) and make a point to introduce yourself to any neighbors you see. Go out at different times of day and see which times more people are out and about.
- **Start new traditions.** Start a neighborhood special event tradition (like a neighborhood summer block party, progressive dinner event, or holiday party) and see if this brings people together more.
- **Host a get-together.** Consider hosting a casual backyard get-together to meet the neighbors. In the winter, you could try a fire pit gathering on your driveway and set out s'mores and hot chocolate. In the summer, you could do a fun BBQ and set out a sprinkler for the kids.
- **Form a new group.** Send out an email to your neighborhood listserv asking if anyone would be interested in meeting up for a walking group, book club, or some other group. You might be able to meet some neighbors who are looking for friends too.
- **Host a playdate.** Send out an email to your neighborhood listserv saying that you'd like to host a neighborhood playdate in your backyard for all elementary school kids (or whatever age range your only child is) and see who responds. This can be a good way to meet neighbors you didn't know have a child your only's age.
- **Stay out front.** Start hanging out in your front yard a lot more so you can wave, say hi, and chat with neighbors who walk by. It's much easier to meet people this way than if you always hang out in your backyard.
- **Beautify your yard.** Try working on your front yard landscaping often—planting flowers, raking leaves, or watering plants.

Neighbors will see you and wave more often. They may even come by to compliment your landscaping and stay to chat a bit.

- **Do something thoughtful.** If your garden has a bounty of cucumbers or peppers, gather them in a basket and bring them over to your neighbor as a friendly gesture. If it's holiday time, bake a tin of cookies and take them over to your neighbor.
- **Help out.** Offer to help an elderly neighbor clear their driveway of snow or rake leaves in the fall. You could also help out with the neighborhood common spaces. Is there a community garden or neighborhood entrance sign that could use some sprucing up? Offer your gardening skills to make your neighborhood more aesthetically pleasing.
- **Socialize at the bus stop.** If there's a school bus stop, focus on making an effort there. Wait outside with your only for the school bus, socialize with others, and then stay after a little while to chat with the neighborhood parents who wait there with you.

If it's the house itself that you have buyer's remorse over because it doesn't fit your family's needs the way you had originally thought, think about what you might be able to change through renovations. Renovating can make your home more functional and is usually much less expensive than moving! If you are a DIY family, you or your spouse might be able to watch some YouTube videos and learn how to do your own simple renovations, like retiling a bathroom floor or replacing carpet.

Also think about repurposing rooms that don't work for your family. For instance, many traditional homes have a formal living room. If having a living room space doesn't seem appealing because you rarely entertain, maybe you could turn that space into a playroom or office space that would get more use. Or if your home has a tiny laundry room and no mudroom, consider relocating the laundry room and turning the existing laundry room into a mudroom. A simple change like this can make your house much more functional and easily solve what can seem like a big issue with the home. Think about what issues make your house less than ideal and brainstorm solutions that can make the spaces more functional.

Conclusion

As we have seen in this chapter, there are many factors that only-child families consider when looking for a new home and neighborhood. By clarifying your needs before you start your housing search, you can ensure that you find the home and neighborhood that is the perfect fit for your family, which will provide many wonderful memories for years to come.

REFLECTION QUESTIONS

1. Think back to your childhood home(s). What did you like best about the home you grew up in, and what did you like the least? Are there any characteristics of your childhood home that you would like to have in your current home?

2. Think back to your childhood neighborhood. Was your neighborhood family-friendly? Was it social? Do you have positive memories of your neighborhood? Would you like a similar type of neighborhood for your own family or something completely different?

3. Think about the home you are currently in. What do you think your child likes most/least about your current home? What are some special features of your home that are most meaningful or important for your child?

4. What makes a living space feel like home to you? Is it a type of architecture, decorating style, location of the home, type of neighborhood, outdoor space, or the style of the home itself? Does your current house feel like home to you? If not, how can you make your current house feel more homey?

CHAPTER 14

Finding Enriching and Meaningful Activities for Your Only

Many parents value extracurricular activities outside of school for their only child because they provide several wonderful benefits, including giving onlies a chance to socialize with other kids, learn new skills, build mastery in an interest, and have fun. Activities also help kids become more well-rounded and try new things.

But with so many activities out there, the options can be mind-boggling. Where do you start and how do you choose? This chapter helps ease the extracurricular overwhelm by giving parents a roadmap of how to evaluate potential activities and then best match activities to their child's interests.

The Benefits of Extracurricular Activities

Let's start by talking more indepth about the countless benefits extracurricular activities provide for only children.

First, participating in an activity is an opportunity to socialize with a new group of kids outside of school. If your child is having difficulty making friends at school, hasn't yet found a group of friends, or doesn't have many friends in the neighborhood, participating in an extracurricular activity is a great opportunity to meet a whole new peer group. It may turn out that your child's new best friend is from dance class or chess club!

Second, participating in an activity is a chance to focus more intensely on an area of interest, like LEGO engineering or violin, that your child would not otherwise get the chance to engage in at school. For kids who aren't that enthusiastic about school but are searching for their "passion," this is a great way to help them develop an interest in something outside of school that will build self-esteem and self-confidence simultaneously.

Third, participating in an activity is a good opportunity to develop important character traits like discipline, grit, and teamwork. Working toward a goal, such as learning to play a particular song well on the piano or becoming proficient in coding, takes time, patience, and practice. There can be a steep learning curve at first, but if your child perseveres and eventually becomes proficient, they will develop the increased self-confidence and self-esteem that comes from successfully tackling a challenging task and sticking with it.

Participating in an extracurricular activity is also a great way to work on self-discipline, time management, and executive functioning skills, which benefit all children. For example, if your son is into a martial art and learns how to control his body and channel aggression constructively, it develops personal discipline. Or if your daughter is on a soccer team and makes the effort to get to practices on time, practices the sport outside of scheduled practices, and balances schoowork along with the demands of the sport, her efforts all come together to build important executive functioning skills that will serve her well for the rest of her life.

Fourth, your child's activities can become whole family activities if you take an active role, which can help you both build a sense of community. Coaching your child's Little League team, being a Scout troop leader, or volunteering to bring snacks to sport practices are all great ways for you to get involved in activities and meet other parents. In addition, your child will form strong ties with other kids through participation, especially through activities like a team sport, dance studio, or Scouts.

Finally, participating in activities is an opportunity to incorporate additional structure into your child's evenings or weekends, which can be helpful if your child thrives on more of a structured schedule. Enrolling your child in activities can be valuable if you're trying to keep your child off screens or if you don't usually have much going on after school or during weekends. It can also be helpful if your child wants more social time with other kids after school but you're having difficulty scheduling enough playdates. Doing a Saturday morning swim class and a Sunday morning fencing class can provide a productive structure to your weekends and extra social time for your child.

Amanda, mom of an only child and a teacher in Pennsylvania, said that extracurricular activities are important because a child learns how to follow directions from other adults, as well as how to take turns, cooperate, and build team skills. She also believes that activities can help kids who aren't as interested in school. "Some kids don't want to sit still at a desk and use all of their talents. Not everyone wants to learn through a book, but maybe they're great at track or basketball or violin. That can give them a sense of self-accomplishment, belonging, and [the ability] to excel at something that they choose."

Evaluating Types of Extracurricular Activities

There are many different categories of extracurricular activities your child can participate in, and it can be overwhelming to figure out where to start and which to choose. First, let's discuss each category in order to give you a better sense of which activities might best fit your child's interests and needs.

ARTS

Visual arts, music, performing arts, and writing are all different types of art-related activities. They are great opportunities for your child to learn a new skill or develop mastery in something they're already good at. You can find art classes, music classes for every instrument, theater classes, writing classes, and more.

There are also many art activity options beyond traditional drawing, painting, and piano lessons. How about a class to learn comic book illustration? A botanical drawing class? A drumming class? A creative writing class? A dance or gymnastics class? Classes in the arts let your child's creativity soar. You can find these kinds of classes through independent enrichment centers, music schools, arts studios, rec centers, dance studios, community centers, or in-home local teachers.

Also note that there can be many different options in each category. For example, if your child is interested in dance, there are many options to explore: classical ballet, tap, jazz, modern dance, folk dance, Irish dance, and more. You can try one type of dance class and see how your child likes it before branching out into other types. You can also find summer camps focusing on the arts, many of which are held at schools, studios, and community rec centers.

SPORTS

There are all kinds of sports your child can participate in: weekend soccer, T-ball, tennis, ice hockey, ice skating, football, rugby, biking, and more. Your child can benefit in many ways from participating in sports, like learning new athletic skills, developing large motor skills, improving overall fitness, getting regular exercise, learning discipline, and having a lot of fun.

When deciding on a sport to try, think about a few sports that your child has expressed interest in. Maybe your child has mentioned wanting to learn how to ice skate. You can check out your local ice rink to find a variety of ice-skating classes. And if your child has never skated before, you can start with the beginner's class.

Amanda, mom of an only child, said that solitary sports, such as swimming or cross-country, can also be great activities for some kids because it's a team sport that's based on your own child's personal achievements.

If your child isn't athletic but still would like to participate in a sport, what about a Ping-Pong, golf, or fencing class for something a little more outside the box? You can find these sports classes through youth sports leagues, independent sports companies, rec centers, or gyms. You can also get your child interested in sports by having them watch a sports game or the Olympics on TV and see what appeals to them.

TEAMS

Your child has the option to join different types of teams, ranging from sports teams like soccer, ice hockey, and swim teams, to non-sports teams like chess, math, and LEGO building teams. Teams are great for creating a family-like atmosphere and a sense of community because participants are practicing together often and travel together for games, tournaments, or meets. They also help build important character skills like discipline, perseverance, and teamwork.

I wish I had participated on a team growing up because team participation provides so many benefits, such as helping kids feel a sense of community and camaraderie with others sharing the same goals. I wanted my son to experience all of this, so he started participating on a team as soon as he was old enough. He took ice skating lessons at a young age then ice hockey lessons, and he has loved playing on an elementary school ice hockey team for several years.

If this sounds like a good fit for your only child, check out the teams offered through your child's school, rec centers, youth sports leagues, swim centers, and independent centers (like chess or fencing schools).

SCOUTS

Cub Scouts, Boy Scouts, and Girl Scouts are all fun scouting groups you and your child can join. It's a great opportunity to meet other kids and build friendships because your child stays in the same group for a few years and they usually meet monthly, so there is ample time to get to know the other kids in the troop. Scouts also helps you meet other families through pack activities that are family outings, allowing plenty of opportunities for parents to participate with their child. It's really an activity for the entire family.

Plus all the time out in nature, the emphasis on community service, and the opportunity to learn nature- and STEM-related skills is very beneficial for positive character growth. We thoroughly enjoyed our experiences in Cub Scouts when my son was in early elementary school.

ACADEMIC ENRICHMENT

You may also consider trying out some academic enrichment extracurricular activities, from language classes to math clubs to science teams—all with the goal of helping kids keep up with their schoolwork, get ahead, learn interesting new concepts in their preferred areas of interest, or compete against other teams.

Some kids take advanced math classes on the weekends to maintain current skills or get ahead. Other kids take academic enrichment classes because they're not being challenged enough in school. A math club could be a great way for your child to get extra experience with math and socialize with other kids who love math too. You can also find summer school classes that are focused on various academic enrichment topics.

SOCIAL SKILLS CLASSES

There are many situations where a child might need a little extra help with social skills. Perhaps your child is struggling with making or keeping friends and could use some extra practice working on these skills. Maybe their conversation starter skills could benefit from a little extra help.

The great news is that there are many different kinds of social skills classes available for your child to work on improving their social skills. Learning good interpersonal skills (like conversation starters, teamwork skills, friendship skills, and problem-solving skills) are all important for kids to learn and practice in a comfortable setting with other kids who are working on the same set of skills. Having a strong grasp of basic social skills can change kids' lives for the better because it helps them make new friends and maintain friendships more easily.

Many kids take social skills classes after school or on the weekends. Some classes may be covered by your health insurance if you have mental health coverage (check with your insurance provider). You will find these classes most often through counseling centers, social skills centers, therapy offices, and community centers. Your school's guidance counselor may also offer a lunch bunch or other social skills groups that your child can participate in during school hours.

MOMMY-AND-ME CLASSES

Mommy-and-Me classes are great social opportunities for parents and young children, usually benefitting ages infant through three years old. You can find Mommy-and-Me music and art classes, gymnastics, sports, swim classes, library activities, and many others. There are even Mommy-and-Me preschool-type classes for toddlers, which are a wonderful introduction to the preschool environment.

My son and I did a year-long Mommy-and-Me introduction to preschool class once a week when he was a toddler, which was a great way for me to get to know other moms because the class met weekly for an entire year. It was also a wonderful way for my son to get used to the preschool environment because it took place in a preschool classroom. For three hours every Thursday morning, he got to play with the class toys, play on the school playground, and become familiar with preschool expectations. I look back very fondly on our Mommy-and-Me preschool class experience.

You can find a variety of Mommy-and-Me parent/child classes through local rec centers, preschools, and libraries, including music, gymnastics, swimming, story time, and preschool readiness classes.

MOMS' GROUPS/PLAYGROUPS

Moms' groups and playgroups are excellent activities for infants up through around age three, before kids get busy with preschool. (And even still, you'll find some up until kindergarten.) Moms' groups/playgroups are many parents' first experience meeting other parents, socializing their babies and toddlers in a group setting, and building a parenting community. There are local groups to join, as well as a few national moms' groups, like the MOMS Club and MOPS (Mothers of Preschoolers).

I joined a number of different moms' groups when my son was a baby, toddler, and preschooler, mainly through meetup.com and

Facebook groups. I found these groups to be invaluable for meeting other moms in the same parenting stage, for sharing recommendations and resources, and for the camaraderie and support. Because everyone had kids around the same age, these groups were such a nice opportunity to talk about what we were experiencing in our parenting journey with others who completely understood. I even started two moms' groups myself—one was for babies and toddlers in my local area, and the other was for only-child families. Both were successful, and one grew to have more than three hundred members.

You can find moms' groups through meetup.com, Facebook, recommendations from friends, your OB-GYN office, the hospital where you delivered, and through preschools and religious congregations. If you don't find a moms' group that will work for you, consider starting one of your own through any social media network!

STEM/STEAM CLASSES

STEM classes are very popular right now because there is an emphasis on kids learning about science and technology concepts early on. "STEM" stands for science, technology, engineering, and math, while "STEAM" adds in the arts. There are a variety of STEM and STEAM classes to try—you can look into chess clubs, LEGO engineering classes, computer coding, robotics classes, mad science classes, art classes, and more. These are great for academic enrichment or just for fun.

You can find these types of classes through academic enrichment centers, local rec centers, after-school programs, libraries, community centers, and indoor play spaces.

VOLUNTEERING

Older onlies may be interested in finding meaningful volunteer positions in the community, which can be wonderful after-school, weekend, or summer activities. For instance, middle school and high school kids might find a volunteer position at an assisted living facility, science or art museum, animal shelter, farm, or nonprofit organization. There are even opportunities for virtual volunteering (through your computer or at home), which became popular during the COVID-19 pandemic.

Volunteering can help teens and kids give back to their community; become more aware of important social issues; learn more about an interest; learn practical, job-related skills; work with people of all ages; and make meaningful new friendships.

When I was in middle school and high school and aged out of summer day camp but was too young for a summer job, I spent many of my summers volunteering at a local assisted living facility, which I loved. I got to know the residents, helped out with creative projects, and learned about event planning by helping out with different events. I also volunteered at a local science museum in middle school, which had a summer volunteer program for kids. Both were amazing experiences that I look back on fondly and were great opportunities to meet new people and gain new skills.

You can find similar opportunities for your child through sites like volunteermatch.org, your local county or town website (which lists local volunteer positions), or the app JustServe. You can also contact individual nonprofits directly to inquire about volunteer opportunities open to kids.

INTERNSHIPS

Internships are great for older onlies because they provide an opportunity to learn about different professions, gain new skills, give back to the community, and make new friends. Internships can be done after school, on weekends, or during the summer.

Where can you find out about internships? Middle and high school–aged kids can usually find internships at many of the places that accept volunteers, if they also have an internship program for kids. Some of the places you can look for internships include animal shelters, nonprofits, newspapers, and community centers. Check out idealist.org and volunteermatch.org to look for specific places in your area that offer internships.

I did several internships as a kid and teen, and I found them to be meaningful and fulfilling experiences. When I was in middle school, I did a summer internship program at a local science museum. Then in high school, I had an internship during the school year at a newspaper writing a monthly column. I also did a high school summer internship at a local community newspaper. Both of these internship opportunities led to a strong interest in writing as a career.

Similar to volunteering, internships are fantastic ways to help kids explore a potential career interest, learn professional workplace skills, gain experience working with people of all ages, and make new friends. As an extra bonus, they also look great on future college and job applications.

PART-TIME JOBS

Older onlies can apply for a part-time job for after school, on weekends, or during summers. Keep in mind that the Fair Labor Standards Act states that teens have to be fourteen years old in order to work a nonagricultural, part-time job, and there are specific regulations about how many hours teens can work. And different states have varying rules about the minimum age for babysitting jobs. (Check with your state about specific regulations.)

A part-time or summer job is a great way to make new friends, work with people of all ages, learn new skills, and learn basic financial skills (like budgeting and maintaining a first bank account).

Having a part-time job also fosters independence and greater financial savvy because teens who make their own money tend to develop more responsible saving and spending habits. Holding a part-time job even helps kids with executive functioning skills because they will need to be on time to their job, show a good work ethic, and complete work in a timely fashion in order to keep a job. In addition, it can help foster skills of working well with others and positive teamwork.

I loved my jobs in high school, which I did during summers and on weekends, working at a movie theater and as a hostess at a popular restaurant chain. I made a whole new friend group from these jobs, which was a social benefit alongside the work experience. I also liked the independence and self-confidence that having a job as a teen provided.

What to Consider for a Child with Special Needs

Danielle Peters, LMFT, a therapist in California specializing in emotionally supporting parents of kids who are neurodiverse and with special needs, has a few suggestions for finding activities for only children with special needs in particular. If your child has autism, she suggests looking for an activity where there is a lot of social interaction, such as Boy Scouts or Girl Scouts. If your child with autism has a special interest, like Pokémon or art, she suggests looking for clubs around your child's interest. If your child has ADHD, physical activities like a Ninja obstacle course or soccer would work best.

Once you've found an activity that seems like a good fit, Peters suggests talking to the leaders of the activity. "I would want to talk to the leaders and have them be aware of my child's disability. I would want to know how they will handle problems, like if the child doesn't want to participate or transition, and I would want to see them taking a flexible approach."

Peters continues that she would be sure to ask the leaders some additional questions that would help a parent decide if an activity is the right fit for their child. "My first question would be: how much do the adults understand what is going on with your child, and are they able to make accommodations? My second question would be: it would be best if the child would be able to do the activity without parent involvement, but if a parent needs to be involved for support or the physical aspect, would they allow a parent to be involved?"

Peters recommends asking the activity leader about necessary accommodations and then trying out the group activity and seeing what happens before committing.

Start with the Most Important Skills First

With such an abundance of activities to choose from, it can feel overwhelming to decide which activities are the most important for your only. Where do you start, and how do you choose? One approach you can take is to determine which extracurricular activities teach the most important skills you want your child to learn and then participate in those first.

For many parents, a survival skills class, like swimming, is at the top of the list. Many parents feel that water safety is a top priority, so they want to enroll their child in a swim class as early as possible. Many parents don't feel that they can adequately teach their child how to swim, so they look for a class at a rec center or swim school. Swim classes can start early in age, even as young as Mommy-and-Me classes for babies.

Other parents feel that it's important for their child to take music lessons so that their child can learn how to play a musical instrument well. They feel that learning a musical instrument is part of a well-rounded childhood, as well as an important life skill.

Others believe it's most important for their child to learn how to play a sport, valuing athletic and large motor skills development, so they sign their child up to join a soccer, hockey, baseball, rugby, football, fencing, wrestling, or other type of sports class or team. Individual sports, like karate, diving, or gymnastics, could also be included here.

All of these are great options. One approach to handling extracurricular activities is to start with an important survival skills class, such as swimming, and then add one or two other fun classes based on your child's age and interests, like sports, gymnastics, chess, a language, or music.

Amanda, mom of an only child and a teacher in Pennsylvania, believes that the best activities for only children are those that are individualized but folded into the façade of a group. She gives the example of swim team and band as two great activities for onlies. "In swimming, you can compete on your own, but you still belong to a swim team that trains together, so you get that sense of community [while] it comes down to your own individual accomplishments. That sense of autonomy is important to an only child [when] they might not be ready to jump in right away to where it requires constant team cooperation. Band is another example— you have the chance to do solos, but you're also folded into the larger orchestra."

The best way to evaluate your options is to sit down with your spouse/ partner and come up with a list of the most important skills you would like your child to learn. Then think about the time you have available to take your child to activities and whether there is a budget for activities you need to stick with. This will help you narrow down your list.

To Gain or Improve Skills

Some parents choose an activity by determining whether they would like their child to gain new skills or improve existing skills. If you prefer to focus on activities where your child gains new skills, you might, for example, decide to focus on swimming lessons if your child doesn't know yet how to swim. If you would like your child to improve their physical fitness, you might get them involved in a new sport.

If you'd like your child to improve their current skills, think about what classes or activities they've already done and how they could continue to build upon those skills with higher-level classes, a team, or private lessons. For example, if your child has been in soccer classes for a few years already, maybe it's a good time to try a summer soccer camp or try out for a competitive soccer team. Or if your child has taken piano lessons in a group class for the last few years and shows lots of interest in improving their skills, it could be a good time to hire a teacher for private lessons.

Amanda, mom of an only child, believes the best way to choose activities is to look at the domains your child already shows interest in first. She said, "If your only is an active child, they might prefer an activity that's athletic. I think kids should try an activity three times before deciding it's not for them."

Involve your child in the decision-making process to see what they're interested in doing. Come up with a few options that can help achieve these goals and let your child determine which activities interest them the most.

Try a Variety and See What Sticks

Some parents want their child to sample a cornucopia of activities to see what sparks their only's interest. If they try enough activities, eventually they will find one that really interests them and, most likely, they'll want to stick with it long-term to build mastery. The important thing is to let your child lead the way on this. Ask your child what activities they would like to try. Their answers might surprise you.

Consider trying a trial class of different activities before you commit to an entire session. You might be able to try one class before officially signing up, or you might even take advantage of a free class. If that's not possible, commit to one short session to see if your only likes the activity. Then, if your child shows continued interest, you can commit to signing up for longer sessions.

When Your Only Loses Interest in an Activity: Quit or Persist?

Many children try an activity, get all excited about it, and then quickly lose interest. They may decide they don't want to go anymore or complain often about the activity. You might sign them up for a semester of fencing classes that they initially seemed excited about, but then on week two, they decide they don't like fencing and refuse to go anymore. For some kids, this becomes a pattern with every activity they try. So the big question is: Should you allow your child to quit, or should you make sure they continue with what they signed up for?

If your child is trying an activity for the first time, consider doing a trial class or two, where your child can try it out to see if they like it. If your child likes it and says they want to participate in the rest of the session, they may try it for a while and then suddenly want to quit. When this happens, some families adhere to the philosophy that their child must stick with the duration of the classes and follow through on their commitment. They value the concepts of grit and perseverance and believe these are important skills for kids to learn. This stick-with-it mentality will serve kids well over the long run, rather than teaching them that it's okay to give up if something starts to feel hard.

But sometimes an activity is just not the right fit, even if your child has participated in it for a while. Their interests may have changed, or they may lose interest in an activity after a period of time and want to try something new. If they've given it a fair try and put forth a good effort, consider the possibility that changing directions and trying something else may be the best choice.

It can be hard to know when kids should stick with an activity or change gears to something else. Follow your child's lead and figure out what they may be telling you through their actions. If they've already given it a good try but flat-out say that they don't want to play basketball anymore, or if they never practices the flute after a year of flute lessons, it may be time to reconsider whether this really is the best activity choice.

Do an Activity with a Friend

Letting your only take a class with a friend can be a fabulous way to get them interested in a new activity, spend more time with a friend, and learn a new skill in the process.

Think about what your child and a friend might like to do—perhaps a dance class would be fun, or a martial arts class. Do they already have a shared interest or hobby? If so, it will make finding a class they both like much easier. It will probably be one of the highlights of their week to take a class with their BFF, not to mention it'll be a great way for you to get to know another parent as well.

How Many Activities Are Enough?

Many parents wonder how many activities are enough for their only. A lot of this depends on your child's age, your ability to drive your child around and stay during the activity, and your overall weekday/weekend structure. If you have a really busy schedule already, you may want to focus on fewer activities closer to home in order to limit time commuting. On the other hand, if your schedule is wide open and you don't mind driving all over town, then your schedule can probably accommodate more activities.

Amanda, mom and teacher in Pennsylvania, believes that three extracurricular activities is the magic number. "I'd like my child to participate in at least three different activities per school year, one in each developmental domain: physical, mental, and creative. Three activities gives a sense of balance, where it doesn't overwhelm them, and speaks to each developmental domain. And three is still less than half the days in a week."

Some families like to be busier, while others prefer a more open, relaxed schedule. There are families who value family time on the weekends and don't want to have anything scheduled (which might leave activities for weekday evenings only). Other families like to have something structured to do each day and value multiple weekend activities. Think about your ideal family time/schedule/activity balance when you decide how many activities is the right fit.

A younger child may need fewer activities than an older child. Many parents believe that doing one activity per week during the toddler and preschool years is plenty. They may want to stick with one activity per week during elementary school as well, while others decide to increase that number to two or three activities. It all depends on how busy you want your child to be (and how busy you are taking them to those activities). If your child does better with the structure of activities so they stay off screens, you might want to enroll them in several activities. If your child does better with free play and unstructured time, then one activity per week might be the right number.

If your only has more than one activity, you can also consider how they are adjusting to a busier schedule. With multiple activities, can they get their schoolwork done, participate in family time, and still have enough time for free play or downtime? If so, then the number of activities they're doing might be the right number. But if your child seems cranky or tired, can't get all their schoolwork done, or doesn't have enough free play/downtime, then perhaps reducing the number of activities is a better choice.

Also consider your personal philosophy on structured activities versus free play/downtime. Some families prefer a more relaxed, unstructured approach to their child's schedule, with mostly unfilled time for free play, whereas others like the structure that scheduled activities provide.

Ask yourself the question: what is your philosophy on kids being overscheduled? Some parents consider being overscheduled a bad thing, whereas others see it as a good thing. Parents who view being overscheduled negatively may worry that their child misses out on other, more valuable childhood experiences and opportunities because of being overscheduled, or that their child becomes stressed from too many commitments. On the other hand, those who view a busy schedule positively prefer their child to be more scheduled because it entertains their child, provides structure to their evenings and weekends, and provides additional opportunities to socialize outside of school.

Also think about the structure of your week and weekend. Do you want to be driving to multiple activities after work on weekdays? Or do you prefer to keep your evening family time unstructured? On the weekends, some families appreciate the structure that multiple activities provide, especially if they don't have much going on during weekends.

For example, if you have no local family, have few friends, and don't have many weekend plans in general, you might appreciate the structure that doing weekend activities provides. As we all know, entertaining an only child all weekend can be challenging. When you have an activity on a Saturday and one on a Sunday, some families find that it provides the perfect balanced structure to your weekend and takes some of the pressure off of you to provide the sole entertainment.

On the other hand, having weekend activities as a part of your plans can make it feel like your weekend schedule is too full, when instead you'd rather relax as a family or have plenty of time available to clean the house and take care of chores and errands. If your weekends are always busy visiting local family and getting together with friends for playdates and activities, then having a less structured schedule may be more appealing.

Unstructured Hobbies for Your Only

If your only isn't into structured activities or classes, another alternative is finding a hobby instead. A hobby is more of a casual activity that your only can do anytime for fun. The nice thing about hobbies is that they have the potential to turn into areas where your child wants to seek additional mastery. For instance, if your child starts painting as a hobby, and enjoys it and develops a talent for it, they may decide they would like to enroll in painting classes and learn more. Or, if your child plays chess against Grandpa as a hobby, they may decide they want to join a chess club to improve their skills.

There are tons of hobbies out there that might interest your only. In fact, there are so many hobbies, it can be overwhelming! You can start by looking through lists of hobbies online and choosing a few that might be a good fit. You can also check out books about hobbies from the library to learn more about different or unique ones, or you can browse through a hobby or craft store to find something that sparks your child's interests.

The Value of Summer Camps for Onlies

Many parents choose to send their onlies to a summer camp as an activity that they can do when school is out. Summer camp can be an opportunity for your child to do something fun and structured with their summer, make new friends, stay busy, and try new interests. Many kids return to the same summer camps, year after year, to reconnect with their "camp friends."

There are two types of summer camps: summer day camps and sleepaway camps. Day camps are usually full-day or half-day and are typically held at community centers, rec centers, schools, religious congregations, art studios, dance studios, or music schools. They can run for one to eight weeks in the summer. Sleepaway camps are where the child goes to an overnight camp for either just a long weekend, a few weeks, or the entire summer. Usually younger kids go to sleepaway camp for a weekend or a week, and older kids go for one to two months. Summer overnight camps can be single-sex or coed and often focus on a theme.

If summer day camps or sleepaway camps appeal to you and your child, you can explore different weeklong camps where you can mix and match sessions, or you can choose longer-term camps, like a four- to eight-week session. Keep in mind that camps vary on cost, and it's likely you will be able to find a summer camp that fits your budget.

Conclusion

This chapter discussed a variety of ways your child can explore their interests by participating in different extracurricular activities. While it can be initially overwhelming to decide on an activity to start with from all of the possible options, once your child does find the perfect fit, it is a joy to watch them using their skills and interests to develop their talents.

REFLECTION QUESTIONS

1. Think back to the activities you did as a child. Did you like the activities you participated in? Did your parents insist you participate in an activity that wasn't the right fit for you? If so, how did that impact you?

2. What extracurricular activities do you and your spouse/partner value the most and why? For example, perhaps your spouse grew up playing a particular sport and wants your child to do the same. Or maybe you have always had a particular hobby and would like your child to also learn that skill.

3. Has your child had difficulty committing to a particular activity after an initial period of interest? If so, what do you think were the main challenges? Did your child end up quitting the activity or sticking with it a bit longer? What criteria do you have for your child to try an activity before they are allowed to quit, if they're still not showing interest?

CHAPTER 15

Connecting with Other Only-Child Families

O ne of the most meaningful ways to make new friends for both you and your child is to connect with other families who also have only children. Imagine how gratifying it would be to find another parent whose only child becomes great friends with yours and who you can relate to on multiple levels because they also have experienced a similar parenting journey. It would be amazing to connect with another only-child family who has similar perspectives on the importance of playdates and building community.

Sometimes only-child families can feel alone in their parenting journey and could benefit from a supportive village of other parents who can empathize with the blessings and challenges of raising an only child. Parents often find they can relate better to other parents with only children because they are in a comparable life stage and dealing with similar issues and concerns.

Amy Weber, LCSW, a licensed clinical social worker in New York who specializes in therapy for children and their families, said it's very important for parents of only children to connect with other parents of onlies so they can compare notes and trade stories because they're in similar boats. "It's important to have people you're connected to who are coming from a similar place."

She continues that if parents of only children feel alone or isolated, try to find "your people." The internet can be a fantastic tool for this. "It makes the world smaller and brings us closer together. I think it's important to seek out people that you have things in common with—whatever your concern is, there is a group for you somewhere. Finding online friends can be a good source of support while you're building your network."

Some parents instinctively tend to befriend other parents of only children, perhaps because they sense that parents of only children tend to value similar things, like frequent playdates and fostering deep friendships. Most of Rashmi's friends in Virginia are also mothers of onlies. She said, "I get along better with moms of only children than moms of siblings." She continued, "As parents, we bond together . . . We gravitate towards playdates with other only-child families because we have that in common."

Kids can have a natural affinity for friendships with other onlies. I remember in my son's kindergarten class, his best friends were also only children. These were families who happened to be the most interested in after-school playdates, so the kids got to know each other well and fast friendships formed.

Rashmi said that her daughter's friendships naturally gravitate toward onlies like her. "Most of my daughter's friends are also only children— her best friend is an only child. I think she is subconsciously drawn to [them]. Maybe they're looking for the same things in terms of social interaction. In general, only-child families are the families that we reach out the most to."

Along with the commonalities you feel with other one and done parents, it's also possible that your child may have more in common with another only child. When I was growing up, most of my closest friends happened to also be only children. Perhaps it's because we could relate to each other's experiences better and we were all looking for close friendships. My only child friends and I had an extremely close bond—truly like sisters.

Finding another only-child family to connect with can make all the difference between feeling lonely and isolated and gaining a sense of camaraderie and community.

The Importance of Connecting

Building a relationship with other only-child families is important for a few different reasons. The first is that it helps you feel less alone in your parenting journey if you have another parent you can relate to, particularly in terms of the struggles they're experiencing, the milestones they're going through, and the similar life stage they're living. For example, another only child parent will be able to relate to what it feels like to experience a specific milestone (like the first day of kindergarten or losing a first tooth) for the first and only time, which can be a poignant combination of joy and sadness.

Sometimes it can feel isolating if you're the only one in your friend group who has an only child, especially if you are one and done, not by choice. You might feel left out when your friends discuss sibling relationships or baby/toddler stages (if your child is older). You might feel like the odd one out if you're at a playdate with multiple families and everyone else has two or more kids who are all playing together.

Feeling excluded by your friend group can be rough—I know because I've been there. It's not a great feeling. But what can help is connecting with other only-child families. Something magical happens when you connect with another mom who also has an only child and you two are simpatico. It's genuinely comforting and empowering when you feel totally understood and accepted by another mom who has walked in similar shoes.

If you are the only single-child family in your preschool, daycare, or neighborhood, finding and connecting with other families of onlies will help you feel less isolated in a world where families with only children can be few and far between. It can make all the difference to find the one parent friend who understands you, as well as another only-child family to get together with for activities and playdates.

Another reason why it's helpful to connect with other only-child families is because it's often easier logistically to get together with another family who also has an only child. Many only-child families are interested in frequent playdates, and they can have difficulty finding a family with multiple kids who has the same level of interest in get-togethers. When they find another only-child family who also wants to do a lot of playdates, they know they've found a kindred spirit. Many only-child families are on the same page when it comes to playdates—they are interested in playdates and friend meetups, and lots of them!

One phenomenon I noticed during the preschool and early elementary years was that, in general, families gravitated to other families with the same number of similarly aged kids. It's usually nothing personal; most playdates for young kids are whole family playdates, where one parent brings all the siblings who aren't yet in school, so it's more about parents wanting all of their kids to have a friend to play with. If one family has three kids and you have an only child, it's likely that two of their kids might feel left out during a playdate. This causes parents of multiples to seek out other families with similar dynamics; however, it can leave only-child families feeling left out and excluded. One solution is to find more only-child families to connect with!

Keep in mind, however, that this dynamic of whole family playdates usually changes once kids are old enough to consistently have drop-off playdates, because parents don't need to stay and bring along younger siblings. This usually occurs around kindergarten or first grade, when the kid-to-kid friendship becomes most important and kids start making their own friends (usually through school).

Being friends with another family of an only is also wonderful beyond the opportunity to do more playdates; it's a good way to find another family to spend holidays with or even travel together. It's much easier to plan to spend holidays together with another only-child family, and it's possible that those who don't have any holiday plans might be interested in spending holidays with your family in order to make things more fun and exciting for their only. It is also much easier to travel with another only-child family when you don't have to worry about finding age-appropriate activities for sibling(s) or planning around another sibling's nap times—the two only children can just hang out together.

Another reason to connect with other only-child families is that it's especially helpful emotionally if you find another parent to talk to who is one and done by choice, or one and done, not by choice, depending on your status. Having another parent to connect with who is in a similar situation can really help you feel less alone and more understood.

Where Can You Find Them?

Now that we've established how it would be ideal to find another family with an only child to be friends with, let's discuss how you can find these families in order to connect.

How many other only-child families do you know in your local area? In general, if you live in a big city, it's likely you know more only-child families, but only-child families seem to be fewer and farther between in the distant suburbs, a rural area, or a small town.

The demographics of your geographic area matter when it comes to whether or not there are more one and done families in your local area. Only-child families are more commonly found in larger cities for several reasons. One reason for this is that geographic regions where women are more likely to have a college degree tend to have older first-time mothers, because having a college degree is the biggest factor for having a first child later (according to a recent report in *The New York*

Times). According to the report, big cities (like NYC, Boston, Seattle, San Francisco, and DC) tend to have a population of women who are highly educated, are focused on their careers, and decide to wait to have their first child. Infertility, pregnancy issues, health concerns, high cost of living in cities, or advanced maternal age may cause these families to stop at one child.

Another reason is that big cities tend to have smaller housing accommodations, such as two- and three-bedroom apartments, condos, or townhomes. You'll find more only-child families staying in the city because they gravitate to homes with fewer bedrooms and less space because they don't need the extra room. With housing prices being so expensive in cities, if a larger family needs three to four bedrooms, most decide it's cheaper and easier to just move out to the suburbs.

If you've moved to the distant suburbs into a house with four to five bedrooms, it's going to be less likely that you'll find another only-child family in your neighborhood, as opposed to living in a townhouse or condo in or near a city. It's also expensive to live in a city with a higher cost of living, but families with a single child may be better able to afford these expenses. So one way to be around more only-child families is to consider putting down roots in a smaller house in an area that tends to have more only-child families, like urban areas and closer-in suburbs.

In Rebekah's city in the UK, she has found this to be true. She also noticed how she is surrounded by a lot of older one and done moms, just like her. "It's been good living here. There are a lot of OAD mums in my city. The parenting population is older here. When I was pregnant at twenty-nine [years old], my midwife told me I was really young to be having a baby. And my closest friends with kids the same age are in their late forties or fifties."

She continued, "I met one of my best friends when my daughter was four. The kids now are really good friends, but it was me and the mum that made that happen. . . . [My daughter also] has three other friends who are onlies, and it's very common at her school to be an only child."

But regardless of whether you live in a big city, the suburbs, or a small town, there are ways to reach out to other only-child families. Social media is a great way to do this. Search meetup.com or Facebook groups to see if your local area has an only-child family social group. You can also post on the larger only child Facebook groups to see if anyone in your local area would be interested in meeting up. There are many only-child family groups to join, such as "One and Done: a Group for Parents of an Only Child," "Moms of Only Children—Inclusive Space," and "One and Done—Single Child Families." Try searching for any variations of "only-child families," and see what you can find.

When you join an online group, consider writing a post to introduce yourself because it's a great way to meet other only-child families in your local area. You could write something like: "Hi! I'm a mom with a five-year-old only child in Nashville, TN. I'd love to meet other only-child families in the area. If you're looking to make new friends, comment below or PM me!" If you do this in a few groups, it is likely you'll get a few people who contact you and are interested, and maybe you will make a new friend. It does take some courage to put yourself out there, but because it's online and not in person, it can be a little easier to initially reach out.

Besides the specific only child social/support groups, also try posting in local social media parenting or neighborhood groups. If you're in a local moms Facebook group (and there are many), like Philadelphia Moms or Orlando Moms, you could write a post saying that you're looking to make new friends in the area, mentioning the age of your child, and asking if anyone would like to connect. It's likely you will get some interest and meet other only child moms this way. People in local Facebook groups are usually very friendly and supportive, and these groups are a great way to make new connections.

Amanda, mom of an only child in Pennsylvania, has mainly met mom friends in two ways: at early intervention therapy groups and in her local Buy Nothing neighborhood group. She said, "We have a local neighborhood group where toys are cycled through, and it's like a lending library. We start to get to know each other's children and preferences, as they are similar in age."

Also check on Facebook, meetup.com, or other social media platforms to see if your local area has an only child social group. If so, this can be a great and easy way to meet other families. If not, consider starting one! Starting an only-child family social group is incredibly easy, and in a few minutes you can have your group up and running. While it can be hard to take the initiative to start a group, it is totally worth it when you build a community of other only-child families in your local area. Soon you'll be inundated with new members and can get started planning fun events!

Also, don't forget to check your social media to see if anyone you already know has an only child. Consider asking your friends if they know of anyone with an only child who might be looking to make new connections. Friends love to introduce their friends to new people! And it's often easier to make connections with friends of friends rather than with strangers or completely on your own.

Another way to find only-child families to befriend is to figure out if there are any in your child's class at school. You can do that by volunteering at school and attending school events. Chaperoning field trips and talking to the other parents at school events, becoming the room parent, and class playdates are good ways to get to know the other parents and find out if there are other only-child families.

In my son's small preschool, there were generally four or five only-child families in the entire school. You might find this is also the case at your child's school if it is small. But when you move to a larger school, it's more likely you will find a greater number of only-child families. When we got to kindergarten, and the school was a bigger public school, I was happy to learn that his homeroom class alone had five other only children, and he became best friends with several of them.

You can also seek out other only-child families through your child's extracurricular activities. If you notice another mom sitting in the waiting area alone, without any other kids, she might be a mom of an only. Consider going up to her and chatting. You may come to find out that she has an only child too. Wonderful friendships can start this way, and all it takes is the courage to reach out.

In addition, do you belong to a religious congregation? If so, think about only-child families you might be able to connect with there. If your child attends Sunday school or Hebrew school, perhaps there's another only-child family in the class that you can connect with. You could volunteer and get to know other families that way, or stick around during drop-off or pick-up and chat with the other parents. Some great new connections could result!

After going through all of these suggestions, even if you initially thought you didn't know any other only-child families, it's very likely you will find that your child knows at least a few other only children. Connecting with another only-child family or two will help you feel more connected and build your community.

How to Nurture New Friendships

Once you've found a great only-child family to be friends with, think about how to best nurture this new relationship. Perhaps it's been a while since you've made a new friend and you might feel a bit rusty. Let's talk a bit about the process of getting to know and making a new friend.

The first step in making a new friend is to chat and get to know them. As you're talking, do you feel like you have some things in common? Do you feel like you naturally "click" and like you never run out of things to talk about, or does it seem like you're struggling to connect? Does the other parent seem receptive to new friends? Do they often mention how "crazy busy" they are with work and family? If it sounds like they don't have much free time, or that their weekends are jam-packed with other activities and commitments, then they may not be in the market for a new friend.

And that's *okay*, because not everyone is looking to make new friends right now, and that's just something we need to accept. Nicole McNelis, LPC, a maternal mental health therapist in Pennsylvania, said that it's common to have difficulty making friends as an adult. "For people who are introverted or busy, the first thing you can recognize is that there are some people who need lots of friends, and others need just a few." As you get to know each other, you can adjust your expectations of whether or not a potential friend might turn into a real friendship or whether they'll stay a friendly acquaintance.

Sometimes making a new friend can feel intimidating because you're putting yourself out there and are not sure how it will be received. Many people fear rejection and it causes them to wait for others to make the first move. McNelis' advice is to take a risk and reach out. "If you want to go to places and engage in activities that you enjoy, you have to take risks. If you're at the playground and there's a mom you want to strike up a conversation with—go for it! It's okay to fear rejection [because] relationships come with risks. Just try to put yourself out there." Remember that if you don't reach out, and you just sit at home not making any effort, it's unlikely that you will make a new friend. It's up to you to take that first step.

It's also important to have a good sense about what kind of friendship you're looking for and determine whether the other parent is looking for something similar. Are you looking for a friend to meet up with while the kids play? Or are you looking for a friend to meet up for a moms-only get-together? Some women are only interested in meeting up with the kids, others just want adult get-togethers, and some are interested in both. A new friendship works best if the two of you have similar friendship goals and expectations.

If this new friend is receptive to getting together for a playdate with the kids, reach out and invite the other family to do something. Meeting up for something very casual that you were planning to do anyway, like a playdate at a park, is a great first step. You could text something like,

"Hey, we're headed to Center Park on Sunday at 3 p.m., if you'd like to join us." It takes the pressure off a more formal get-together and keeps things casual and light. If they don't accept the invitation, try once or twice more. If they seem disinterested, don't respond right away, or decline and don't suggest alternative dates, then realize that they're probably not interested in a new friend right now.

If they do accept the invitation and you have a great time, continue reaching out again to keep in touch between meetups, either by text or email. Consider inviting them to meet up again after a few weeks have passed. If your kids seem compatible and you like the other parent, you're well on your way to a great new friendship.

Conclusion

In this chapter we've explored many reasons why connecting with other only-child families is so important in your parenting journey. Making friends who can relate to your parenting experience on a variety of different levels can go a long way to helping you feel a sense of belonging and community. If you are able to find other only-child families to be friends with, it can have wonderful benefits for both you and your child as you nurture these amazing new friendships.

REFLECTION QUESTIONS

1. When you were growing up, did your parents have many friends? If so, did they tend to befriend other parents who had a similar family size to yours?
2. Have you found a difference in the receptiveness of other parents to friendships based on their family size?
3. Have you found it easy or difficult to meet other only-child families? If difficult, why do you think that is?
4. If you could make a new friend right now, what qualities would this friend have?

5. Do you find it easy or difficult to connect with others? If it's challenging for you, what tends to get in the way of fulfilling friendships?

Conclusion

Having an only-child family is my life's greatest joy, and most likely is yours too. Parenting my only child has fulfilled me in ways I never imagined, and I cherish all the blessings and challenges of motherhood that I encounter every day.

Writing this book has been an incredible journey, and I have loved connecting with dozens of only-child families around the world, sharing their stories and perspectives in these pages. When I first started interviewing for this book, what stood out to me was how much parents of only children are searching for community and connection with other only-child families. Connecting with other only-child families and building a vibrant community and village of other like-minded parents has been one of the highlights of the parenting experience for me.

My hope is that you felt a sense of community and connection by reading the stories of other only-child families in this book, and that you are inspired to seek out your own community too. May their words and experiences bring wisdom, comfort, and inspiration to your unique only-child family journey.

References

INTRODUCTION

"Pew Research Center Analysis of 1976 and 2014 Current Population Survey June Supplements," Pew Research Center, accessed October 1, 2021, https://www.pewresearch.org/social-trends/2015/12/17/1-the-american-family-today/.

"Historical Families Tables," United States Census Bureau, accessed November 2, 2021, https://www.census.gov/data/tables/time-series/demo/families/families.html.

CHAPTER 1

Alejandra Vallos-Davalos Salazar, in discussion with the author, August 2021.

Keren Wakefield, in discussion with the author, August 2021.

Rashmi Ghei, in discussion with the author, August 2021.

Jessica (last name withheld by request), in discussion with the author, December 2021.

"2015 Expenditures on Children by Families Annual Report," U.S. Department of Agriculture, accessed August 12, 2021, https://www.fns.usda.gov/resource/2015-expenditures-children-families.

Rebekah Fisher, in discussion with the author, August 2021.

Erin McDermott, in discussion with the author, August 2021.

CHAPTER 2

Beth Zunde, in discussion with the author, August 2021.

Danielle Peters, LMFT, in discussion with the author, December 2021.

Amy Weber, LCSW, in discussion with the author, December 2021.

Keren Wakefield, in discussion with the author, August 2021.

Jennifer Sotolongo, LMHC, in discussion with the author, December 2021.

Nikki Shallenberger, in discussion with the author, December 2021.

Danielle Zero, in discussion with the author, December 2021.

Nicoletta Balbo and Bruno Arpino, "The Role of Family Orientations in Shaping the Effect of Fertility on Subjective Well-Being: A Propensity Score Matching Approach," *Demography* 53, no. 4 (2016): 955–78.

Hans-Peter Kohler, Jere R. Behrman, and Axel Skytthe, "Partner + Children = Happiness? The Effects of Partnerships and Fertility on Well-Being," *Population and Development Review* 31, no. 3 (2005): 407–45.

Nicholas J. Beutell and Ursula Wittig-Berman, "Predictors of Work-Family Conflict and Satisfaction with Family, Job, Career, and Life," *Psychological Reports* 85, no. 3 (1999): 893–903.

Jean M. Twenge, W. Keith Campbell, and Craig A. Foster, "Parenthood and Marital Satisfaction: A Meta-Analytic Review," *Journal of Marriage and Family* 65, no. 3 (2003): 574–83.

"2015 Expenditures on Children by Families Annual Report," U.S. Department of Agriculture, accessed August 12, 2021, https://www.fns.usda.gov/resource/2015-expenditures-children-families.

Kristie Nichols, in discussion with the author, December 2021.

Jessica (last name withheld by request), in discussion with the author, December 2021.

CHAPTER 3

Nikki Shallenberger, in discussion with the author, December 2021.

"Historical Families Tables," United States Census Bureau, accessed November 2, 2021, https://www.census.gov/data/tables/time-series/demo/families/families.html.

"Pew Research Center Analysis of 1976 and 2014 Current Population Survey June Supplements," Pew Research Center, accessed October 1, 2021, https://www.pewresearch.org/social-trends/2015/12/17/1-the-american-family-today/.

Vanessa Grigoriadis, "Only Children in New York," *New York Magazine*, October 29, 2004, https://nymag.com/nymetro/urban/family/features/10290/.

"Households with Children in the EU," Eurostat, accessed November 1, 2021, https://ec.europa.eu/eurostat/en/web/products-eurostat-news/-/edn-20190601-1.

"Portrait of Families and Living Arrangements in Canada," Statistics Canada, accessed November 4, 2021, https://www12.statcan.gc.ca/census-recensement/2011/as-sa/98-312-x/98-312-X2011001-eng.cfm.

"Families," Office for National Statistics, accessed November 20, 2021, https://www.ons.gov.uk/peoplepopulationandcommunity/birthsdeathsandmarriages/families.

Nadia Hlebowitsh, "How Many Families Worldwide Have Only One Child?" *Only Child World* (blog), accessed November 2, 2021, https://onlychildworld.com/how-many-families-worldwide-have-only-one-child/.

Danielle Zero, in discussion with the author, December 2021.

Keren Wakefield, in discussion with the author, August 2021.

Amy Weber, LCSW, in discussion with the author, November 2021.

Jacy L. Young, "G. Stanley Hall, Child Study, and the American Public," *The Journal of Genetic Psychology* 177, no. 6 (2016): 195–208.

Sarah Drummond, in discussion with the author, December 2021.

Kristie Nichols, in discussion with the author, November 2021.

Damon E. Jones, Mark Greenberg, and Max Crowley, "Early Social-Emotional Functioning and Public Health: The Relationship Between Kindergarten Social Competence and Future Wellness," *American Journal of Public Health* 105, no. 11 (2015): 2283–90.

Alejandra Vallos-Davalos Salazar, in discussion with the author, August 2021.

CHAPTER 4

Rashmi Ghei, in discussion with the author, August 2021.

Amy Weber, LCSW, in discussion with the author, December 2021.

Beth Zunde, in discussion with the author, August 2021.

Nicole McNelis, LPC, in discussion with the author, September 2021.

Jessica (last name withheld by request), in discussion with the author, December 2021.

Danielle Zero, in discussion with the author, November 2021.

Danielle Peters, LMFT, in discussion with the author, November 2021.

Kristie Nichols, in discussion with the author, November 2021.

CHAPTER 5

Beth Zunde, in discussion with the author, August 2021.

Danielle Peters, LMFT, in discussion with the author, December 2021.

Jennifer Sotolongo, LMHC, in discussion with the author, December 2021.

Nicole McNelis, LPC, in discussion with the author, September 2021.

"Social Isolation & Loneliness," Human Animal Bond Research Institute, accessed October 10, 2021, https://habri.org/research/mental-health/social-isolation/.

CHAPTER 6

Nicole McNelis, LPC, in discussion with the author, September 2021.

Jennifer Sotolongo, LMHC, in discussion with the author, December 2021.

Rebekah Fisher, in discussion with the author, August 2021.

CHAPTER 7

Amanda Adams, in discussion with the author, December 2021.

Danielle Peters, LMFT, in discussion with the author, December 2021.

Jill Belsky, in discussion with the author, August 2021.

Danielle Zero, in discussion with the author, December 2021.

Midori Kawase, in discussion with the author, August 2021.

Nicole McNelis, LPC, in discussion with the author, September 2021.

Amy Weber, LCSW, in discussion with the author, November 2021.

CHAPTER 8

Jill Belsky, in discussion with the author, August 2021.

Nicole McNelis, LPC, in discussion with the author, November 2021.

Kristie Nichols, in discussion with the author, December 2021.

Danielle Zero, in discussion with the author, November 2021.

CHAPTER 9

"2019–2020 National Pet Owners Survey," American Pet Products Association (APPA), accessed November 10, 2021, https://www.americanpetproducts.org/press_industrytrends.asp.

"Social Isolation & Loneliness," Human Animal Bond Research Institute, accessed October 10, 2021, https://habri.org/research/mental-health/social-isolation/.

"The Power of Pets: Health Benefits of Human-Animal Interactions," NIH News in Health, February 2018, accessed October 1, 2021, https://newsinhealth.nih.gov/2018/02/power-pets.

Danielle Peters, LMFT, in discussion with the author, December 2021.

Kristie Nichols, in discussion with the author, December 2021.

Rebecca Purewal, Robert Christley, Katarzyna Kordas, Carol Joinson, Kerstin Meints, Nancy Gee, and Carri Westgarth, "Companion Animals and Child/Adolescent Development: A Systematic Review of the Evidence," *International Journal of Environmental Research and Public Health* 14, no. 3 (2017): 234.

Jill Belsky, in discussion with the author, October 2021.

CHAPTER 10

Nikki Shallenberger, in discussion with the author, December 2021.

Kristie Nichols, in discussion with the author, December 2021.

Danielle Zero, in discussion with the author, December 2021.

CHAPTER 11

Keren Wakefield, in discussion with the author, August 2021.

CHAPTER 12

Danielle Zero, in discussion with the author, December 2021.

Sarah Drummond, in discussion with the author, December 2021.

Alejandra Vallos-Davalos Salazar, in discussion with the author, August 2021.

Rashmi Ghei, in discussion with the author, August 2021.

Kristie Nichols, in discussion with the author, December 2021.

Nicole McNelis, LPC, in discussion with the author, September 2021.

Amy Weber, LCSW, in discussion with the author, November 2021.

Jessica (last name withheld by request), in discussion with the author, December 2021.

Nikki Shallenberger, in discussion with the author, December 2021.

CHAPTER 13

Name withheld by request for privacy, in discussion with the author, September 2021.

Alejandra Vallos-Davalos Salazar, in discussion with the author, August 2021.

Jessica (last name withheld by request), in discussion with the author, December 2021.

Nicole McNelis, LPC, in discussion with the author, September 2021.

CHAPTER 14

Amanda Adams, in discussion with the author, December 2021.

Danielle Peters, LMFT, in discussion with the author, December 2021.

CHAPTER 15

Amy Weber, LCSW, in discussion with the author, December 2021.

Rashmi Ghei, in discussion with the author, August 2021.

Amanda Adams, in discussion with the author, November 2021.

Quoctrung Bui and Claire Cain Miller, "The Age That Women Have Babies: How a Gap Divides America," *The New York Times*, August 4, 2018, https://www.nytimes.com /interactive/2018/08/04/upshot/up-birth-age-gap.html.

Michelle Robertson, "San Francisco Women Have Children Later Than Anywhere Else in the U.S. Here's Why," *SFGate*, August 6, 2018, https://www.sfgate.com/mommyfiles/article /women-sf-children-mother-motherhood-later-age-13136540.php.

Rebekah Fisher, in discussion with the author, August 2021.

Nicole McNelis, LPC, in discussion with the author, September 2021.

ACKNOWLEDGMENTS

Writing this book was one of the most rewarding, most intellectually challenging endeavors I have ever undertaken. Hours upon hours of writing, researching, and interviewing went into this book, as well as extensive thought and planning to make sure that every major topic pertinent to raising an only child was covered. This book wouldn't be possible without those who contributed their insight and supported me through the process of its development.

I first want to thank all the amazing only-child families and mental health professionals who provided their thought-provoking insights for this book, and without whom this book would not be possible: Rashmi Ghei, Jill Belsky, Nicole McNelis, Jennifer Sotolongo, Keren Wakefield, Danielle Peters, Amy Weber, Kristie Nichols, Amanda Adams, Midori Kawase, Nikki Shallenberger, Alejandra Vallos-Davalos Salazar, Erin McDermott, Danielle Zero, Beth Zunde, Jessica (last name withheld by request), Rebekah Fisher, and Sarah Drummond. I also want to thank Jessica Myhre for writing such a beautiful and moving foreword to the book and for supporting thousands of only-child families with her inspirational podcast, *Only You: A One and Done Podcast*.

I would like to thank my incredible editor, Laurie Duersch, for her brilliant editing skills and organizational insights that polished the manuscript and made it shine. She provided outstanding feedback and support throughout the entire editing process. I also want to express my gratitude to my extraordinary publisher, Christopher Robbins, and the entire publishing team at Familius, who have expertly guided this book from idea to publication.

And, most importantly, I offer my heartfelt thanks to my amazing husband, Brian, for always enthusiastically supporting me and my writing, and to my son, Alex, my wonderful one and only, who inspires me every day.

About the Author

Rebecca Greene, MSW, LMSW, is an only child raising an only child, and a mental health professional who has many years of experience counseling kids, teens, and families. She is also an award-winning author who writes nonfiction, self-help, and parenting books, as well as children's books about developing social-emotional skills and overcoming challenges. Her recent children's book, *My Perfect Cupcake*, won first place for best health book in the 2021 Purple Dragonfly Book Awards contest.

Rebecca grew up in Columbus, Ohio, and now resides in the Washington, DC, metro area. She lives with her husband, young son, and two curious Cornish Rex cats. When she's not writing or counseling, you can find Rebecca looking for shells at the beach, cheering on her son at his soccer and ice hockey games, and volunteering in the community.

One & Done is Rebecca's seventh published book. You can learn more about Rebecca's work and forthcoming titles through her website: www.rebeccagreeneauthor.com.

About Familius

VISIT OUR WEBSITE: WWW.FAMILIUS.COM

Familius is a global trade publishing company that publishes books and other content to help families be happy. We believe that the family is the fundamental unit of society and that happy families are the foundation of a happy life. We recognize that every family looks different, and we passionately believe in helping all families find greater joy. To that end, we publish books for children and adults that invite families to live the Familius Ten Habits of Happy Families: *love together, play together, learn together, work together, talk together, heal together, read together, eat together, give together,* and *laugh together.* Founded in 2012, Familius is located in Sanger, California.

CONNECT

Facebook: www.facebook.com/familiustalk
Twitter: @familiustalk, @paterfamilius1
Pinterest: www.pinterest.com/familius
Instagram: @familiustalk

FAMILIUS

The most important work you ever do will be
within the walls of your own home.